AN INTRODUCTION TO
CHRISTIAN
ETHICS

Goals, Duties, and Virtues

ROBIN W.
LOVIN

Abingdon Press
Nashville

AN INTRODUCTION TO CHRISTIAN ETHICS

This book is printed on acid-free paper.

Library of Congress Cataloging-in-Publication Data

Lovin, Robin W.
  An introduction to Christian ethics : goals, duties, virtues / Robin W. Lovin
    p.   cm.
  Includes bibliographical references (p.   ) and index.
  ISBN 978-0-687-46736-5 (pbk. : alk. paper)   1. Christian ethics—Textbooks.   I. Title.
  BJ1251.L695 2011
  241—dc23

                                                                    2011032927

All scripture quotations are taken from the New Revised Standard Version of the Bible, copyright 1989, Division of Christian Education of the National Council of the Churches of Christ in the United States of America. Used by permission. All rights reserved.

11 12 13 14 15 16 17 18 19 20—10 9 8 7 6 5 4 3 2 1

MANUFACTURED IN THE UNITED STATES OF AMERICA

CONTENTS

Contents

A PREFACE FOR THE STUDENT

The book you are reading is an introduction to Christian ethics. You may be reading it because it was assigned in a class that is also called "Introduction to Christian Ethics" or perhaps "Moral Theology" or "Religious Ethics" or "Theological Ethics." The different names indicate differences in scope and content, but in any of these courses, you will be reading this book as part of an introduction to the way that people think about moral questions from a Christian perspective.

But if you are reading this book, you have already been introduced to ethics. You have been taught from childhood to follow some kind of moral code, and you have ideas about right and wrong which reflect your own experience, the moral standards of the people around you, and the values of the society in which you live. You have also been introduced to ethics in the sense that you have done some critical reflection on the moral code you have been taught. You have wondered whether its standards of right and wrong are correct. You have asked whether its values have any basis in reality, or whether they simply reflect the prejudices of the people who taught them to you. You may already have decided that the ethics you were taught is not the ethics you want to live by. You may have changed your religion, your political ideas, or your vocational goals to bring them more in line with the results of your own thinking. Or you may have decided that the way you were taught to live really is the way you ought to live, and you have taken these rules on for yourself. Your religion, politics, and way of life are now your own, and not just something you were told to follow.

Either way, you were introduced to ethics without a textbook, assignments, or exams—except maybe for the real-life tests that come along when you find out whether you are actually going to live by the rules and values you say you accept. Ethics is like that. The introduction is part of life, before you open a book or sit in a classroom. So an introduction to ethics is not like an introduction to quantum physics, where you learn ideas and equations that belong to a world very different from the world of ordinary experience. In fact, you are not really ready to begin the academic study of ethics until you have had some experiences like the ones I just described.

So an introduction to ethics is not designed to lead you through solving your first moral problems in the way that an algebra textbook leads you through solving your first equations. The point is to help you organize your thinking, provide a vocabulary for some questions that you are probably already asking, and show you how others have dealt with those same questions in the past. Unlike introductions to algebra or quantum physics, every student in an introduction to ethics already has a lot of knowledge about the subject. To make sense of the course, you will have to draw on that knowledge and connect the kind of thinking that you already do every day to ways of thinking that began in ancient Athens, in the early days of Christianity, or in a medieval university.

To say that everybody in an introduction to ethics already has a lot of knowledge about the subject is not to say that anyone knows all of it. You will encounter new problems, new ways of thinking, and a new vocabulary. All of these have to be mastered in order for you to understand your own thinking in relation to the ways of moral thinking that this text explores. Nor does your previous knowledge and experience of ethics mean that your thinking cannot be challenged. The popular idea that everyone is entitled to his or her own opinion on moral questions is less than half true. It would be more accurate to say that because everyone knows a lot about ethics already, everyone is competent to challenge anyone else's judgment. Professors of ethics have to get used to responding to that kind of challenge, but ethics students have to expect it, too. One of the most important uses of an introduction to ethics is to provide a vocabulary and a framework of ideas which people can use to question each other about their moral thinking. If that discussion goes well, everyone's ideas will become clearer. If it goes badly, the voices just become louder.

Christian Ethics

It is important that this book is not just an introduction to ethics, but an introduction to *Christian* ethics. To some readers, adding that qualifier will seem like an admission that there is something peculiar about this approach. Emphasizing that this is specifically Christian ethics suggests that somewhere there is neutral, plain-vanilla ethics for everybody, while Christians do ethics in a way that is somehow different, maybe even incomprehensible, to those who do not share their beliefs. This, too, is less than half true.

Everybody wants to live a good life, and nearly everybody thinks about how to do it. In that sense, we all participate in the same moral discussion, and it would be strange for Christians to stand aside and say, "We want to talk about ethics, too, but we don't want to talk about those questions." But when people answer the questions of ethics, they do it from a particular point of view. Their ideas about what it means to live a good life are shaped by their ideas about human nature, whether life has a purpose, and what they expect from the future. A Christian who believes that all things come from God will answer questions about living a good human life differently from a scientific materialist who believes that everything is just matter in motion. In that sense, Christian ethics *is* different. But all ways of answering the questions of ethics differ in that way. Moral thinking may be shaped by a religious tradition, by ideas drawn from philosophy, by political or economic values, or simply by the conviction that what is right is what works for me. There are Buddhist ethics, existentialist ethics, free-market ethics, Muslim ethics, and even egocentric ethics alongside of Christian ethics, but there is never just plain ethics. Some moral thinkers have been so concerned about the conflicts between these ways of doing ethics that they have insisted that what we need is a set of neutral assumptions on which all reasonable people could agree as the basis for their moral thinking. The idea would be that everyone would set aside contentious beliefs about how the world began, how it will end, and how it is going, and rely only on the neutral moral principles that all had agreed to follow. But even if such a set of assumptions could be devised, it would have to include the assumption that religious and political beliefs can be fenced off in a way that keeps them from influencing the moral discussion.

The Christian Stance

In this book, we will call these different ways of looking at the world *stances*, borrowing a term from Charles Curran.[1] The Christian stance is an approach to moral problems that begins from a set of beliefs that are generally shared among Christians, including beliefs about God and about how God's presence in Jesus of Nazareth reshapes human lives and indicates the direction of human history. In thinking about the stance of Christian ethics, however, we will not be concerned with the precise formulation of those beliefs, nor with the arguments for and against them. Our concern is with the ways these beliefs shape the perspective of Christians as they approach moral choices. A stance provides a way of thinking about your place in history and in the world, and that is how we will want to understand the beliefs that constitute the stance of Christian ethics.

As Christianity spread through the Roman world and beyond it, into Persia and Central Asia, and among the peoples who lived on the edges of Roman culture in Europe, Christian ideas about God, the world, and human history shaped the encounter with other religions and schools of philosophy. We will consider just a few of these encounters, primarily with the Stoic, Epicurean, and Neoplatonist philosophers whose moral systems influenced early Christian thinking. We will also learn something about Manichean religion, which challenged the Jewish and Christian belief in one God who created all things. There are many other stances we could consider, both in the ancient world where Christianity grew and in the modern world, where Christians everywhere live among a rich variety of religions, cultures, political systems, traditions, and values. The important thing to understand is that Christians have never made their moral choices in isolation from other beliefs and other ways of thinking. They have understood what is distinctive about their Christian stance by seeing it in relation to other stances.

Neither have all Christians seen their stance in the same way. Early in its history, Christianity split into Eastern and Western churches. Later, the Western church split into Roman Catholic and Protestant communions, with the Protestants themselves divided into several different ways of understanding the Christian stance. If we were to follow these different families of Christian faith through history and into all the places where they now find themselves, we would see even more variations, as each group responded to the cultural settings, systems of government, and particular mix of religions in the places where they lived. No one way of doing Christian ethics fits all of these situations. Each deserves its own introduction to its own idea of Christian ethics. But that would make a very long book.

In this introduction, we will follow the development of ethics in Western Christianity as it grew from the teaching of Jesus, through persecution and acceptance, to the work of Augustine of Hippo (354–430), a North African bishop whose life and teaching encompassed many of the possibilities for relating the Christian stance to a complex social reality. Like our own world, the society in which Augustine lived was made up of many different peoples and religions. It faced serious questions about its future, and it was alternately grateful for the Christian presence in its midst and suspicious of that presence. Augustine, in turn, sometimes embraced the community where he lived, teaching Christians to serve their neighbors as a way of serving God; and sometimes he drew a sharp line to preserve the integrity of Christian faith, distinguishing Christians from those who served other gods or made a god of themselves. In Augustine's explorations of the Christian stance, we will become familiar with ideas that influenced many later thinkers, from Thomas Aquinas (1225–1274), who combined faith and reason in a great synthesis that brought human knowledge and love of God together, to Martin Luther (1483–1546), who reasserted the difference between the Christian community ruled by love and a society ruled by sin and controlled by force. Modern Western Christianity has inherited this history, and in the third chapter we will find its tensions still present in four versions of the Christian stance that shape the ways that Christians in more recent times have seen their moral problems.

Goals, Duties, and Virtues

Learning how to see the world, however, is not the same thing as solving moral problems. Augustine sometimes suggested that if everyone were united in a common love for God, they would all agree on the answers to all their moral questions. That may be true, but getting everyone to agree on the same stance, or even getting all Christians to agree on the same version of the Christian stance, is not a very efficient way to arrive at a decision.

The moral question is not, *What do I believe?* It is, *What should I do?* Stance will influence that answer, but stance alone does not determine it. Christians also shape their moral choices by bringing some form of moral reasoning to bear on the problems they face. Here, Christian ethics comes into conversation with other ways of thinking about ethics, for although there are many stances, there are three primary ways of arriving at a moral decision: You can use reason to set goals and determine the course of action most likely to achieve them. You can think about what your duty is and ask what you must do to fulfill it. You can determine what kind of person you should be and how to acquire the personal characteristics or virtues that enable you to be that kind of person.

Each of these forms of moral reasoning has a long history that begins before the beginnings of Christianity. Christianity has contributed its own understanding of goals, duties, and virtues, but other ideas have developed alongside these Christian ways of doing ethics, or in opposition to them. In the later parts of this book, we will explore the history of Christian thinking about goals, duties, and virtues (chapters 4, 6, and 8) and consider the ways that contemporary Christian ethics makes use of goals, duties, and virtues (chapters 5, 7, and 9). By the time you have worked your way through all nine of the chapters that follow, you will know a good deal more about how Christians through history have thought about ethics and how contemporary Christian ethicists make use of that history in their own systematic ways of thinking about moral problems.

Usually, at the end of an introduction to Christian ethics, there is an exam of some sort. Perhaps it will ask you to identify some of the figures you have studied and write brief essays about their work. Or it may give you a problem and ask you how you would solve it, thinking about goals, duties, and virtues. There are many ways to give an exam in ethics, but all of them are a bit artificial. You have to have an introduction to ethics in your own experience before a book titled *An Introduction to Christian Ethics* can be of any use to you, and in any course in ethics, it is always your own experience that administers the final exam. The date and time of that exam are not announced, and even your instructor cannot predict what the questions will be, but I hope that when the test comes, something you read in these pages will help you to write your own answers.

Part 1
Christian Ethics

CHAPTER ONE

THE ORIGINS OF ETHICS

The study of ethics begins with critical reflection on a way of life. Christian ethics has its roots in the work of the Hebrew prophets, who called people to renew their covenant with God by living with justice, kindness, and humility. It grows from the teaching of Jesus, who taught love of God and neighbor. Christian ethics is also closely connected with another tradition of critical reflection that begins with Greek philosophy and asks what it is that everybody is seeking. Thus, Christian thinking about ethics develops as shared human questions find specifically Christian answers.

At some point, most people begin to ask questions about the way of life they have lived. They start to wonder whether they really should obey the rules they have been told to follow. They ask whether the ideas they have been taught about the world and their own place in it are really true. They look at the dreams and the goals they have been pursuing, and they have to decide whether the life they have or the life they want really is a good life. Many things lead to this kind of critical thinking. Sometimes, it happens as a person matures and leaves the familiar surroundings of home and family for further education, marriage, or a new career. People encounter new cultures, new religions, or new neighbors, and as a result, they see their own lives and beliefs in a different way. Illness, war, or natural disaster can change lives suddenly and so completely that people ask whether they can return to the life they were living before, and whether they want to. Sometimes, too, the questions come slowly, out of quiet reflection, as we recognize the choices we have already made about our own lives and begin to discern the possibilities still ahead of us.

However the questions arise, the people who ask these questions have begun doing ethics, even if they do not know what to call it. They are thinking critically about their own lives and the social world in which they live. They are asking how they can be *good* people and how they can make the *right* choices. They are thinking about how they *ought* to treat the other people around them, and how they can together build a *just* society, where everyone will have a fair chance to ask these questions and find the answers. The words themselves—*good, right, ought, just*—are signals that moral thinking is going on. We can do what we have always been told to do, or we can decide for ourselves what things are really important and what deeds are worth doing.

Something like that happens in history, too. For as far back as we can go, people have had rules to tell them what to do and what not to do, ideas about things that are good and worth pursuing, and words for character and virtue to tell them what kind of people they ought to be. For most of human history, people would not have thought to separate some of these ideas from the rest of what they did and believed and call those beliefs "ethics," any more than they would have thought to identify some of their ideas and activities as "religious." Most human beings have lived their lives as part of a culture, where they learned how to grow their crops, pray to the gods, ward off diseases, deal with their neighbors, and keep track of the seasons, all as part of a unified way of life. Modern thinkers might divide these practices into agriculture, religion, medicine, magic, science, etiquette, and ethics, but those distinctions probably would not occur to people for whom the whole way of life came as a package.[1] To an Israelite praying in Solomon's temple, a Native American hunter, or a scribe copying magical and medical information onto a scroll in ancient Egypt, our categories would probably have seemed a strange way to divide up a life they experienced as a unified whole.

At some point, however, the accumulation of cultural memories, the growth of literacy and written records, and contacts with other people and other ways of life through warfare, trade, and travel reached a point at which questions became inevitable. Globalization moves at a very rapid pace in our world of Internet connections and air travel, but globalization happens even when the exchanges are by way of handwritten scrolls and camel caravans. People begin to reflect on their way of life. They start asking what is really important among all the rules, stories, and rituals that make up the way they live. They want to know if there is something that holds this way of life together across time, something to which they might remain faithful, or from which they might drift away. Is this just the way we do it? Or is there some deeper connection to reality behind all of these practices?

We might say that the history of ethics begins when there are records that allow us to follow this critical reflection on a way of life. Out of the whole array of customs, courtesies, rules, and rituals, people start to identify some as really important. These are the things that make them who they are, the beliefs and actions that help them find their place in the universe. These beliefs and actions also give individuals their own character, so that others around them think of them as good when they live according to these practices and as bad when they do not. These things are so important to identity and relationships that people hold on to them, even when they are no longer easy to follow; but they can also become the basis for a new way of life, when the details of the old life no longer work.

That kind of critical reflection grew out of changes in many cultures and religious traditions that began about 800 years before the time of Jesus. During this period in history, India, China, and Greece developed their characteristic systems of philosophy. The religious movements that became Buddhism and Zoroastrianism began, along with many other religions whose rituals and beliefs spread along the trade routes that connected Asia, the Middle East, and the Mediterranean world.

During this time, too, the Hebrew prophets transformed the religious life of their people by focusing on the requirements of justice in relations with fellow Israelites and reverence for God before all other loyalties. Through centuries of upheaval that divided rich against poor, subjected the people of Israel and Judah to foreign rulers, and introduced them to foreign gods, their prophets and teachers challenged them to return to the Law of Moses and to the covenant that formed them as a people. Central to this covenant was a relationship between persons that also involved a right relationship to God.

He has told you, O mortal, what is good;
  and what does the LORD require of you
but to do justice, and to love kindness,
  and to walk humbly with your God? (Micah 6:8)

Jesus of Nazareth continued this prophetic criticism, announcing the nearness of the Reign of God, which would be open to all people and not only to those who had been part of the covenant and the Law of Moses. For Jesus' followers, it was more than ever essential to see what had been really important in that old way of life, so that everyone could shape a new life by it. In a memorable summary in the Gospel of Matthew, Jesus reduces the Law to just two commandments:

> One of them, a lawyer, asked him a question to test him. "Teacher, which commandment in the law is the greatest?" He said to him, " 'You shall love the Lord your God with all your heart, and with all your soul, and with all your mind.' This is the greatest and first commandment. And a second is like it: 'You shall love your neighbor as yourself.' On these two commandments hang all the law and the prophets." (Matthew 22:35-40)

For Jesus' disciples, his teaching inaugurated a new covenant, even a whole new creation. That was how Paul, the most important of the early Christian teachers, explained it to his readers in the Greek city of Corinth. "So if anyone is in Christ, there is a new creation: everything old has passed away; see, everything has become new!" (2 Corinthians 5:17). Paul could also speak of this new creation as a profound personal change of thinking, in which Christians are no longer conformed to this world, but transformed in mind so as to be able to discern the will of God. At that point, they no longer require guardians and tutors to tell them what to do.

This teaching provided a critical way of seeing not only life lived according to the Law of Moses, but all of the other ways of life that Christians encountered as they carried their message around the Mediterranean. Paul pointed out the differences in his letter to Christians in Galatia, a Roman province in what is now central Turkey:

> Now the works of the flesh are obvious: fornication, impurity, licentiousness, idolatry, sorcery, enmities, strife, jealousy, anger, quarrels, dissensions, factions, envy, drunkenness, carousing, and things like these. I am warning you, as I warned you before: those who do such

things will not inherit the kingdom of God. By contrast, the fruit of the Spirit is love, joy, peace, patience, kindness, generosity, faithfulness, gentleness, and self-control. There is no law against such things. (Galatians 5:19-23)

Early Christian texts are filled with such contrasts: living by the flesh or living by the Spirit; walking in the light or walking in darkness; the way of life or the way of death.[2] These sources offer advice on the details of Christian life and daily prayers. They talk about family life and relations between husbands and wives, and they also offer guidance on how to relate to the pagan rituals and sacrifices that were an inescapable part of life in the cities of the Roman world. Through it all runs the theme that the roles and distinctions that once shaped relationships lose their importance in comparison to the new way of life that Christians follow. "There is no longer Jew or Greek," Paul writes, "there is no longer slave or free, there is no longer male and female; for all of you are one in Christ Jesus" (Galatians 3:28).

We have said that ethics begins with this critical reflection on a way of life, when people condemn its failures, challenge its accepted rules, identify what is really important, and set out guidelines by which life can be lived as it was meant to be and not just as we have known it in the past. Christian ethics, then, takes its start from the Hebrew prophets and the teaching of Jesus, and especially from this idea that the most important thing is to connect justice and kindness to a right relationship with God. Those two commandments hold all of life together, so that there is no difference between what you love and what you do and how you relate to God.

The Greeks Had a Word for It

Neither the Hebrew prophets nor the early Christians would have called this reflection on a way of life *ethics*. That term comes to us from the Greeks, who also experienced historical changes that led to critical reflection on traditional customs and culminated in new ways of understanding life as it should be lived. But the Greeks posed the questions in a different way. Instead of thinking about right relationships, both to God and neighbor, the Greeks asked how to make the right choices when we face decisions about how to live.

They could, of course, simply follow their desires, but they noticed that desires change from day to day, and they realized that the first thing we pursue often turns out not at all to be what we really want. Another way they had available to make their choices was to consult an oracle or use magic, hoping to find out what fate had in store for them. Lacking any texts quite like the Hebrew scriptures, the Greeks did not have a definitive set of divine commandments to follow, but they might try to emulate the heroes in the poems of Homer, or the characters in ancient stories that were being retold by their contemporary poets like Aeschylus, Sophocles, and Euripides.

Some four hundred years before the time of Jesus, a series of Greek philosophers offered a different answer: Right choices are guided by reason. Socrates seems to have originated this movement in Athens, raising hard questions for his pupils, and for the rest of the Athenians, by pointing out that they did not really know what they meant by key ideas like truth, goodness, or justice. Plato, a student and follower of Socrates, wrote out dialogues that recalled his teacher's way of asking questions, but Plato also argued that reason could supply the answers. Reason is what enables us to recognize what is really real, as distinct from desires and illusions, so that those who are guided by reason will make their choices in accordance with reality.

A third key figure in this development was Aristotle, who wrote what was perhaps Western civilization's first systematic treatise on ethics. Aristotle suggested that rational decisions about action begin by identifying the purpose or goal (*telos*) at which we are aiming. Everything in nature has a natural direction, from rocks, which fall downward—never sideways or upwards—when released, to oak trees, which pursue their goal as they grow from acorns, to animals, which follow very complex patterns of behavior to achieve their goals of survival, mating, and rearing their young. What distinguishes human beings in this goal-oriented world of nature is that they use reason to identify their goals. Animals just do what they do, but human beings have to think about their choices. They can inquire into what makes a good person or a good life and direct their actions to that end.

Ordinary people think about goals all the time. A navigator asks what makes for a good voyage, or an athletic trainer asks what makes for good physical conditioning. The philosopher, however, asks what makes a good person. What goal does a person aim at, not to accomplish some particular thing, but to live life as it ought to be lived? For the Greek philosophers, this is the first question of ethics.[3]

ETHICS AND MORALS

Our English word *ethics* comes from the Greek word *ēthos*, which means the customs by which a people guide their behavior. The ancient Greeks used a number of different words for what we would call "ethics," including some that we might today translate as "politics," since they considered the ways that communities seek a good life as part of the same subject as the study of the good life for individuals. In Latin translation, *ēthos* could be rendered *"mos,"* or *"mores"* (pl.), which gives us our English word *morals*. Modern writers sometimes make a distinction between *ethics*, as critical thinking about a way of life, and *morals*, as the ordinary beliefs that people hold about right and wrong before they get around to thinking critically. This is, however, an artificial distinction. *Ethics* and *morals* are interchangeable terms, distinguished only by their respective Greek and Latin origins.

Ethics also happens to be a singular noun that ends in *s*—like *physics* or *economics*. So we should usually say, "Ethics is" rather than, "Ethics are..."

Aristotle suggests a number of possibilities as the goal of the good life, including pleasure and honor, both of which were very important to the aristocratic Greek men who were the students at Aristotle's lectures on ethics. It probably would not have occurred to him to include relationship to God, or piety, as a candidate for the most important goal. Religious rituals and reverence for the gods mattered to the Greeks, but were hardly central to their lives in the way that Jesus regarded love of God as central.

Aristotle concludes that all of the obvious goals have their limitations. For one thing, most people fail to see the difference between what they want as a means to something else and what they want because it is good in itself. People spend a lot of time pursuing money, success, or power because these things seem to be part of the life they want, and they are hard to get. But it turns out that most of those obvious goals are not things that we really want for themselves. We want them because we believe that they will give us something else. There is, however, one thing that all people seek, and they seek it for its own sake. That goal is happiness.[4]

HEBREW PROPHETS, GREEK PHILOSOPHERS, AND THE BEGINNINGS OF CHRISTIANITY

ca. 1000 BCE	Beginning of the Kingdom of Israel
ca. 800–700 BCE	Writings of Homer; the beginning of Greek culture
ca. 800–500 BCE	Major writings of the Hebrew prophets
ca. 450 BCE	Beginning of Greek ethics
	Socrates (469–399 BCE)
	Plato (428–348 BCE)
	Aristotle (384–322 BCE)
ca. 200 BCE– 200 CE	Development and spread of Stoic, Epicurean, and Neoplatonist Philosophy
30 CE–100 CE	Teaching of Jesus and spread of Christianity

Eudaimonia

Aristotle's word, actually, is *eudaimonia*, and happiness is perhaps too weak a translation for it. Happiness sometimes suggests little more than a momentary feeling of pleasure or satisfaction. For Aristotle, *eudaimonia* is a long-term achievement that involves not merely feeling good, but actually living well. Some modern scholars translate *eudaimonia* as "well-being" or "flourishing." *Eudaimonia* also involves sustaining that kind of happiness over the course of a lifetime. Ethics, then, for these Greek philosophers, is thinking critically about their society's ideas of happiness, determining what happiness really is and how to achieve it in a lasting way.

Notice that Aristotle does not make the sharp distinction that we sometimes make between *moral* goodness and other good qualities. The good, *to kalon*, is also the noble and the beautiful, and *arete*, virtue, is the same word that the Greeks would use for any kind of human excellence, the courage of a soldier, the skill of a musician, or the strength of an athlete.

Another difference between Aristotle's understanding of ethics and ours is that when we think of ethics today, we often think of questions about what a specific person should do in a specific situation: Should I report a fellow student who cheats on an exam? If Mary finds a large sum of money, how hard does she have to work to find the rightful owner before she can claim it as her own? Should Carl ask an influential family friend, whom he does not really know, to write a recommendation for him? A popular column by *New York Times* writer Ariel Kaminer called "The Ethicist" answers readers' questions like these, and we might suppose that the study of ethics is just a long series of such questions and answers. But Aristotle seems to have assumed that most people already know these answers. The more important questions are about how these individual decisions, taken one at a time, fit together in a whole way of life. Once you understand the good life, *eudaimonia*, you will know why it is important to follow the rules that govern specific choices—do not lie, complete your assignments, fulfill your promises, and so on. When you get in the habit of making the right choices, you acquire the virtues that make you a good person.

Eudaimonia, then, is a particularly rich and long-lasting kind of happiness. It is the satisfaction of knowing that you have given your best effort, and that you have made those efforts using your highest and best abilities. You have made the best use of your opportunities and developed your human capacities and talents to their fullest. *Eudaimonia* is not the happiness of a day off with friends that perhaps includes winning a mildly challenging game of tennis. Think, instead, of the happiness of a math whiz in the midst of acing a calculus test.

Now, imagine that satisfaction extended over a whole lifetime. Not a lifetime of calculus tests, mind you, but a life in which you have done well on a whole variety of challenges by meeting each of them with careful thought, real ability, and courageous effort. Your life goes well because you have made thoughtful, reasoned choices at every point and thus lived a complete and balanced life. Other people who consider your life share your satisfaction in it, and they recognize in you someone they can look to for an example and guide. You enjoy health, wealth, and respect, not because you seek them for themselves, but because you live the kind of life that brings those good things along with it.

Was Aristotle right that *eudaimonia* is what everyone is seeking? He knew perfectly well that many of the people around him did not appear to be making these sorts of choices. They were pursuing short-term pleasures and trying to figure out how to avoid the consequences, or they did not know themselves well enough to understand their own highest and best abilities. It takes a while to figure out what happiness really is, and it may take even longer to acquire the understanding and self-discipline to put yourself in secure possession of it. Even after you have it, there is always a risk of losing it through a bad choice or bad luck. Aristotle warns us that young people are not always ready for the study of ethics; and at one point, he wonders whether we can call anyone happy while he is still alive.[5] *Eudaimonia* is the achievement of a lifetime, and although everyone wants it, it is difficult to acquire and difficult to hold on to once you have it.

Aristotle was also aware that many people are simply not situated to achieve happiness in this full sense. Women and slaves cannot exercise their highest and best abilities, because they have to do what other people tell them to do. People who have to work for a living and lack the wealth to pursue their interests and abilities are unlikely to be happy. Foreigners have difficulty living fully developed lives, because they are ineligible to participate in the political activities that lead to honor and public recognition. (Interestingly, Aristotle himself was a foreigner in Athens, since he came from Macedonia.) Even among free male citizens with some means and the leisure to pursue *eudaimonia*, there will be those who are sick, or a little slow-witted, or just too ugly to achieve real happiness. By the time all these disqualifications are considered, Aristotle's ethics must have been written with a very small part of the Athenian population in mind as its audience. But Aristotle does not seem to be particularly concerned with these problems. His idea of justice has to do with treating everyone appropriately with regard to rank and place in society, and he assumes that the way that ranks and places are assigned in traditional Greek society is, for the most part, just fine.

Nevertheless, Aristotle does think about society and how it should be organized. Many times, when we would use the word *ethics* for the subject matter Aristotle is discussing, the underlying Greek word is closer to *politics* or *political science*. Unlike people today who think that politics is a matter of keeping government and society from interfering with the pursuit of happiness, Aristotle argued that the conditions that make happiness possible have to be sustained by politics. It may be true that only a few people really have possibilities for happiness, but none of them is going to achieve it alone. To be happy, people require the opportunities and security that only an organized community can provide. Besides, if happiness is about using your best abilities at their highest level, that really is not possible if you are always working for your own advancement and only thinking about how to stay ahead of the competition. Our most important skills come into play, Aristotle believed, when we are working for the good of the whole community.

Aristotle and Christian Ethics

Aristotle's systematic treatment of ethics asks questions that are still important today. But does it provide a point of connection with Christian ethics? Or is ancient Greek society so different from our own and is its conception of happiness so alien to Christianity that Aristotle's ethics and the philosophical systems descended from it are engaged in an entirely different task? If these two ways of critical reflection are connected, we might think of Christian ethics as a distinctive set of answers to questions that others are asking, too. If Aristotle's reasoned pursuit of happiness is alien to Christian thought, then Christian ethics may have little or nothing in common with the ways that other people think about ethics, and critical reflection on the Christian way of life will have to proceed on its own, entirely different terms.

Both answers have been given in the course of history and in contemporary Christian thought. We will consider some of them in the next two chapters, and you will probably still be asking yourself these questions when you come to the end of this book. A tentative assessment, however, would be that Aristotle and the philosophers who have built on his work provide us with a framework for understanding questions that people are still asking today. It makes sense to say that happiness, rather than pleasure, fame, or wealth, is what everyone seeks as the goal of life. It makes even more sense to say that when we reflect critically on the idea of happiness, we come up with something like Aristotle's idea of what true happiness is. We want to use our best abilities at the highest level we can, and we want to sustain that pattern of activity through a whole lifetime of balanced achievements, so that when we enjoy rewards, recognition, and success, these are not just momentary pleasures or lucky accidents, but the side-effects of a life well lived. This seems to be something we learn not only from the pages of Aristotle, but also from the people around us who are trying to live a good life and who achieve it, at least occasionally.

We may raise questions about the fairness of Aristotle's society and ask whether a system in which opportunities for happiness are distributed so unevenly can be a model for us in any way. It will be worthwhile to ask as we go along whether these questions about fairness come chiefly from the modern, democratic idea that everybody should have equal opportunity, or from the Christian idea that everyone is equally a child of God and created in God's image. Or perhaps, as liberation theologians suggest, we learn quite different things about what happiness means and what a good life is when we pay attention to the experiences of people who have been excluded from the kind of opportunities on which Aristotle's good life depends. We will consider those questions further in later chapters.

We can expect, however, that most people will want something like the happiness that Aristotle described and that most Christians will see that as part of their aspirations, too. People generally will want to live in a society that provides opportunities for that kind of happiness and allows them to feel secure in whatever measure of happiness they have been able to achieve. Christians will be able to engage with others in thinking about how to bring about the opportunities and security that happiness requires.

That is not to say that Christians will find that a shared interest in happiness, opportunity, and security covers everything that is involved in loving God and your neighbor, or that they will agree with everything they hear in discussions of ethics that begin from other starting points. But our brief examination of Aristotle's ethics suggests at least that questions about the good life and the good society are of general human interest. Those questions and their answers are part of Christian ethics, too.

Other Questions, Other Philosophers

Aristotle's philosophical ethics is a fairly complete guide to making moral decisions, but there are other things that we want to know about a good life that Aristotle does not tell us. For example, why is it that happiness is so easily lost, and why is it that people who lead good lives nevertheless suffer from illness, or accidents, or the loss of people who are close to them? Can I protect myself from those threats to happiness, and is there any kind of happiness that is not so vulnerable to these losses? What becomes of the good I have achieved, if I lose it to bad luck or bad choices? Why is it that doing the right thing sometimes seems to lead to no results at all? Does my effort to live a good life make a difference to God, or to humanity in general, or is the meaning of my pursuit of happiness confined to myself and the other people who pursue it with me? If happiness is the achievement of a lifetime, what happens to it after my death?

Other writers paid more attention to these problems than Aristotle did, and we might say that in the centuries between Aristotle and the spread of Christianity, these became the most important questions of ethics. How can you know how to live a good life, people asked, unless you know what is truly real and lasting? How can you expect to sustain happiness over the course of a lifetime, unless you understand how your life fits into this larger reality?

Plato, the pupil of Socrates who was also the teacher of Aristotle, put more emphasis on contemplation of true reality as the only reliable source of happiness. Reason is important not only for determining goals and making right decisions, but for grasping the truth; and if reason has its proper role in guiding our lives, doing the right thing follows directly from knowing the truth. Like other Greek writers, Plato emphasized four virtues—prudence, courage, temperance (self-control), and justice[6]—which he organized systematically by saying that temperance should rule the part of us that is concerned with desire, courage the part that defends our lives, homes, and families, and prudence the part of us that uses reason. Justice, in turn, organizes life as a whole by making sure that each of the other virtues occupies its proper place.

True happiness, for Plato, is the result of this kind of balanced, reasoned life. But Plato is more clear than Aristotle that happiness endures, despite bad luck and ill health and other unfortunate circumstances. As long as reason keeps us aware of the unchanging realities, we are not vulnerable to the changing fortunes that threaten human life. In the end, this conviction that sure happiness was connected with true knowledge depended on Plato's conviction that the rational part of the person is immortal, distinct from the body and not subject to the pains and losses that occur in the world of changing things.

During the early centuries of Christianity, this Platonic philosophy became a highly developed understanding of the soul and its relation to unchanging realities in the heavens, distant from the changing world of sense experience. Neoplatonism, which grew from the work of the philosopher Plotinus (204–270 CE) and his disciple, Porphyry, offered a complete understanding of how the material world comes into existence and mirrors the ordered beauty of the world of ideas.[7] With this grasp of true reality, the aim of life becomes more than good decisions that lead to happiness. Through disciplined meditation, the soul can actually regain its place amid the unchanging realities. Neoplatonism was an important influence on Christian theology and provided a channel through which many of Plato's ideas found their way into later thinking about ethics.

Tragedians, Epicureans, Cynics, and Stoics

Plato's contemporaries seem to have been less confident that reason and contemplation could provide security against the loss of happiness. The tragedies of Aeschylus, Sophocles, and Euripides provided a dramatic retelling of old stories that were part of the traditions of Greek culture, but they also gave the Athenians a chilling reminder of how good lives could be undone by hidden flaws in a noble character or by ironic twists of fate. Oedipus uses courage to save a city and becomes its king, but he unwittingly kills his father and marries his own mother. Medea murders her children in a jealous rage. What contemplation of eternal reality could possibly restore happiness to such a life? Tragedy is always lurking in the background in Greek ethics, threatening to destroy a good life that depends on luck as much as it does on reason.[8]

A different approach was taken by the Epicureans, who took their starting point from the work of the philosopher Epicurus (341–270 BCE). Epicurus was what modern philosophers would call a "materialist." He believed that reality consists of small atoms of matter. The gods, if they exist, are powerless to affect these material realities. Ceaseless changes bring birth and death in an inevitable, endless succession. We have no more control over the endless years that will follow our death than we do over the time that was before our birth, and no more reason to regret the one than the other. The key to happiness, then, is a calm contentment that faces these inevitable losses without fear and does not give in to superstitious ideas about why these bad things happen or how they might be prevented. According to the Acts of the Apostles, Paul debated with Epicurean and Stoic philosophers when he carried his message of the resurrection of Jesus to Athens (Acts 17). The Epicureans, at least, would have found that idea quite implausible. The poet Lucretius (ca. 99–55

BCE) wrote a long poem, *On the Nature of Things*, which seems to combine an almost Platonic contemplation of natural reality with an Epicurean reminder that life is no more than atoms in motion, with no way for the soul to survive the dissolution of the body.[9]

Of all those who developed Aristotle's idea of ethics in these new ways, the most important for subsequent thought were the Stoics. While this large and varied group of thinkers dates back to Athens around 300 BCE, the surviving texts are all from later, Roman times. At the outset, Stoics and their predecessors, the Cynics, seem to have been countercultural figures, rejecting wealth and social conventions and living simple lives in accordance with nature. Diogenes the Cynic reputedly lived in Athens in a tub, and his biting wit directed at his more conventional neighbors is probably the origin of the modern meaning of *cynicism*. The early Stoics took up these ideas of simplicity and harmony with nature and developed a school of philosophy to teach them, taking their name from the *stoa*, or public colonnade, where they taught.

MAJOR SCHOOLS OF GREEK PHILOSOPHY

Neoplatonists developed Platonic ideas in the third century CE. Plotinus (204–270), his disciple Porphyry (232–305), and their followers believed that the good life is achieved when the soul reaches its proper place among unchanging realities through disciplined meditation.

Epicureans were influenced by the atomist philosophy of Democritus, and believed that happiness is found in enjoying the pleasures of this life. They believed that atoms are the basic substance of reality, including the soul. At death the atoms of the soul will be dispersed, so that the soul ceases to exist at death. Important thinkers include especially Epicurus (341–270 BCE) and Lucretius, who lived during the first century BCE.

Stoics believed the good life should be guided by reason, and they held the distinctive view that reason is equally present in all people. Important Stoic philosophers include Cicero (106–43 BCE), Seneca (4 BCE–65 CE), Epictetus (55–135), and Marcus Aurelius (121–180).

By Roman times, Stoic ideas about nature, character, and ethics were widely shared among educated lawyers and political leaders, as well as among philosophers. Stoics shared the conviction of all Greek philosophers that the good life must be guided by reason, but unlike most other philosophers, they believed that reason is equally present in all people. Since anyone can reason, and since reason is more important for leading a good life than any external circumstances, the Stoics believed that the opportunity for a good life was available to everyone. Stoic ideas can be found in the writings of Roman statesmen, including Cicero and Seneca, in the works of Epictetus, the former slave turned philosopher, and in the *Meditations* of a Roman emperor, Marcus Aurelius.

Stoic ideas of a life guided by reason drew on those four virtues of prudence, courage, self-control, and justice that were identified as particularly important by Plato. However, the Stoics tended to focus, as Aristotle did, on making decisions that would lead to a virtuous and contented life in the midst of everyday challenges, rather than on a Platonic contemplation of eternal truths. Stoics were also aware of the tragedies, accidents, and conflicts that could quickly bring an end to an Aristotelian life of virtuous enjoyment. We learn from history that both Cicero and Seneca met their deaths after they ended up on the wrong side in Roman political controversies. Other Stoic texts point out that unhappiness can result from longing for success and for the honors that were so essential to the good life of an Aristotelian aristocrat. The only sure defense against these disasters is not to rely on what other people can do *for* you, and not to fear what they can do *to* you. Events are often controlled by others, but how you respond is always under your own control. Epictetus summed up this Stoic wisdom in this way:

> What should we have ready at hand in a situation like this? The knowledge of what is mine and what is not mine, what I can and cannot do. I die. But must I die bawling? I must be put in chains—but moaning and groaning too? I must be exiled; but is there anything to keep me from going with a smile, calm and self-composed?
> "Tell us your secrets."
> "I refuse, as this is up to me."
> "I will put you in chains."
> "What's that you say, friend? It's only my leg you will chain, not even God can conquer my will."
> "I will throw you into prison."
> "Correction—it is my body you will throw there."
> "I will behead you."

"Well, when did I ever claim that mine was the only neck that couldn't be severed?"

That's the kind of attitude you need to cultivate if you would be a philosopher, the sort of sentiments you should write down every day and put in practice.[10]

Stoics generally rejected the Platonic and Neoplatonist idea that reason gives us access to a true reality that is separate from the world of change and decay, but they had a strong belief that reason is the connection between mind and nature. Because our minds give us access to reason and reason in turn gives order to nature, we are able to know true reality without needing to escape the world of nature to do it. If we allow our minds to be guided by reason, we can live in harmony with nature. Because everyone lives in the same nature and shares the same reason, there are some laws that everyone knows and everyone should live by, no matter how distant or different their cultures may be. The Stoics thus provided a starting point for the idea of "natural law," which became important in later Christian ethics.[11]

Stoic ideas had a particular resonance in the Greek-speaking Jewish community that grew in the city of Alexandria, in Egypt, two or three centuries before the time of Jesus. Here, the Hebrew Scriptures that would become the Christian Old Testament were translated into Greek, and Jewish scholars began to connect their ideas about God with the vocabulary of the Greek philosophers. Terms that the Greeks used for reason and for the order of nature could also be used for the wisdom by which God shaped creation. In Jewish thought, the link the Stoics made between the human mind and nature could become part of a three-way relationship between mind, nature, and God, all connected by reason. Even those four virtues of Plato and the Stoics made their way into Jewish writings like The Wisdom of Solomon. In this long discourse in praise of divine wisdom, God is unmistakably the God made known in the Hebrew Scriptures, the Creator of all things. Much of the moral advice in The Wisdom of Solomon, however, would have sounded very familiar to a Stoic.

If riches are a desirable possession in life,
what is richer than wisdom, the active cause of all things?
And if understanding is effective,
who more than she is fashioner of what exists?

And if anyone loves righteousness,
her labors are virtues;
for she teaches self-control and prudence,
justice and courage;
nothing in life is more profitable for mortals than these. (Wisdom of
Solomon 8:5-7)

Ethics, Then and Now

This brief survey of how the study of ethics developed from its beginnings in Greek philosophy reminds us that Christianity grew in a world that was already crowded with ideas about how to live a good life. There were many different ways to think about good and bad choices, and various ways of understanding how those choices relate to the world of nature or the purposes of God. All of these schools of ethics involved some criticism of common ideas about happiness. They warned people who spent their lives in pursuit of pleasure, wealth, or power that these things cannot provide the secure, lasting satisfaction that everyone is really seeking; but from that starting point, they moved in many directions to explain what a life that is worth living is really like. Stoics stressed self-control. Epicureans focused on enjoyment and moderation. Platonists praised contemplation, while Aristotelians sought a balanced life that avoided extremes.

The philosophers and religious teachers of that time did not shy away from hard questions about tragedy and failure, about the certainty of death, and about the meaning of the short span of human life in the vastness of time and space. Exactly how they understood the ultimate conditions under which we all have to live made all the difference in how they said we ought to live. If everything is atoms in motion and nothing remains of a person when life's activities cease, then the Epicureans had to say that we should enjoy things while they are happening and spend no time worrying about illusions of divine judgment or punishments after death. If goodness and truth are more real than any changing, material things and we have access to those realities through our reason, then the Platonists had to say that we should find satisfaction in thinking about the things that last and spend no time on the illusions that most people mistake for happiness.

All of these views are important for understanding Christian ethics, because they provided the background for early Christian thinking about what it meant to live as a follower of Jesus Christ in a world where God is bringing about a new creation. What the philosophers believed about the world and human life might lead them to think the Christians were admirable, or it might lead them to think that the Christians were delusional. What the Christians read in the philosophers was sometimes so different from their Christian ideas about God and the world that they rejected what those philosophers said about the good life with the same force that they rejected the worship of idols. But sometimes what they read was not so far from their own understanding of the truth, and sometimes it even provided words and ideas that could help to explain the Christian message.

This early history of ethics is important, too, because these ideas about the good life and about reality are still very much with us. People who today insist everything is reducible to the reality that science can measure and study often have much in common with the ancient Epicureans and their ideas about how we should live. What matters to these people are pleasures and pains that we can feel, and ideas that cannot be tested against material reality cannot give us a reason to decide one way or the other about a course of action. Others today are more like the Stoics, approaching life with calm detachment and trying to live in harmony with nature. Others seek the balanced life of achievement that Aristotle thought could sustain happiness over the course of a lifetime. Some people today still read and admire the works of the ancient philosophers, but their philosophies are also followed by many more who have only a vague notion of where the ideas they live by originated.

New ideas have been added over the centuries, of course. Some neuroscientists and evolutionary biologists now argue that the way morality developed from the beginning of human life can tell us how to think about the moral life today. For others, the modern worldview is more political. A commitment to democracy, which had few followers among the ancient philosophers, determines for some people not only how their society should be organized, but also how they should live their own lives. Still others follow a Marxist understanding of history and society, which sees the world in materialist terms, but sees it moving toward economic as well as political equality. Many of the religions which would have been known in the cities where Stoics, Epicureans, and Neoplatonists lived have disappeared, but Judaism remains, and it has been joined in the lands of the old Roman world not only by Christianity, but also by Islam. Buddhism and Hinduism are older than the story we are following here, and they, too, have made a place for themselves in the Western world in which Christianity grew.

As it was for the early church, so it is today. Christian thinking about ethics takes place against a background of other ways of asking and answering the same questions. Despite vast differences in these ways of thinking, most people who live in parts of the modern world shaped by this cultural history share enough in their thinking about how to live a good life to live together in peace, and even to encourage one another in their efforts. Still, the differences are real, and they sometimes lead to real conflict.

Stance

All of our thinking about how to live takes place against a background of these ideas about the whole of reality and our place in it. When we think about what makes a good choice or what makes a good life, we are usually focused on problems and possibilities that are immediately before us, but the larger ideas are always there for us, too, just as they have been from the beginning of the study of ethics. Religious ethics is particularly concerned with this connection between immediate questions and ultimate reality, including an understanding of how human life is related to God. "Within Judaism," as Louis E. Newman explains, "the moral life in its entirety is lived in the context of the covenantal relationship between the Jews and God. This means, at the very least, that all moral obligations are responsibilities, not only to other persons, but also to the God who created all people and who is the source of all value."[12] Given the close relationships between Judaism and Christianity, we should not be surprised that the Christian perspective on morality and ultimate reality is very similar, especially as it describes God as creator and as one to whom we can have responsibilities and relationships. Other religions and philosophies might formulate their own perspectives very differently. The point is that for each of them, core beliefs about reality and the human place in it provide the context for thinking about ethics and the moral life.

Christian thinkers have often described the relationship between Christian beliefs and ethics in this way. Protestant theologian James Gustafson says that Christianity provides an "orientation" or a "posture" toward the world.[13] Charles Curran, in his study of the Catholic moral tradition, calls this way of locating oneself in reality a "stance."[14] Curran's way of putting it is perhaps more vivid. "Stance" suggests a person who has taken a position that is prepared for action, like a tennis player waiting for an opponent's serve. Her stance is informed by everything she knows about the game and how it is played, but she is preparing to respond to the way the ball comes at her just now.

Stance, Curran says, "gives us the angle of vision from which we can put all the aspects of reality together and give some unity and order to what we see."[15] It is important to understand that a Christian stance is not simply a statement of belief, although it can be shaped by the words of scripture, liturgy, hymns, and creeds in which Christians express their faith in worship. It is rather a set of convictions that work together to guide action by giving us an idea of the whole reality in which that action takes place and pointing out what it is within that reality that is most valuable and important. A stance "must be broad enough to encompass all reality but narrow enough to provide some critical understanding of how all aspects of reality fit together."[16]

Stance is a modern idea, but it helps to explain how Christian ethics developed in the midst of the many different philosophies and religions in the ancient world where Christianity grew and spread. Christianity caught up all sorts of different people and different ways of life into its movement. By the late second century, Christians were making the point that they were largely indistinguishable from their neighbors in dress, manners, and customs.[17] What made Christians different was that they understood all of their decisions about how to live and what to do in light of what God had done in the life, death, and resurrection of Jesus Christ.

That stance is what distinguishes Christian ethics from all the other ways of thinking about ethics that were available in the world in which the early Christians lived. It is also what holds Christian ethics together today, in all its diversity and disagreement, and connects it to the history that leads back to the beginning of Christianity. It is now time to turn our attention to the Christian stance and see how it shaped the ethics of one of the most important early Christian thinkers.

Additional Reading

Bostock, David. *Aristotle's Ethics*. Oxford: Oxford University Press, 2000.

Coleman, Janet. *A History of Political Thought from Ancient Greece to Early Christianity*. Oxford: Blackwell Publishing, 2000.

Garver, Eugene. *Confronting Aristotle's Ethics: Ancient and Modern Morality*. Chicago: University of Chicago Press, 2006.

Irwin, Terence. *The Development of Ethics: Volume I. From Socrates to the Reformation*. Oxford: Oxford University Press, 2007.

MacIntyre, Alasdair. *A Short History of Ethics: A History of Moral Philosophy from the Homeric Age to the Twentieth Century*. 2nd ed. Notre Dame, IN: University of Notre Dame Press, 1998.

McDonald, J. Ian H. *The Crucible of Christian Morality*. London: Routledge, 1998.

Taylor, C. C. W. *Socrates: A Very Short Introduction*. Oxford: Oxford University Press, 2001.

CHAPTER TWO

THE GOOD LIFE AND THE CHRISTIAN LIFE

From the beginning, Christians have shared in the search for a good life that Aristotle regarded as the main object of ethics. For Christians, a distinctive understanding of God's relationship to humanity and history reshapes the Aristotelian idea of secure and lasting happiness around five key themes that we will call the Christian stance. The work of Augustine, bishop in the Roman city of Hippo, in North Africa, gives us an example of how Christian writers dealt with the resulting tension between the Christian life and the human search for the good life.

As we learned from Aristotle, ethics often begins by setting choices and goals in a larger context. Instead of seeking happiness in immediate pleasures and short-term success, a good person makes choices that sustain happiness over a whole lifetime. Most people share this Aristotelian search for a good life that will last, but there are very different ways of thinking about the world in which that search goes on. Stoics warned that those who enjoy the success and honors that human society can provide are staking their happiness on things they cannot control. They will live better lives if they avoid attachments to people and things and depend on the order of reason and nature, which does not vary from place to place and time to time. Epicureans, by contrast, figured that happiness depends on seizing the opportunities that we have and not worrying about what will happen when the temporary arrangement of matter that is our life dissolves. After reviewing several of these philosophies developed by Aristotle and his successors, we gave the name "stance" to those ways of orienting particular choices toward a larger framework of understanding.

The early Christians, too, had a stance that set their decisions in a larger context, but in their case, the framework was a narrative of God's dealings with humanity through the whole course of history. Understanding choices and goals thus required more than seeing an individual life as a whole, as Aristotle did. It required more, even, than seeing life as part of a natural order, as the Stoics and Epicureans did in their different ways. The whole of nature is God's creation, and the order in nature must be understood in relation to God's purposes. For the Christians, those purposes were known in a powerful way in the life of Jesus, but even his story was not yet the whole story. In Paul's account, as we have seen, Jesus was the beginning of a new creation, and Christians had to understand themselves as part of that order, too.[1]

It will be important to keep this stance in mind as we consider how Christian ethics has developed and the different forms it has taken. We will need a summary that is easy to remember, but also one that can encompass the diversity of Christian ethics through history. Our summary of the Christian stance must identify what Christians have in common, but it must also be complex enough to explain why they often differ among themselves.

Charles Curran summarizes the stance of Catholic moral theology with five key points in Christian teaching about God, humanity, and history.[2] These are big ideas, and each of them has received a variety of interpretations, even within the framework of Catholic theology. Cast the net more widely to include other Christian traditions and the range of ideas will be quite broad, and disagreements will be obvious. Nevertheless, these ideas are widely shared among Christians. Any account of the Christian faith must include all five of them, and they provide one way to identify what Christians have in common as well as what distinguishes them from other faiths. So in this book, we will use these five themes as a summary of the stance with which Christians approach their moral choices and decisions.

They are: creation, sin, incarnation, redemption, and resurrection destiny.

Understanding what these terms mean for Christian ethics requires some background in the Bible, history, and the traditions of the Christian faith. They are not just words we could look up in a dictionary and know their meaning. Christians learn them by a lifetime of using them in worship, reading, discussion, and prayer. Nevertheless, we can give a brief summary that will serve as a reminder, or as an introduction, to these elements of the Christian stance.

Creation sees the will of God as the beginning of all things. Christians believed that God created the world *ex nihilo*, out of nothing. This was very different from the belief of Neoplatonist philosophers that a divine power had formed the world out of eternal matter that was already there at the beginning of creation. It was also different from dualistic religions and philosophies that divided the world between a good power, often associated with mind or spirit, and an evil power, sometimes associated with the material world. Creation *ex nihilo* implies that everything comes from God, and because everything comes from God, everything is in some way good. We will see later in this chapter that this biblical understanding of creation was very important to Augustine, the bishop and theologian who argued that something completely evil, entirely opposed to God's creation, could not exist.

Because creation comes from God, Christians also concluded that the world is orderly and knowable by reason. Human life has a special place in creation because men and women are created "in the image of God" (Genesis 1:27). Human beings can be aware of the order God has created, and unlike other animals that know what to do by following their instincts, human beings must decide to participate in the created order, rather than struggling to escape it or trying to dominate it for their own purposes. Through the choices that women and men make, the order that is part of creation extends not just to the physical, natural world, but also into the world of human nature and conduct. As we will see, this perspective helped give rise to Christian ideas of *natural law* and to the belief that people who use their reason can discover this order and follow it. What makes a good person or a right action is not determined only by the goals and values of the people who are making the judgment. It is part of the order given in creation.

Remembering this part of the Christian stance helps build connections between those who share the Christian faith and those who do not. Because all persons share the image of God, all have some knowledge of this larger reality, and anyone may live well by living in accordance with this natural moral order.

Sin, by contrast, becomes the Christian's primary explanation for the way that evil enters the world. Creation suggests that everything which comes from God is good, but when people deny their relationship to God or try to live outside of it, they lose the goodness they should have as part of God's creation. They begin to seek what they want for themselves and ignore the good of their neighbors. So the things people do and the institutions they create become sources of new evils. Eventually, even nature itself can be changed and corrupted by human sin, so that it no longer provides the good things intended in God's creation.

It is very important for the Christian idea of sin that these effects cannot be easily reversed, as though people could just decide that they are going to do better next time. Once evil is introduced, the world is a different place. So Christians speak not only of sin, but also of the *Fall*, interpreting the story of Adam and Eve in Genesis as a reminder that the whole of human history has been cut off from the good intended in creation.

People who see the world from this perspective might be moralistic and censorious, prone to depressing examinations of their own faults and quick to condemn the failures of others. Today, even some Christians suggest that the idea of sin has outlived its usefulness to Christian faith.[3] But the understanding of sin in Christian theology as a whole takes a more balanced view. Sin and the Fall point to a human propensity to do wrong, but they also recall an original right relationship to God that can be a source of hope. Most important, sin and the Fall remind Christians that no one escapes these human limitations. Remembering that is supposed to make Christians into realists, not into judgmental critics. Their stance reminds them not to expect too much of others, not to trust too much in the wisdom of their leaders, and not to become too confident in their own righteousness.

Incarnation is God "being born in human likeness" (Philippians 2:7) in Jesus of Nazareth. Jesus, of course, was a great teacher whose wisdom, humility, and compassion have touched many people beyond just Christians. The idea of the incarnation, however, is more than a way of honoring Jesus. It is a statement about God's relationship to the world and to all of humanity. God's unique way of being present in Jesus resolves the ambiguity of the human condition after the Fall, for it demonstrates that God has not abandoned sinful humanity, but intends to reclaim them for that original right relationship to God for which they were created.

Incarnation is for Christians the decisive act of God in history, and it is the part of the Christian stance that is most distinctive to the Christian faith. At the same time, incarnation is so central to the Christian understanding of God's relationship to history and humanity that it reshapes the rest of the Christian stance. Because of incarnation, the other elements of the stance take on different meanings from those they have in the closely related faiths of Judaism and Islam, which have their own ideas about creation, sin, redemption, and resurrection destiny.

God's presence in Jesus explains why his teaching, recorded in the four Gospels, has a special authority for Christians, but other parts of the New Testament are less concerned with what Jesus did and taught than with what he reveals about God. In Jesus Christ, God takes the initiative to undo the effects of sin. Jesus' death by crucifixion marks not defeat, but the triumph of God's loving and reconciling purpose, and the Resurrection confirms that God did not abandon Jesus, or humanity, to the cross and death.

God's initiative remains decisive, whether or not people respond to it. We would expect those who know this to be changed by that knowledge and to live better lives because of it, but many theologians have insisted that such moral improvement is beside the point. Incarnation is a perspective on the world that sees that only God is capable of freeing humanity from the effects of sin and affirms that God has, in fact, chosen to do that in Jesus Christ.

Redemption puts God's decision for humanity into effect, transforming human lives and the world so that they once more become fit for the relationship with God that was intended in creation. In redemption, as in incarnation, it is God who takes the initiative. We sometimes tell a person who has failed a test or violated a trust that "you need to redeem yourself," but it is important to understand that in the Christian stance, God is the agent of redemption. The verb used for redemption in the New Testament refers literally to a transaction like ransoming a prisoner. That is not the sort of thing you can do for yourself.

That much is clear, but beyond that, redemption is one of the most debated concepts in Christian thought. Redemption is God's action, but does it require our cooperation? Does it happen only to individuals, or are whole societies and perhaps even nature itself involved in the process of redemption? Does redemption happen gradually in ways that can be seen over time, or do the effects of sin just continue to get worse until God brings about a final, climactic judgment? Christians have tried again and again to reduce redemption to a series of understandable steps, but they have never found one account on which they could all agree. Redemption defies simple formulations. It is God's action, but human beings are involved in its completion. It happens to each individual, maybe even beginning at a specific point in life that a person can identify, and yet it is something that is always already happening to the whole creation.

Whatever account of redemption a Christian holds, those beliefs profoundly shape his or her perspective on the world. Some Christians see redemption in every sign of change and progress, so that events promise much more than a mere recitation of the facts would suggest. Redemption allows these Christians to apply the certainty of God's promise to the changes of history, and they find signs of reconciliation between God and humanity in events. Other Christians interpret redemption in a way that withholds hope in anticipation of final judgment, so that it is only when things get really bad that redemption seems near at hand. Most Christians see redemption in terms somewhere in between these extremes, but however they think about it, redemption changes their expectations and gives them a hope that transcends what the facts alone predict.

Resurrection destiny completes the Christian understanding of God's relationship to humanity and history that begins with creation. Taken by itself, resurrection is the conclusion to the story of Jesus that begins with the incarnation. Jesus' life does not end with his death on the cross. It continues in a resurrected life witnessed by his disciples. Resurrection, however, is more than a statement about how Jesus' life ends, just as incarnation is more than a statement about his birth. For Paul and other New Testament writers, Jesus' resurrection marks the beginning of the new creation. It is the lens through which Christians view their expectations for the future as well as their understanding of the past. Resurrection begins with Jesus, but it comes to completion only at the end of history.

For the Hebrew prophets, the end of history was connected with the Reign of God, a restored kingdom in which justice and right judgment would replace the corrupt and unfaithful rulers who had brought disaster upon God's people. In Mark's Gospel, Jesus begins his ministry by announcing that this Reign of God has come near (Mark 1:15). But the early church quickly concluded that this Reign of God should not be confused with a new version of ordinary political power, any more than the resurrected body could be confused with a physical one (1 Corinthians 15:35-58). The Reign of God is already present where Jesus' resurrection shows that justice and right judgment prevail over all attempts to subvert the order of God's creation. Resurrection destiny assures Christians that moral choices remain meaningful, even when they are not successful. Those who see history in this way cannot acquiesce to a tragic view of life, in which good people are destroyed by events that bring their lives to a meaningless end. Resurrection destiny reminds Christians that the whole of history, from beginning to end, the world and everything in it, serves the purpose for which God created it.

Augustine

This understanding of God's relationship to humanity and history has been part of Christianity from the beginning. Concepts develop, language varies over time, and Christians argue over interpretations, but the Christian stance provides a way to understand how Christians generally think about human life as they approach the questions of ethics. It also raises a new issue about how to relate Christian ethics to other ways of thinking about humanity and history. We have been treating the questions of ethics as shared questions, problems that all people face in their effort to lead a good life. But do the questions of ethics really remain the same when they are approached from different stances? Perhaps the frameworks of understanding are so different that the good life and the Christian life have nothing in common. If it is true, as Aristotle thought, that the search for the good life culminates in a political understanding of how citizens can pursue good lives together, how is that possible when the citizens have different stances?

Conflict between Christians and the wider society made this question urgent in the early years of Christianity. Periodic efforts by Roman officials to suppress the new religion kept Christians aware that martyrdom was a real possibility, and even when there was no active persecution, there was the hostility that people always meet when they belong to a religion that is seen as different or subversive. Christians were often on trial, figuratively or actually, and their leaders warned them that they should expect to suffer for their faith. Still, other writers tell us that Christians were admired for the good things they did, and the letters of Paul that they had begun to read as scriptures in their churches told them to obey the governing authorities, precisely because those authorities hold power from God to reward good and punish evil (Romans 13:1-7).

As Christianity spread more widely and Christians became more numerous, the bishops who led their churches became public figures in the major cities, and some Christian teachers became widely known, like the Greek philosophers of earlier times. But the increasing acceptance, even popularity, of Christianity in cities like Alexandria led other Christians to go into the desert, where they could live lives of poverty and self-denial, far from the temptations of what most people thought of as the good life. From these origins grew the monastic communities of men and women which became a prominent part of Christianity in the Middle Ages and which continue everywhere Christianity is found to this day.

Christians, then, have been divided over whether their faith permits them to participate in the cities where they live and share in the good things those societies provide, or whether it requires them to isolate themselves and carefully avoid what counts as good for other people. Is the Christian life similar to, partly overlapping with, or completely different from other people's ideas of the good life? Those who share the Christian stance have found in it different answers to this question.

This has been true almost from the beginning of Christian history, and it did not change very much when Constantine became the first Christian emperor early in the fourth century. Of course, Christian churches and their bishops could now play a more prominent public role, and the attitude of the authorities gradually shifted from hostility to approval. Still, those who held to the old religions and philosophies doubted that Christians could ever be full participants in Roman civic life, and Christians continued to head for the deserts and the monasteries in large numbers. The relationship between the good life and the Christian life continued to be a question, even in a society that was increasingly led by Christian rulers and guided by Christian clergy.

One of the most important Christian leaders to consider this question was Augustine, Bishop of Hippo. Augustine was born in Roman North Africa in 354, in Thagaste, a small city located in what is now Algeria. Like other Christians of his time, he grew up in a very complex social world. Christians now enjoyed official favor, but they were sharply divided among themselves into different churches, following conflicting theological interpretations and led by rival bishops. Many people, especially in the ancient city of Rome, lamented the loss of the old religion and blamed Christians for the weakness of the empire, which was increasingly beset by barbarian invaders who would set up their own kingdoms in what later became Germany, France, Italy, and Spain. By the time Augustine was well established in his career as a bishop, in 410, the barbarians actually took the city of Rome itself, and by the time of his death in 430, they were at the gates of Hippo. To add to the confusion, many of the barbarians were themselves Christians, though often they were from a different group and were regarded as heretics by the Roman Christians whose territory they were invading.

Despite these increasingly unsettled conditions, Augustine received a good education and enjoyed a very successful career, arriving by 384 in Milan, the administrative center of the Western Roman Empire, where he became an influential teacher of rhetoric. Positions like his were often steppingstones to high political office, but this son of a Christian mother and a pagan father was deeply interested in philosophy and religion. For a time, he was a follower of Manichaeism, a new religion which, like Christianity, was spreading rapidly through the Roman world. Manichean teachers practiced strict asceticism and viewed the world as a scene of conflict between good, spiritual powers and the evil powers of material reality. They explained their doctrines as a more complete, more spiritual version of what Jesus had taught, and it appears that Augustine was impressed by the contrast between the philosophical refinement of Manichaeism and what he then regarded as the crudeness of the texts in the Christian Bible.[4]

Augustine became increasingly devoted to his philosophical and religious studies. Through his mother, Monica, he also came into contact with Ambrose, the learned and politically powerful bishop of Milan. Under these influences, Augustine began to see Christianity as a more effective answer to his own moral failings and a more adequate explanation of the evil in the world. In 387 he received Christian baptism, quit his teaching position, and shortly thereafter returned to Africa. There he became a priest and then bishop in the city of Hippo, not far from where he was born.

AUGUSTINE OF HIPPO	
354	Born at Thagaste in North Africa
373–380	Follower of Manichaeism
374–383	Teacher of rhetoric at Carthage
384	Assumes teaching position in rhetoric and philosophy in Milan
386	Converts to Christianity
387	Baptized at Milan
391	Ordained priest at Hippo
396	Becomes Bishop of Hippo
430	Dies at Hippo

The former teacher of rhetoric became a popular preacher, and his writings vigorously defended the Christian faith he had previously criticized. Among the elements of the Christian stance we have outlined, creation became particularly important to Augustine. The Manichean idea of a perpetual conflict between good and evil no longer made sense to him in light of his Christian conviction that God had created all things out of nothing. Everything that God made must have been good at its beginning, and for Augustine, everything in creation retains at least some of that goodness, no matter how reduced or distorted. Otherwise, it could not exist at all.[5]

The evil in the world, in Augustine's interpretation of the Christian stance, is not part of God's creation. It is primarily the result of human sin. In contrast to philosophers who argued that rational human beings could always make the right choices, Augustine insisted that sinful people often choose what they know is wrong. These choices distort both human lives and the good creation. They make it impossible for people to relate to God as they should. Sin requires incarnation and redemption to restore human life and bring history to the conclusion God intends.

We might expect sharp differences between Augustine, the Christian bishop, and the other religions and schools of philosophy that were so much a part of the world in which he lived. What, then, does Augustine say about ethics? Is it true, as the philosophers taught, that everyone seeks lasting happiness, or were they wrong about that, too? If it is true, how should we think about that search in light of the Christian stance? What about Aristotle's idea that politics concerns the way that people organize communities around this shared search for happiness? Augustine's answers are somewhat surprising. He accepts the philosophers' idea that everyone seeks happiness, and he agrees that many of the things they want as part of that happiness are good. Loving families, secure homes, important ideas, and friends with whom to discuss faith and philosophy are all good things. So are many of the other pleasures that seem to be part of a happy life. The problem with happiness is not that the world is full of bad things that people want. The problem is the same one that many Greek philosophers and poets who came after Aristotle also noticed: The good things that people think essential to happiness are so easily lost.

Of course, the Stoics thought we could solve that problem by taking control of our attitude toward our losses. If we have to go into exile or suffer imprisonment, we can do it "with a smile, calm and self-composed," as Epictetus says.[6] But Augustine was an acute observer of human psychology, as well as a theologian. He noticed that the most unhappy people are often those who seem to have everything they could want. Other people, by contrast, suffer the actual experience of illness or loss with surprisingly good spirits. Augustine concluded from this that happiness has less to do with the actual experience of life than with anxiety about what might happen. What makes us unhappy is not just the loss of good things, but the fear that we might lose them. It is the possibility of exile and prison that clouds our happiness, even when we are sitting at home in freedom. Perhaps, then, Aristotle was right in quoting the saying that we cannot call someone happy until that person is dead. Then, at least, the risk of loss is safely past. Or perhaps people can be happy in prison or exile because at that point they have nothing else to lose. That would, however, be an odd kind of happiness to seek.

Augustine followed this insight in a way that set his understanding of the Christian life apart from other accounts of the good life available in his day. Philosophers might develop their ideas about which good things in what combinations provide the key to happiness, but Augustine saw that the search for happiness on those terms is self-defeating. Whatever we think will make us happy ends up making us unhappy, because we fear we might lose it.

Anything that could make anxious humanity truly happy would have to meet two conditions. First, it would have to be a good that is higher and more complete than any other. To know that we had found this good, we would have to be sure that there was nothing better and nothing missing that we might still require to be happy. But if there were something so good that it could make us truly and completely happy, we would immediately start to fear the loss of it. Hence the second condition: This good would have to be something that cannot be lost, unless a person deliberately throws it away.[7] Anyone should be able to figure out these two conditions, Augustine argued, by paying attention to the way people really experience happiness and unhappiness. But the only good thing that fits this description is not so easily gained by reason alone. It is the relationship to God known by Christian faith.

In this way, Augustine both establishes a connection between the good life and the Christian life and sets some distance between them. He accepts the questions that everyone is asking about what makes for a really good human life. He even agrees that lasting happiness based on the highest good we know is a pretty good description of what it is that everyone is seeking. But once Augustine has analyzed the requirements that are set by the search for the human good, it is the Christian stance that provides his understanding of God, who alone satisfies those requirements. The God who is present in Jesus Christ is both creator and redeemer, and for Christians, God's action in history and the search for human happiness both end in resurrection destiny.

The Two Cities

Just how Christians go about living this life in a world where others seek happiness in other ways occupied much of Augustine's attention over his long career, and he thought about it in different ways at different times. Two approaches can be found in his greatest work, *City of God*, which he wrote between 413 and 426 to answer those who held Christians responsible for the decline of Roman power. In the course of the book, which traces a Christian view of history from creation to resurrection destiny, Augustine criticizes the other religions and schools of philosophy known in his day and explains how Christians should relate to these other ways of living that they see around them all the time.

One approach echoes those early teachers who fled the growing comfort of Christian life in the cities to live a life of devotion and self-denial in the desert. As Christianity became an accepted and powerful influence in the Roman world, this ascetic movement continued to grow, and organized monasteries for men and women replaced the solitary dwellings of the early hermits. Augustine himself was attracted to this way of life, and although he continued in his active, public role as a bishop, he organized the clergy under his care into a kind of monastic community. This separation from the world and from the things that other people seek becomes part of his ideal for all Christians, and it helps to explain the contrast between the city of God and the human city that is central to his book. "Two cities, then, have been created by two loves: that is, the earthly by love of self extending even to contempt of God, and the heavenly by love of God extending to contempt of self."[8]

Augustine sees the whole of human history in light of the Christian stance, but in this aspect of his work, he emphasizes sin and the fallen world of human society, where many people have, indeed, deliberately rejected that relationship to God on which true happiness depends. Augustine warns Christians not to be too sure of themselves on this point, since it is possible that some who are now part of the earthly city will repent and be part of the heavenly city in the end, while others who are in the church at the moment will turn away from the faith and join the earthly city in time to share its final condemnation. Christians should not be smug about which side of the line they are on, but the line itself is real. Christians thus live in a kind of wary watchfulness, knowing that sin has mixed them up with the citizens of the earthly city until the final judgment makes the differences between them evident. Meanwhile, there is really nothing that they share except the space in which they find themselves, for the time being, all mixed up together.

Those in the earthly city love all kinds of different things. All of these things are perishable, and they are so different from one another that people find themselves confused by conflicting loves—love of family gets in the way of love of success; love of country conflicts with love of peace, and so on. Faced with these competing loves, Augustine sometimes relies on a distinction that he made in his early writings between *loving* things and *using* them. The contempt that Christians bear toward themselves in order to love God must extend to the things they might seek for their own satisfaction. Christians cannot get along entirely without the goods that other people seek, but they must be careful not to undermine the love for God in which true happiness depends. "God alone, therefore, should be loved, but this whole world, that is, all sensible things, should be held in contempt. We must, however, use them for the needs of this life."[9]

One way to think about the moral life in Christian terms, then, is to see it as a process of separation and distinction that mirrors the separation of the two cities. Despite some common vocabulary about virtue and happiness, the goal of the Christian life is so different from the goals that people seek in a confused, fallen, and sinful world that it is impossible that these two ways of life could have anything in common.

We see this separation and distinction most clearly in politics. For Aristotle, politics was an essential part of the good life, in which people seeking their own good share in creating the conditions that make this pursuit possible. For the Stoics, the virtues that make an individual a good person were also essential to good leadership. Rome liked to think of itself as a "commonwealth," where citizens live together in peace because they have a patriotic devotion to the society they all share. In all these cases, the individual good finds fulfillment in a larger whole. For Augustine, however, this political unity was an illusion. People who are seeking their own good will inevitably be divided and competing with one another. The only true commonwealth would be one in which people were united by a common love for God, the one good in which they all could share. The only true commonwealth, it seems, is the heavenly city itself.[10]

Meanwhile, in the earthly city, people relate to one another in search of mutual advantage and strive to get the best of one another when they can. Because they really have nothing in common, disagreements are frequent, and peace can be kept only by force. Political responsibility is a heavy burden, and good people take it up only because they see that there is no other way to prevent even worse evils. Augustine expects Christians to share the burden of politics, too, but certainly not because they see it as the way that a community seeks the good life together. The Christian who agrees to sit in the judge's seat prays, "From my necessities deliver Thou me."[11]

AUGUSTINE'S MAJOR WORKS	
388	*The Catholic Way of Life and the Manichean Way of Life* (often known as *On the Morals of the Catholic Church*)
397–400	*Confessions*
413–426	*City of God*

God, Self, and Neighbor

There is another side to Augustine's thinking on these questions, however. While he sometimes sees the world divided into two cities separated by sin, a world in which Christians dare not love anything but God alone, he also sees the world as God's creation, inhabited by neighbors whom Jesus said that we should also love. From this point of view, the good things that people seek are truly good, because they are part of God's creation.

> God, therefore, is the most wise Creator and just Ordainer of all natures, Who has established the mortal human race as the greatest adornment of things earthly, and Who has given to men certain good things appropriate to this life. These are: temporal peace in proportion to the short span of a mortal life, consisting in bodily health and soundness, and the society of one's own kind; and all things necessary for the preservation and recovery of this peace.[12]

We must use these things because they are necessary to life, but when Augustine is thinking in terms of creation, he does not equate using things with holding them in contempt. Using them means understanding how they are related to God's creation as well as how they satisfy human desires. The conflicts between goods that confuse people who are pursuing them only for their own purposes largely disappear when things are seen as good in relation to God. Understanding how things are good in relation to God also shows us how to relate them to one another and how to use them so that we attain our own highest good.

And these things are given under a most fair condition: that every mortal who makes right use of these goods suited to the peace of mortal men shall receive ampler and better goods, namely the peace of immortality and the glory and honour appropriate to it, in an eternal life made fit for the enjoyment of God and of one's neighbour in God. He who uses temporal goods ill, however, shall lose them, and shall not receive eternal goods either.[13]

The good things of this life thus have a place in redemption that challenges the self-centered pursuits of the earthly city, but it also challenges Augustine's own idea that love for God requires contempt for these things and contempt for self. God, who is to be loved above all things, loves the human creation, and when Jesus commanded his disciples to love God, he also commanded them to love their neighbors as they love themselves.[14] It is hard to see how people who have contempt for themselves and for anything that their neighbors might enjoy could fulfill this commandment. Loving the neighbor does not mean wanting for the neighbor exactly what the neighbor wants, but it surely requires wanting for the neighbor and for oneself those things that God has created for human good. Augustine draws the conclusion: "In these precepts, a man finds three things which he is to love: God, himself, and his neighbour; for a man who loves God does not err in loving himself."[15]

The wary watchfulness that sometimes marks Augustine's attitude toward the sinful world around him gives way here to a genuine love for others and a sense that the good things of this life are part of God's larger purposes in creation and redemption. Love for God shows Christians how to love themselves and their neighbors in the right way, and this in turn gives a certain freedom. For someone who truly loves God, one "short precept" contains all that needs to be said: "Love, and do what you want."[16]

Those who love God, their neighbors, and themselves in this way will also love the society in which they live, as Augustine's references to temporal peace suggest. Although he recognizes that everyone is not yet united in the love of God that, for him, defines a true commonwealth, there are values that Christians share in common with their neighbors. Especially, they value the things that enable them to live together in a peaceful, orderly society. So he is willing in some sense to call the Roman world in which he lives a "commonwealth" that Christians share with their neighbors. The Roman claims to have created a true commonwealth are pretentious, just as the complaints that Christians have spoiled this commonwealth are false. But in another sense, it is true that all the societies that people through history have built together have been commonwealths. Christians may live in any of these places, Augustine says, just as the Bible says that exiles from Jerusalem once lived in Babylon. They are not at home there, but they pray for the peace of the community where they live, and they share its burdens. It is not the city of God, but for the time being, it is their city, too, and its peace is their peace.[17]

Augustine's Influence

Augustine's work was important for the shaping of Christian ethics. He lived at a crucial time in Christian history, especially for the church in Western Europe, which would eventually give us the forms of Catholic and Protestant thought that are still familiar today. Just as Aristotle gives us the first systematic treatise on ethics, Augustine sets the direction for Western Christian ethics, beginning with his first criticisms of the moral teachings of the Manicheans and continuing through the great, sweeping account of God's purposes in history in his *City of God*.

Augustine has left us his questions and uncertainties, as well as his answers. Even he, it seems, could not represent the whole Christian stance all at once, to arrive at a single understanding of its meaning for human life that could apply to any historical situation. His work emphasizes different themes in the Christian stance at different points. Sometimes, the realities of sin require Christians to separate themselves from the other people among whom they live. At other times, the good creation in which all share draws Christians into a society which allows them to enjoy these goods together. Sometimes, the sense of resurrection destiny is so immediate that it requires a sharp distinction between the city of God and the earthly city. Sometimes, the ultimate end of history remains hidden in God's purposes, and the more immediate human task involves shared responsibility for the fragile peace that is still possible under conditions of human sin.

Later Christian writers have inherited these issues from Augustine. They have studied his writings, adopted his ideas, and re-invented his questions to fit their own circumstances. We will see that radical preachers during the Protestant Reformation renewed the call for Christians to form new, separate communities, where they could live their faith without compromise. We will also see that some theologians today, while they live fully within the institutions of modern society, see the church as a distinctive Christian community, which shapes its members according to virtues and values that have little in common with the values by which others live. Others, by contrast, think that the important moral questions are the ones that everyone can discuss, using ideas drawn from reason or from natural law to devise policies that shape a whole society. In the course of history, the tension between Christian identity and social responsibility that runs through Augustine's works has resolved itself into multiple, opposing forms of Christian ethics based on different versions of the Christian stance.

It is important to understand the differences between these competing systems, but it is also important to remember what they have in common. Though they put the emphasis in different places, what marks these systems as versions of Christian ethics is that they share the Christian stance, with its five themes of creation, sin, incarnation, redemption, and resurrection destiny. When you encounter a new author or a new idea that seems not to fit with the rest of what you know about Christian ethics, it is often useful to ask, "Where does this person put the emphasis within the Christian stance?" Creation and sin both have a place in the long arc of God's purposes for humanity and history, but as we have seen in Augustine's work, focusing on one or the other of them can lead you in quite different directions. Understanding where a particular author's interest lies between creation and resurrection destiny will often help you understand why this person's ideas seem different, but it should also help you see how those ideas are connected to the rest of Christian ethics.

In the later chapters of this introduction to Christian ethics, we will return to Augustine's thinking about goals and goods in the Christian life, and we will follow the development of his ideas in later Christian thought, from medieval concepts of natural law through the Reformation emphasis on scripture to modern ideas of personal and political freedom. First, however, we turn to four ways of understanding the Christian stance that provide the most important starting points for Christian ethics today.

Additional Reading

Brown, Peter. *Augustine of Hippo: A Biography.* Berkeley: University of California Press, 2000.

Chadwick, Henry. *Augustine of Hippo: A Life.* Oxford: Oxford University Press, 2009.

Meeks, Wayne. *The Origins of Christian Morality: The First Two Centuries.* New Haven: Yale University Press, 1993.

O'Donnell, James J. *Augustine: A New Biography.* New York: Ecco, 2005.

TeSelle, Eugene. *Augustine.* Nashville: Abingdon Press, 2006.

Wogaman, J. Philip. *Christian Ethics: A Historical Interpretation.* Louisville: Westminster John Knox Press, 1993.

CHAPTER THREE

VARIATIONS ON THE CHRISTIAN STANCE

The Christian stance unites Christians across the centuries. It also provides a framework for their disagreements. In this chapter, we will consider four contemporary versions of the Christian stance that provide different ways of relating to the surrounding society and human efforts to shape good lives and good communities. Each of these versions is shared by many Christians today, but each one also has its critics. A complete understanding of the Christian stance must consider moral problems from all four of these perspectives, but making moral decisions also requires making choices between them.

What made Augustine a great Christian theologian was the comprehensiveness of his understanding of the Christian stance. Whether he was interpreting his own life in his *Confessions* or the whole of human history in *City of God*, he saw reality in light of Christian faith as a whole, from creation through resurrection destiny. That comprehensive vision is appealing, but even Augustine could not hold on to all of it, all the time. His confidence in the goodness of God's creation led him to see beauty in the world around him, but his insight into the subtleties of human sin warned him that created things should be used, but not loved. His sense that all people naturally seek peace led him to think that Christians should take a part in government in the places where they live, but the pervasiveness of self-love suggested that a realistic Christian politics might have to consist mainly in using force to resist evil. The whole of his Christian faith went into his understanding of the problems that he saw, but his solutions to those problems inevitably required emphasizing some aspects of that faith and minimizing others.

Augustine was never entirely satisfied with those choices, and so he passed on to future generations his uncertainties: love of God, neighbor, and self *or* love of God and contempt for self; building a human commonwealth around common objects of love *or* using force to compel obedience. Western Christian ethics has taken shape around these unresolved choices.

Christian theologians and ethicists today still work with this Augustinian legacy. They affirm the Christian stance as a whole, but the particular problems they see around them lead them to emphasize some parts of it more than others. In the rest of this chapter, we will consider four important ways of relating the Christian stance to contemporary society. To identify them briefly, we will give each of them a name:

- • SYNERGY seeks ways for Christians to work together with other understandings of human good.
- • INTEGRITY maintains a distinctive Christian witness.
- • REALISM warns Christians against overestimating their own power and virtue.
- • LIBERATION stresses that freedom from oppression is central to the Christian message.

Synergy

John Courtney Murray (1904–1967) was a scholar who wrote about church and society in ways that changed thinking both in the Catholic Church and in the wider society. At the middle of the twentieth century, many American Protestants still looked with suspicion on Catholicism, which they saw as foreign and undemocratic. The candidacy of John F. Kennedy, who became the first Catholic President of the United States, brought these questions into public discussion and prompted Murray to write about the connections between Catholic faith and American democracy.[1] He also privately advised candidate Kennedy about how to respond to his Protestant critics. As the Catholic Church under Pope John XXIII undertook important changes at the Second Vatican Council (1962–1965), Murray also became a leader in interpreting the church's commitment to human rights and religious freedom.

Murray drew heavily on what he called the "public consensus" to explain the synergy between Catholic faith and American democracy. People in society use their reason to decide how they are going to live in order to create good lives for themselves. They do not need to share the same faith to do this. What they share is a commitment to civil argument. They do not settle their differences by force. They do not just hold elections, so that whoever wins the vote decides the question without further discussion. Rather, they agree to continue reasoning together about what contributes to the common good and what kind of constitutional framework is required to sustain it. Murray's articulation of this public consensus was his most important contribution to his church and to society. His view connects American democracy and the much older tradition of natural law.[2]

From Murray's perspective, public consensus is not just a lucky accident that occurs when people happen to agree. Because they all live in God's creation, they have a common human nature that orients them toward shared goals, and they can use their reason to understand what their human nature requires. Everyone needs a society that provides security, opportunities to form families, education, meaningful work, and the freedom to express ideas and faith in community with others. Christians believe that this shared nature is part of God's creation, but people who have quite different stances can also understand that we need to organize our common life in ways that make these good things possible. Thomas Aquinas (ca. 1225–1274) taught that human law and human society are guided on these points by natural law, so that despite differences in detail and changes over time, people come to agreement on how to live together, what they owe to one another, and even how to fight fairly with one another, when fighting becomes necessary.[3]

These ideas were formulated by medieval theologians, but they became part of the way that philosophers and political leaders understood what government is supposed to do. So when modern democracy took shape in the eighteenth century, ideas drawn from natural law about the rights of the people and the limits of government became part of how democracy was understood. If Americans were suspicious of Catholicism, Murray argued, it was because they had forgotten the roots of their own political system. Likewise, Catholics who were suspicious of democracy failed to see how commitments to freedom and human rights grew from ideas about human nature that were part of Catholic teaching. The synergy between Christianity and democracy is no accident. It is part of the history of both religion and politics.

Natural law does not settle all questions in advance, but it does make it possible for people to engage in civil argument about them, instead of letting those with the most power or the most votes decide every question their own way. Differences do not simply disappear in the "public consensus." As a Catholic in a society that was historically and culturally Protestant, Murray shared the common concern of minority groups that talk about an American "melting pot" where peoples and traditions blend into one conceals an expectation that they will all think like Anglo-Saxon Protestants when the blending is over. He wanted to retain the differences, but his knowledge of history and his confidence in human reason convinced him that different groups can work together.

In the America of his day, that meant especially the cooperation of four groups: Protestants, Catholics, Jews, and secularists. Murray called them four "conspiracies."[4] His choice of that term was an ironic nod to Protestants who kept insisting that Catholicism was a foreign conspiracy, but he gave the accusation a positive spin. A conspiracy, after all, is when people are so closely united in a common purpose that they "breathe together." They "con-spire" to achieve their common goal. "Perhaps, then," Murray wrote, "our problem today is somehow to make the four great conspiracies among us conspire into one conspiracy that will be American society—civil, just, free, peaceful, one."[5]

SYNERGY

emphasizes the connections between Christian faith and other understandings of human good and seeks ways to work together with them.

Representative works in recent Christian ethics include:

Lisa Sowle Cahill, *Between the Sexes: Foundations for a Christian Ethics of Sexuality.*

Franklin Gamwell, *Politics as a Christian Vocation.*

Robin Gill, *Health Care and Christian Ethics.*

David Hollenbach, *The Global Face of Public Faith: Politics, Human Rights, and Christian Ethics.*

Peter Paris, *The Spirituality of African Peoples: The Search for a Common Moral Discourse.*

Jean Porter, *Nature as Reason: A Thomistic Theory of Natural Law.*

Theodore Walker, Jr. *Mothership Connections: A Black Atlantic Synthesis of Neoclassical Metaphysics and Black Theology.*

Murray's vision of a free and unified society is appealing, but it occurs to us at once that it would have to include many more "conspiracies" in order to reach a public consensus today. Buddhist, Hindu, and Muslim groups have become important parts of American religious life, and all of our religious and cultural communities are more connected globally than they were when Murray was writing.[6] Some of the old conspiracies seem to have fragmented, too. Catholics and Protestants are often divided into traditionalist and progressive factions, with conservative Catholics and evangelical Protestants sharing more with each other than they share with Catholic progressives or Protestant peace activists from their own traditions. The Catholic progressives and the Protestant peace activists may march and pray together too, with few worries about who belongs to which church.

Growing religious diversity and conflict within traditions allow more voices to be heard in the civil argument, but they cast some doubt on the claim that there is one system of natural law that can be known to all who think about it reasonably. We become more aware that what seems reasonable to us is also a product of our history and our culture. This is true for matters that are close to our relationships and personal identity, like gender and sexuality, as Lisa Sowle Cahill has pointed out.[7] It is also true for political loyalties. As we will see in a moment when we consider the work of Reinhold Niebuhr, Christian realists remind us that we are always biased to see our own group or our own nation as representative of rational humanity. We should not be surprised that those whose experience differs from ours have different ideas about what natural law requires, and we should not expect that even people who are trying to be rational will come to the same conclusions unless they also share some traditions that shape them to share common values. That is one reason why recent Catholic ethics puts more emphasis than Murray did on worship, prayer, and scripture as part of the moral life.[8]

Nevertheless, synergy between religious traditions and public consensus remains an important idea, even after we have recognized some of its limitations. People do reason about their differences and settle disputes without resorting to force. The answers may not be obvious to everyone, even when everyone is trying to be reasonable, but it is hard to imagine a diverse society continuing for very long without some confidence that its people share a capacity to think about their problems in ways that overcome the differences in their backgrounds. For those who share the Christian stance, the experience of what Murray calls "civil argument" connects with the belief that God has created an ordered world that sustains human life and leads those who try to understand that order toward the human good. A thoughtful synergist will not expect the natural law to be obvious, especially given the different experiences that we all bring to the search for it. Nor is it likely that the requirements of natural law, once we reason out what they are, will simply coincide with what we expect or what we want. Nevertheless, for the synergist, confidence in the moral order is part of confidence in God's creation, and everyone can come to some understanding of that order.

Integrity

Stanley Hauerwas is a theologian whose career exemplifies the ecumenism of contemporary Christian ethics. After growing up as a

Protestant in Texas, Hauerwas studied theology in the nondenominational setting of Yale Divinity School. He began his teaching career in a Catholic institution, Notre Dame, where he was heavily influenced by John Howard Yoder, a senior colleague who was a Mennonite. In 1984, he joined the faculty at Duke Divinity School, a theological school of the United Methodist Church. This broad experience makes Hauerwas reluctant to classify himself as a "Catholic" or a "Protestant" theologian. "The object of the theologian's inquiry is quite simply God—not Catholicism or Protestantism. The proper object of the qualifier 'catholic' is the church, not theology or theologians.... Thus I hope my theology is catholic inasmuch as it is true to those Protestants and Roman Catholics who constitute the church catholic."[9]

This wide experience also leads Hauerwas to a distinctive way of thinking about Christian ethics. Historically speaking, it is a perspective that owes much to the radical freedom from government and society that Mennonites and other radical Protestant groups sought during the Reformation. Hauerwas shares their pacifism, their emphasis on local Christian congregations rather than hierarchical church authority, and their suspicion of Christian entanglement with government, wealth, and social prestige. The emphasis is strongly, almost exclusively, on Christian witness to a society from which the Christian stands apart. This sets Hauerwas at odds with most interpretations of Christian ethics by synergist, realist, or liberationist authors.

Despite the efforts of many Christians to get comfortable with their surroundings, Hauerwas insists that we live in a fragmented and violent world. Where John Courtney Murray emphasized the possibility of reasoned agreement, Hauerwas says that the main way people in society resolve their differences is by using force to coerce everyone into a single way of thinking and acting, imposed by those with power. Governments do this in their relations with other governments and also in the ways that they control their own people. But churches also use coercion in the ways that they use authority to ensure conformity. History shows us that churches will use violence, too, if they have the opportunity.

Hauerwas finds little in the ways that other writers approach Christian ethics to help us deal with this fragmented and violent world. Most of them offer what Hauerwas calls "quandary ethics," which focuses on specific problems where people may arrive at temporary agreements.

Quandary ethics supposes that we can reduce our moral conflicts to specific questions: Should we go to war in Iraq? Should the government guarantee everyone access to health care? Does freedom of speech include the freedom to spread misinformation or encourage prejudice? Answering questions like these does not get at the deeper sources of conflict and violence from which the quandaries arise. Resolving one of them for the moment will only make an opportunity for new quandaries to emerge.

Most ethics, too, tries to resolve such questions by appealing to universal moral rules: rules that determine when a war is just; rules that spell out universal human rights; rules that determine the balance between rights and obligations; and many more. The problem is that these abstract moral generalizations say nothing about the Christian life, which must be lived as a whole and cannot be reduced to individual answers to specific moral problems. Indeed, Christians are most tempted to participate in the violence that troubles a whole society when they think they know the universal rules that everyone ought to follow. Once there are rules that everyone ought to know and obey, it is easy to insist that those who do not seem to know what everyone ought to know and do what everyone ought to do should be coerced into the right way of thinking and acting.

By contrast, Hauerwas argues that Christian ethics must be more specifically Christian. Christian ethics will not tell us what everyone ought to do or answer the questions that everyone is asking, but it will tell us how to live as Christians. Being a Christian is not about solving the world's problems. It is about acquiring the characteristics of peaceableness and patience that sustain a community that can live as Jesus lived, despite the fragmentation and violence of the world.

Integrity, then, focuses on incarnation within the Christian stance, just as Synergy emphasized creation. Christians believe that God was uniquely present in Jesus Christ to reconcile the world's conflicts and to offer a new and different kind of good life for those who are part of the community formed by this story. "Thus to be like Jesus is to join him in the journey through which we are trained to be a people capable of claiming citizenship in God's kingdom of nonviolent love—a love that would overcome the powers of this world, not through coercion and force, but through the power of this one man's death."[10]

With this emphasis on "citizenship in God's kingdom," we would expect Hauerwas to have reservations about citizenship and political participation in the various countries where Christians live and, indeed, he does question the way that most Christians have related to government authority throughout history. Hauerwas rejects what he calls "Constantinianism." Early Christians, he explains, had no illusions about the coercion and violence used by the Roman government of that time, since they were often persecuted by it. However, when the emperor Constantine became a Christian, he connected the success of his policies to the power of Christ and began to give Christians a favored position in the government and society. Christians, in turn, increasingly identified the Kingdom of Christ with the Roman Empire, lost their sense of being a distinctive community of witness apart from the state, and began to take responsibility for society's problems. Most Christians since, Hauerwas believes, have made the same mistake.

In contrast to Murray's expectation that Christians will help to form the public consensus, Hauerwas urges the church to concentrate on a distinctive truth that stands apart from what everyone seems to know about human nature. The Christian life does not fulfill ordinary expectations of the good life. It makes sense only in light of the story of Jesus' reliance on love, rather than power. Likewise, Christian ethics does not provide solutions to moral problems that everyone understands. Christian ethics identifies the human qualities that make it possible for a community to follow Jesus and shows us how those virtues can be sustained. Such a life will make little sense to people who seek other goals, but the aim of Christian witness is neither persuasion nor social transformation. It simply reminds the world that fragmentation and violence do not have the last word on human life. Something else is possible.

Hauerwas does not base his judgments on particular things that societies do or fail to do. He charges that the church at least back to the time of Constantine has been lured away from its real task, and he finds that every society in history has relied on coercion and violence to achieve its goals. The conclusion is the same, whether the government is a democracy or a tyranny, whether the history belongs to the modern United States or to ancient Rome. The judgment is not built up on bits of evidence accumulated from history or sociology or insiders' stories of how government really works. The judgment is theological. The violence at the core of all forms of government, like the non-violent alternative that Jesus himself offers, only becomes evident when we see social order in the light of

Jesus' suffering, death, and resurrection. This is the way the world appears to this Christian stance. It is not that some societies are better or worse than others, or that some regimes are more and others less just. The differences between them may be politically important, but all of them rely on their own power in place of the dependence on God that makes peace possible. Each thus tends toward its own form of idolatry, the nations that proclaim themselves free and Christian no less than those that demand complete allegiance to the state.

INTEGRITY

focuses on the differences that separate Christians from the goals and values of the world around them and seeks to maintain a distinctive Christian way of life.

Representative works in recent Christian ethics include:
William T. Cavanaugh, *Torture and Eucharist: Theology, Politics, and the Body of Christ.*
Stanley Hauerwas, *With the Grain of the Universe.*
D. Stephen Long, *The Goodness of God: Theology, Church, and the Social Order.*
Samuel Wells, *God's Companions: Reimagining Christian Ethics.*

To many critics, this distance from ordinary politics seems irresponsible. The scope of Christian ethics is broad enough to encompass both the judgment that all governments fall short of God's purposes and the judgment that some of them serve human purposes better than others. Failure to make these distinctions leaves to others the task of finding solutions to moral quandaries, which are not just intellectual problems. The ordinary questions of ethics determine who gets medical care and who does not, who goes to prison and who goes free, and whether military force will be used to stop aggression or people will be left in the hands of insurgents and invaders. Ignoring the possibilities for synergy between the Christian stance and these moral questions leaves Christians in the role of critics who point out the limitations of every solution, while others are left with the task of deciding which one of the competing real choices to follow.

In reality, of course, Christians are not only witnesses to their faith.

They hold positions in government and business, participate in community activities with neighbors from other faiths and backgrounds, and worry like everyone else about the state of the economy and the problems of the world. These various identities and commitments interact with Christian faith in complicated ways. Ignoring the ways in which real Christians usually do take responsibility for their society may make Integrity too critical of the compromises and choices on which any society runs. Ignoring the multiple commitments Christians have may in turn lead Integrity to idealize the church. Real churches never quite live up to the ideal of detachment from society and its values that Hauerwas's theology requires.

Understanding the relationship between stance and society requires sociological analysis and knowledge of history, as well as theological integrity. Many different relationships are possible, especially in a modern democratic society that allows for different ways of life and offers freedom of religious expression. But one important point is essential for theological integrity: It is always possible that Christians will find themselves in a society where the prevailing values are a radical denial of Christian truth. While the normal relationship between stance and society allows for varying degrees of accommodation, criticism, and mutual support, the church must still know how to be the church when all possibilities for responsibility in society are closed and no recognition is forthcoming from the power of the state. It is a mistake to treat this as the only relationship between stance and society, and it distorts the complicated facts of religious life in modern democracies to impose this theological model on them. But a church which is unprepared to take its stance as witness to a truth that its society denies or suppresses may become so dependent on social approval that it cannot be responsible under ordinary circumstances, either.

Realism

While Integrity refuses to take responsibility for society and its problems, Realism accepts that responsibility eagerly. For the realist, the first task of Christian ethics is to match the requirements of the Christian stance to the realities of the present situation. The realist would agree with Hauerwas that the narrative of God's dealings with humanity provides a critical perspective on human history and society. Seeing ourselves in light of creation, sin, incarnation, redemption, and resurrection destiny undercuts pride in our achievements and destroys any illusions that we have the power to make them permanent. But the realist insists that it is not enough to bear this witness that our achievements are flawed and our possibilities are limited. Christian ethics must also guide our choices among these limited possibilities, because how we choose makes a real difference in the lives of individuals and nations.

Reinhold Niebuhr (1892–1971), the most important Christian realist of the twentieth century, began his career as a pastor in Detroit, where he watched economic conflict between labor unions and auto manufacturers in the 1920s and saw racial tensions grow as the city's African American population swelled with newcomers from the South. Niebuhr had been close to the Social Gospel movement, which welcomed these changes as opportunities to create the kingdom of peace and justice that Jesus had taught. But by the time Niebuhr left Detroit for New York and the faculty of Union Theological Seminary in 1928, he had abandoned any expectation of easy social transformation. People with power tended to hold on to it, even if they talked about fair wages and racial equality, and the nations of the world seemed to be more interested in preparing for another armed conflict than in fulfilling the promises of peace that followed the First World War. After Japan invaded Manchuria in 1931, Reinhold Niebuhr's brother, the theologian H. Richard Niebuhr, even wondered aloud whether it would be better for the churches to just do nothing, rather than facing the crisis with naïve hopes.[11]

Reinhold Niebuhr shared his brother's gloomy assessment of the world situation, but he was determined to preserve the possibility for a realistic Christian response that would avoid the despair of inaction. American Protestants were disillusioned because they had expected too much, he decided. They had put too little emphasis on sin, and they had estimated their own contribution to the work of redemption too highly. He wrote *Moral Man and Immoral Society* to call attention to the persistence of human self-interest, especially in those structures of politics, race, and nation that the Social Gospel had hoped to transform. In *The Nature and Destiny of Man*, Niebuhr explained this realism in more detail.[12] The Christian ideal of love must be seen in light of a biblical understanding of human nature. The human person is both made in the image of God and separated from God by a sinful urge to seek security and power in the self.

Realism approaches moral problems by maintaining this balance between human freedom and human limitations, between the transforming power of love and the restraining influence of self-interest. Christianity neither sinks into pessimism that thinks it can do nothing, nor allows itself to imagine, as reformers of all sorts have often done, that it can see the future so clearly as to transform this world into a new one.

Niebuhr's social ethics moved in the narrow range of real possibilities, refusing to accept things as they are, but working for modest changes, recognizing that human happiness "is determined by the difference between a little more and a little less justice, a little more and a little less freedom, between varying degrees of imaginative insight with which the self enters the life and understands the interests of the neighbour."[13] Even when taking these modest and limited steps, it is important to be self-critical, because success tends to make us too certain of our own wisdom, while failure still leaves us confident that we are more righteous than our enemies. The important thing about Jesus' teaching of love for God and neighbor is not that we can actually live up to it, but that it provides a standard against which we can measure our achievements without overrating them.

Realism thus emphasizes sin and the Fall in understanding the terms on which we have to make our moral choices. Creation and resurrection destiny are important, too. Creation provides a reference point for thinking about human nature, and resurrection destiny sustains hope, even when sin predictably limits what we can achieve in our own lifetimes. The meaning of the moral life depends not on the success of human efforts, but on the certainty of God's final judgment. Within this framework of creation and resurrection destiny, realists are able to focus on judgments of relative good and evil, with no need to overstate their own wisdom or claim too much for their own part in the work of redemption within history.

Niebuhr developed this realistic way of thinking especially in relation to politics. Like Murray, Niebuhr was concerned for the common good, but he emphasized that we cannot expect sinful human beings to make a commitment to justice based on good will alone. We have to understand their self-interest and the way they use power. We need a form of government that will use force to restrain evil, but we also need to restrain the self-righteousness of those who are in charge of the government. That was why Niebuhr's argument for democracy was different from the way that Americans had historically thought about their system of government. It was, as he said in the subtitle to his book *The Children of Light and the Children of Darkness,* "a vindication of democracy and a critique of its traditional defense."[14] From the time of the American Revolution, political leaders had argued that people are led into war and greed by tyrannical rulers who set them against one another. Do away with the tyrants and the people will live in peace and shared prosperity. The more realistic truth, Niebuhr suggested, is that even good rulers need to be limited, and people left to themselves will pursue their own interests as readily as they pursue the common good. Democracy works because it uses the interests of the people to restrain the power of the rulers and gives the government just enough power to keep the self-interest of the people in check. The kind of government that will work over the long run is one that recognizes the ambiguity in human nature, which is capable of both mutual love and ruthless exploitation of the neighbor. "Man's capacity for justice makes democracy possible," Niebuhr wrote. "But man's inclination to injustice makes democracy necessary."[15] A democracy that operates within those limits may be the best form of government, but it still depends on a balance of forces that requires constant attention and honest self-criticism.

REALISM

recognizes that the effects of sin and the weaknesses of human nature are found everywhere and warns against the human tendencies to overestimate our power to control events and to think too highly of our own virtues.

Representative works in recent Christian ethics include:
Jean Bethke Elshtain, *Augustine and the Limits of Politics.*
Christopher Insole, *The Politics of Human Frailty: A Theological Defense of Political Liberalism.*
Rebekah L. Miles, *The Bonds of Freedom: Feminist Theology and Christian Realism.*
Douglas Ottati, *Hopeful Realism: Recovering the Poetry of Theology.*
William Schweiker, *Theological Ethics and Global Dynamics: In the Time of Many Worlds.*
Max Stackhouse, *Public Theology and Political Economy.*
Ronald Stone, *Prophetic Realism: Beyond Militarism and Pacifism in an Age of Terror.*

Niebuhr was not only an important theologian. He became one of the leading political thinkers of his generation, and his ideas had an important influence on American foreign policy during the long Cold War rivalry with the Soviet Union. Nevertheless, his ideas have been challenged by critics who see the relationship between Christian stance and modern society differently. Stanley Hauerwas, in particular, has argued that Niebuhr's close involvement with politics results in the loss of any distinctive Christian identity. The Christian realist who chooses what is merely the best among the available policy options becomes indistinguishable from everyone else. A genuine Christian witness must often stand against all of the choices, reminding society that even the best policies reflect the use of power and coercion that always marks the modern state. John Courtney Murray, by contrast, thought that Niebuhr's warning that even the most responsible choices are morally ambiguous in God's sight did not engage society and politics closely enough. All of the options may be imperfect, but from Murray's natural law perspective, one of them is right. The synergist will be a full participant in the civil argument that makes that determination, and full participation includes being ready to stand up for the right choice once it is made. Realism's subsequent warnings about the moral ambiguity of the decision are little better than Integrity's decision to stay out of the argument altogether. Of our four variations on the Christian stance, Liberation comes closest to Niebuhr's realistic warnings about the ways that self-interest and power distort our moral judgments. But liberation theologians have also seen evidence of these distortions in Niebuhr's own work. From their point of view, the pre-eminent Christian realist was not realistic enough about his own privileged position.

Niebuhr's understanding of Christian ethics certainly reflects the time in which he lived, and he himself would have been skeptical of any moral reasoning that claimed to provide permanent answers that escape those historical limitations. Nearly four decades after his death, however, journalists, scholars, and political leaders still find his ideas relevant to the very different world we live in today.[16] Realism tries above all to be realistic about human nature. The insights drawn from that kind of realism will be different in each situation, but the effort to be realistic seems to be perennially relevant.

Liberation

Katie Geneva Cannon took a different approach to Christian ethics in the 1980s with her study of the Black woman's literary tradition.[17] In formulating a "Black Womanist ethics," Cannon discovered the importance of attending to the details of social experience of oppressed people and understanding how ethics emerges from that experience. For the Black woman who lives with racial prejudice, gender bias, and poverty, understanding the good human life cannot be a matter of applying some other ethical system to her experience. Moral meaning has to be found within that experience.

That insight led Cannon to intensive study of the work of Zora Neale Hurston, Toni Morrison, Alice Walker, and other Black women writers. In their work, she found a revealing account of the details of Black women's lives and a tradition of moral wisdom quite different from the rules and virtues held up by a society that values success, mobility, and personal choice.

> Black women live out a moral wisdom in their real-lived context that does not appeal to the fixed rules or absolute principles of the White-oriented, male-structured society. Black women's analysis and appraisal of what is right or wrong and good or bad develop out of the various coping mechanisms related to the conditions of their own cultural circumstances. In the face of this, Black women have justly regarded survival against tyrannical systems of triple oppression as a true sphere of moral life.[18]

The result is a moral life quite different from the ideal held up by the historical systems of ethics that emphasize the virtues of courage, prudence, temperance, and justice. Here, the most important virtue is often what Alice Walker identified as "unctuousness." This sly form of courage empowers a person to slip out of difficult situations by lubricating them with just the right amount of believable flattery and feigned humility. It preserves integrity by practicing a carefully targeted deceit.[19] Unctuousness may not seem like a virtue to those who are accustomed to being in charge of their own situations and proud of their reputations for plain speaking, but their virtues are no guide to the moral life you live when you have to maintain your home, your family, and your dignity against those who could destroy you if you challenge their self-assumed superiority. Unctuousness, according to a proverb Cannon learned from her mother, means knowing how to treat the lion when your head is in the lion's mouth.[20]

Cannon's Black Womanist ethics helps us understand other forms of liberation theology that have developed in recent decades. Those who have been kept on the edges of society by politics, poverty, or discrimination have increasingly found their own voices, and describing the moral life in their own terms has been the first step toward political rights and social power. Many theologians had supported movements for civil rights before liberation theology came along. One of the things on which John Courtney Murray and Reinhold Niebuhr agreed was the importance of racial equality for American democracy. But Niebuhr and Murray were theologians who spoke up for the oppressed, not people who spoke about oppression with the voices of experience. Niebuhr also urged caution, lest the pace of change disrupt society and provoke a backlash among those who wanted to hold on to the way things were. Black theology emerged in North America in the late 1960s, as activists began to seek a theology more attuned to their own experience, one that would not postpone the freedom of the oppressed to reassure the privileged. They quickly made connections with Latin American theologians who were trying to relate Catholic moral theology to the struggles of the poor in their own countries. This new "liberation theology" provided a perspective that served Christians engaged in political struggles in South Africa and Asia, as well as among marginalized groups in Europe and North America. *Mujerista* theology, reflecting the experience of Hispanic women, and the *Minjung* theology of Korean political activists are just two prominent examples among many ways that this liberationist approach has become part of Christian life around the world.

While the many different liberation theologies reflect the places where they are found, they share a critical perspective on society and on Christian faith that often challenges the beliefs of other Christians. They remind us that the suffering of the poor is not an accident or an unfortunate fact of nature. It is the result of economic and political systems that deliver wealth and power to the people who control them at the same time that they exploit the poor. Often, it is difficult to understand how these systems work, especially for those in privileged groups whose self-interest lies in not seeing what is happening. Liberation theologians have employed a variety of critical social theories to explain the dynamics of the societies in which they live, including Marxist economics and post-colonial theories that relate the poverty of less developed countries to economic and social patterns that began while they were colonies of the major world powers. The first step toward liberation is to understand the ideas and systems that keep the cycle of exploitation and poverty going.

This critical perspective applies to the church, too, and not just to the church as an institution, but to the ideas in Christian scripture and tradition that have been used to blame the poor for their poverty and keep women, outsiders, and minority groups in subordinate positions. Just as it is necessary to see society in a different way, a liberation ethics will have to rethink Christianity from the perspective of the poor. While a new understanding of society often requires bringing in theories about economics, politics, and history from outside, liberation theologians insist that the key to a new understanding of Christianity is found in the experience of participation and liberation itself. This is especially true for the reading of the Gospels, in which the story of Jesus can only be fully understood as the story of one who was born into a humiliated, colonized people, identified with the poor of the land, and suffered death at the hands of authorities who were determined to keep the order of power and oppression in place. The gospel is not something offered to oppressed people by benevolent outsiders. It is their own story. As James Cone puts it, "The task of black theology, then, is to analyze the nature of the gospel of Jesus Christ in the light of oppressed blacks so they will see the gospel as inseparable from their humiliated condition, and as bestowing on them the necessary power to break the chains of oppression."[21]

Like Integrity, Liberation focuses on incarnation. The presence of God in Jesus Christ among the poor and despised is the central fact that must be understood to grasp the meaning of Christian faith and orient the followers of Jesus for action in the world. For the liberationist, however, incarnation and redemption are directly connected in Christian experience. Where Hauerwas worries that Christians will take too much responsibility for the world onto themselves if they start to emphasize their own involvement in the work of redemption, for Cone the evidence that the gospel has truly been heard is that it supplies people with "the necessary power to break the chains of oppression." Redemption is God's work, but it cannot be done for people by others, or even by God. The restoring of the world that leads toward resurrection destiny begins with the empowerment of those who connect the gospel to the possibility of their own liberation. Of course, incarnation and redemption are still set in the context of God's creation, but liberation theologians are wary of drawing too many conclusions directly from this. Claims about what God intends for creation have been used to justify slavery, the subordination of women, and the authority of kings, overlords, and bosses. Liberation ethics is therefore more likely to criticize natural law than to make use of its ways of moral reasoning.

LIBERATION

stresses that Christian faith frees people from the political, economic, and psychological power of those who oppress them and seeks especially to bring this message of freedom to the poor and those who live on the margins of society.

Representative works in recent Christian ethics include:
James H. Cone, *A Black Theology of Liberation.*
Ada María Isasi-Díaz, *Mujerista Theology: A Theology for the 21st Century.*
Harold Recinos, *Good News from the Barrio: Prophetic Witness for the Church.*
Emilie M. Townes, *In a Blaze of Glory: Womanist Spirituality as Social Witness.*
Traci C. West, *Disruptive Christian Ethics: When Racism and Women's Lives Matter.*

Critics are quick to respond that liberationists have their own set of ideas that they use to support a way of looking at the world that works to their advantage. Their use of Marxist ideas about economic relationships and other critical social theories have led some to suggest that the interest in liberation is not theological at all, but a thinly disguised political movement. However, the end of the Cold War has rendered Marxism less relevant to global politics, and many liberation theologians have moved away from it with no loss to their central ideas. In other places, especially in the

United States, Marxism was not particularly important to liberation theology in the first place. More decades of experience have shown that living among the poor and giving voice to their experience is the central method of liberation theology.

Realists, in turn, worry that liberationists may identify the experience of the poor too closely with Christian faith. A realist understanding of human nature warns us that everyone distorts reality to fit their own needs and interests, and realists do not expect the poor to be any different from the rich in this respect. Today's oppressed are tomorrow's oppressors. Liberationists might well reply that for most of the world's poor, that reversal of roles is still a long way off.

Liberation theology struggles to find an understanding of sin that could apply to all persons, oppressed and oppressors alike, but its real contribution is an articulation of the experience of the poor that all Christians can incorporate into their understanding of incarnation and redemption. Christians should never forget that Jesus was one of the poor and marginalized, not one of the rich and powerful. Against all the forces that deprive the poor of dignity, dismiss them as ignorant, and accuse them of creating their own suffering, liberationists speak of God's "preferential option for the poor." Their ways of mastering their own situation, as Cannon shows us, create a meaningful moral life without waiting for approval from the guardians of tradition and order. Their understanding of what is happening in their own situation is often more penetrating than the economic theories that social scientists and policy makers use to rationalize their exploitation.

Stance and Society

Even this brief survey of four versions of the Christian stance reminds us that a stance is a framework for argument as well as a set of shared beliefs. Christians emphasize different parts of the stance they share, and these differences result in different ways of seeing the moral questions they face, especially when those questions involve their relationships to the wider society in which they live. If they think first about the world as God's creation, encompassing nature, humanity, and history in one order in which all have a part, they will not be surprised to find that different people share similar human needs, limitations, and possibilities. They will probably expect to learn something from the way that other people see the world and from the values by which they try to live. At least they will recognize that they share these questions of ethics with all of their neighbors, even if their own Christian answers to the questions differ. By contrast, Christians who turn first to sin and the Fall may well expect people who live without the guidance of scripture and the insights of faith to have distorted ideas about the human good. Such Christians will approach these alien ideas with caution and use them sparingly. They may even think that the good life, as ethics understands it, is not good at all from a Christian perspective.

Of course, how you see the relationship between stance and society depends on your society as well as on your stance. Even if you think the Christian stance requires obedience to the law and loyalty to the state, if the government that happens to have control of your society is dominated by corrupt leaders or guided by evil purposes, you may well try to accentuate the differences between church and society. During the Second World War, Dietrich Bonhoeffer and other German pastors worked to create a Confessing Church that resisted control by the Nazi state, even though they had inherited a long history of Lutheran theology that stressed obedience to the governing authorities. Bonhoeffer himself took part in an effort to assassinate Hitler. By contrast, if you are convinced your country's political system is uniquely attuned to the possibilities and limitations of human nature, you may conclude that its success is essential to world peace, even if your understanding of sin and the Fall makes you skeptical that any human institution can really represent God's purposes. Reinhold Niebuhr offered that carefully limited religious defense of democracy in the United States at the same time that Bonhoeffer was working to undermine Hitler's dictatorship in Germany.

Given the complexity of these interactions between interpretations of the Christian stance and judgments about particular times and places, it should be no surprise that Christians have found many different ways to live their lives in the societies where they find themselves. They have been good citizens and violent revolutionaries. Sometimes, they have used civil disobedience in efforts to compel their society to live up to the values it claims, and sometimes they have denounced those values as part of a way of life that no Christian should live. Their expectations vary, too, on whether other people who do not share their stance might nonetheless agree with their conclusions, or whether they should expect to stand alone when they are being truly faithful.

The differences between these versions of the Christian stance are real, and the disagreements between them can be sharp, loud, and lasting. It is important to understand those disagreements, but it is also important for our purposes to remember how much the different versions of the Christian stance share. The Christian stance provides an overarching framework in which these arguments take place, as contending positions put the emphasis on different parts of the shared Christian stance and offer different interpretations of the whole. In coming chapters, we will sometimes focus on these differences to explain different positions in Christian ethics, and we may sometimes speak of "the realist stance" or "the liberationist stance" as a shorthand way of referring to what are in fact different versions of the Christian stance, not really different stances. Participants in the arguments may forget this, with Integrity insisting that Realism denies the teaching of Jesus and Synergy and Liberation accusing each other of forgetting the meaning of the Christian message. All four of these positions are needed for a full understanding of Christian ethics, and even when we make choices between them, it is important to see the questions from the other points of view.

Additional Reading

De La Torre, Miguel A. *Doing Christian Ethics from the Margins.* Maryknoll, NY: Orbis Books, 2004.

Dorrien, Gary. *Social Ethics in the Making: Interpreting an American Tradition.* Malden, MA: Wiley-Blackwell, 2009.

Gutierrez, Gustavo. *A Theology of Liberation.* Maryknoll, NY: Orbis Books, 1988.

Hauerwas, Stanley. *The Hauerwas Reader.* Edited by John Berkman and Michael Cartwright. Durham, NC: Duke University Press, 2001.

Hooper, J. Leon. *The Ethics of Discourse: The Social Philosophy of John Courtney Murray.* Washington, DC: Georgetown University Press, 1986.

Yoder, John Howard. *The Politics of Jesus.* 2nd ed. Grand Rapids: Eerdmans Publishing Company, 1994.

Part 2
Goals

CHAPTER FOUR

GOODS, GOALS, AND GOD

Although people face many different moral problems, they typically use three methods of reasoning to make their moral choices. They set goals, they identify their duties, and they ask what virtues they ought to have. Much of our moral thinking begins with teleology, the setting of goals, and this method of moral reasoning is found already in Aristotle's Nicomachean Ethics. *Like Aristotle, Augustine often focused on goals in thinking about the moral life, but his Christian ethics made use of teleology by relating goals to love for God.*

So far in this introduction to Christian ethics, we have focused on the different versions of the Christian stance and understanding how they relate to one another and to other stances. This is an important part of Christian ethics, but it is only a beginning. A stance is a way of thinking about reality as a whole. The moral problems that people face every day are more specific. People face questions about choice and action in particular circumstances, and the study of ethics becomes practical when it begins to talk about those questions. What do I say to a classmate who tells me she bought her term paper on the Internet? What should I say to the professor? How do I respond to a friend who wants help with a family emergency on the night before I have an important exam? What should

I say to a friend who clearly needs help with a drug problem? What should I say to a friend in the next row who clearly needs help with an answer during the exam? These are just some of the moral questions that can come up at any time in our ordinary experiences.

Extend the time frame a little or include more people in the mix and the questions multiply. Should I spend my summer taking extra courses so I can graduate sooner, or would it be better to join a volunteer team repairing houses for poor people? Should I take the job that gives me a chance to develop my musical talents, or should I seek an office job that includes benefits so that my family will not have to pay for my medical insurance? Should I insist that everything be done for a family member in the intensive care unit, or is it time to tell the doctors to cease their efforts and let a natural death occur? Do I support my country's decision to go to war, or should I join the protests against it?

Questions like these are all around us, and sometimes they are very difficult. The Christian stance may offer a way to understand why these problems happen. The Christian stance may assure us of the goodness of the created world, even in the midst of disease and disaster. The Christian stance may help identify God's redemptive work in the events of history or give hope that God's goodness will prevail at the end of history. All this can help us to make hard choices, but the Christian stance alone does not tell us what we ought to do. We have to make a decision.

Stances and Choices

The early Christians were not alone in setting the decisions they had to make within an understanding of human life and history that we call a "stance." Stoics did that too, with their careful distinction between what is within our power and what depends on forces beyond our control. Manicheans had a stance which allowed them to interpret disease and suffering as the work of an evil power who created the material world to oppose the good power who seeks to free us from the constraints of the body. These stances remain part of moral thinking today, even when the people who have them do not always recognize the origins of their ideas. We have modern-day Stoics who have a stance that encourages us to avoid too much reliance on other people. There are modern-day Epicureans, whom we sometimes call "secularists," who warn us not to look for meaning in events that are shaped by natural forces operating without direction.[1]

So it is not that Christians make their choices burdened by a complicated set of beliefs about the world that other people manage to avoid. Everyone has a stance. These stances are quite different, of course. We saw that already with our quick review of the tragedians, Cynics, Stoics, and Epicureans in chapter 1. Even within the same stance, a way of thinking about the world that has been around for a long time will develop significant variations, as we saw with the Christian stance in chapter 3. One of the things that study of the history of ethics makes clear is that all ethics is shaped by a particular way of looking at the world and the human place in it. We might think that it would be easier to make our choices, or at least easier to explain them to others, if we could set these beliefs aside and look at our problems "objectively," but this does not work. Without the stance that orients me to the world and gives me an identity, the decision I make cannot be my decision.

Having a stance is part of what makes a moral choice possible, but the differences between stances make agreement on those choices more difficult. It is possible that if two people shared exactly the same stance, they would agree on all their important decisions. They might choose different things for dinner—provided that the entrée did not raise issues about ecology or animal rights—but on the big questions, it could well be that their common view of the world and their place in it would lead them to the same conclusions. Their stance would have to be a strong set of beliefs, covering many aspects of their shared experience, and they would have to have thought about it for some time, to make sure that they understood all of its implications. For some people, moral and religious traditions are supposed to function this way, since a tradition is a set of ideas and practices worked out over many generations, and people turn to it with the expectation that they will find answers they can use from those who share their beliefs and who have dealt with problems similar to their own.

Bringing everyone to the same stance, however, is not a very practical way to resolve most of the moral choices we have to make. Choices often have to be made quickly, and people come to their stances over the course of a lifetime. Decisions often involve many people, and unless these people are members of a family or a small religious community, it is unlikely that they will all share a common stance or a common tradition. Deciding on the right thing to do is less a matter of everyone ending up in the same place and more a question of knowing where to begin. When you face a difficult problem like those outlined at the beginning of this chapter, what do you look to first, in order to decide what you ought to do?

Ways of Reasoning

You could choose randomly, of course. Sometimes, people flip a coin to determine what to do. Sometimes, people who face a difficult decision are quite sure that God has shown them what to do. Sometimes, they turn to an authority they trust, and they do whatever the authority tells them. Aristotle would remind us, however, that ethics is using reason in our decisions, so that thinking guides our actions. Prayer and meditation may help us do that thinking clearly, and discussing our choices with people whom we trust can be an important part of decision making, but what makes a decision moral is that you use reason to identify the right choice. Then, when you have identified the right choice, you act on it.

What we are looking for are ways of thinking that we can apply consistently when we face new decisions. It is not just a matter of wanting a guide to this particular decision. We want to know how to connect it to all the other decisions we have to make, so that any particular decision will be one that fits with the rest of our life, not something that leaves us saying, "I don't know why I did it. I don't usually act that way." So we try to find ways of thinking that connect this choice to others we have made. "The people I admire," we tell ourselves, "make sacrifices for the team, so that's what I'm going to do, too." "It's just wrong for anybody to tell a lie, so I'm not going to do it." "Things always go wrong when people borrow money from their friends, so I'm not going to do it."

That, broadly speaking, is moral reasoning. There is nothing mysterious about it. We all do it all the time. Notice, however, that those three simple examples actually suggest three very different ways of thinking about choices. In the first case, the decision turns on personal characteristics that we find good or admirable. We try to make the choices which that kind of person would make, and our moral lives become consistent as we acquire those admirable qualities and shape the rest of our decisions by them. We become the kind of person who makes sacrifices for the team. We have a virtue that we might call loyalty, or reliability, or just "being a team player." The second example is a decision based on duty. There are some things that all of us ought to do, or some rules that apply to everybody, and when we can identify what those rules are, we know that they apply to us, too. Consistency in the moral life comes from following the rules and doing our duty, even when it is difficult and we do not want to do it. When we do the right thing in that way, our own conduct is reliable from case to case, and because we are all following the same rules, our choices are consistent with those of other people who are trying to do the right thing, too. In the third case, attention centers on results. Bad things happen when people borrow money from their friends, so that is the wrong thing to do. We might say that our goal is avoiding the bad results we expect when friends borrow money from friends. If we thought about it a little longer, we might say that the goal is actually preserving friendship, since friendships often break up when people go into debt to their friends. Or perhaps the goal is more personal, like preserving an image of independence and self-sufficiency. Your friends might think less of you, even if you paid the money back, and you do not want that to happen. However you formulate the goal, consistency in the moral life comes from pursuing worthwhile goals that you know you will continue to follow and that are consistent with the other goals that guide your decisions. There are many different moral choices, but our ways of thinking about them tend to take these three forms. Sometimes, we think in terms of duties, which tell us what we should and should not do. Sometimes we consider goals, which tell us what our actions should accomplish. Sometimes, we focus on virtues, which describe the kind of person we ought to be. Of course, it is possible to jump from one kind of guideline to another until you find one that invites you to do what you wanted to do in the first place. That may be little better than flipping a coin. If you are going to reason about your choices, one of the first things you have to decide is how to match the consideration of duties, goals, and virtues to the particular problems you face.

Those who study ethics systematically organize the subject in this way, too. They speak of *deontology*, a system of ethics based on duties, and *teleology*, a system of ethics based on goals. They also use the term *areteology*, or more simply, *virtue ethics*, to name systems of ethics based on important personal characteristics like humility, generosity, honesty, and courage. Some systems of ethics rely exclusively on one of these three starting points. Others try, as most people do in daily life, to make some consistent use of all three of them.

THREE WAYS OF MORAL REASONING

Deontology is a modern term that comes from *deon*, the Greek word for that which is right or necessary, and *logos*, a Greek word frequently used to name the study of something. So *deontology* is originally the study of what it is right to do, and later, more specifically, the study of rules or duties.

Teleology is derived in the same way from *logos* and *telos*, the Greek word for goal. Contrasted with deontology, it means the study of what we ought to aim for, the results we should seek in making moral choices, as opposed to the rules we should follow.

Areteology, then, is the study of *arete*, Greek for virtue, though the word is a little clumsy to spell or pronounce, and it frequently gives way to the simple *virtue ethics*. Areteology is concerned with the characteristics we must have to be good people.

Seeking Goals

Teleological ethics uses reason to determine the goals or goods at which our actions should aim. The world around us is filled with many different sorts of goods. Some of these are natural, like a mountain range, a beautiful sunset, or a wetland teeming with different kinds of wildlife. These goods are simply there, independent of our personal choices and actions, and often independent of human choices altogether. Many other kinds of goods, however, do depend on us. We can take a moment to enjoy the sunset. We can devise a conservation policy to preserve the wetland. We can decide to take a trip to see the mountains we have always heard about. Some goods, indeed, only come into being when we and others make the choices that bring them about. Books exist only because people write them. Personal traits like honesty, loyalty, and a sense of humor have to be cultivated, even if they depend in part on natural gifts. A government or a corporation may seem so solid and durable that it is practically a part of the natural environment, like a river or a mountain range. But it only takes a political crisis or an economic downturn to remind us that institutions are goods that exist because of choices made by people in the past, and whether they continue into the future or cease to exist depends on choices that other people are making now.

These good things that come into being as a result of our choices and actions are the goals that we pursue. They are related to each other in complex ways. Some are almost entirely *instrumental* goods. As when we perform an unpleasant task or take a bitter medicine, we choose them as goals because they help us get to other goals that we really want. Taking an ethics course, for example, may be an instrumental good toward the goal of being an educated person. Many goods mix instrumental goods and things that are good in themselves, like a brilliant musical performance that is both richly satisfying in itself and a step in the career of an aspiring musician. Some goods support other goods, as a good education can support a career dedicated to public service. But goods can also compete, as they do when the aspiring musician has to choose between financial security and artistic opportunity.

Most of us recognize a number of different kinds of good as very important—relationships, physical and mental health, personal successes, protecting other people and the environment—but we may not know how to relate them to one another until we are forced to choose between them. Some philosophers, like Plato, would say that if we really understood all these different goods, we would know what it is that makes all of them good, and we would know how they are related to one another and how to choose between them. Others, like Augustine, would say that understanding these different goods is a matter of knowing how all of them are related to God. We will consider his ideas about goods and goals later in this chapter. Still others, mostly in more recent centuries, have proposed that everything is good in relation to some basic measure on which all humans, or even all sentient beings, can agree. Things are good because they increase pleasure or reduce pain, and the more pleasure or the less pain, the better they are. Goodness is nothing more complicated than that, these thinkers would say, and there is certainly no goodness in the things themselves that we need to worry about when comparing one good to another.

We will consider these views, which often take the form of a moral philosophy known as *utilitarianism*, in the next chapter.

Because there are so many different goods that can become our goals and the relations between them are so complex, theoretical formulations of teleological ethics can be quite elaborate. In practice, most of our goals are derived from a more simple teleology, constructed of choices between obvious possibilities on the basis of fairly ordinary desires. We want to enjoy the weekend, so we choose friends and activities that seem likely to produce that result. We also want to pass the exam on Monday, so we cut the good times short to allow some time for study, aiming at the best results overall for the week ahead. If asked, we might explain these choices by saying that the good we want is a life that is balanced between work and play, or that our goal is maximum satisfaction in work and personal life as a whole. Corporations, likewise, set goals for production, sales, recruitment, and so on, aiming at the best overall result for the business. Many people spend their working lives in these teleological activities of goal-setting, achieving the goals, and measuring performance in relation to goals. Teleological thinking is such a pervasive part of our lives that often we do not think of these choices as moral decisions, but the goals we set for ourselves and our groups provide some of the clearest indications of what we think a good human life is.

TELEOLOGY

Teleology uses reason to guide action toward the achievement of a good goal.

What makes an action right is that it aims at good results.

What makes a person good is that he or she accomplishes good things.

Christian Teleological Ethics

We have already seen teleological thinking in Aristotle's ethics. Happiness, or *eudaimonia*, is the goal that everyone naturally wants, and according to Aristotle, ethics is about making decisions that lead to that result. Of course, people do not simply decide that they are going to be happy and go directly for the goal. There are many other different kinds of goods that go into happiness, and most of the goals people set will involve achieving those goods, holding on to them, and balancing them with other goods, so that the end result is the good life they are seeking.[2]

For Aristotle, those who are able to have a good life build it step by step, as they come to understand each of the goods available to them and put it in place in relation to all the other goods. They learn this by experience, and the virtues they acquire along the way help them make good decisions in the future. By making the right choices, they achieve a combination of health, wealth, and honor, and they strike the right balance between time spent on political activity and time spent in philosophical contemplation. With courage, prudence, and a little luck, they will sustain these choices over a lifetime, and people will rightly call them *eudaimon*, happy, or *makarios*, blessed. From beginning to end, the good life is about goals. The right choices are the ones that lead to these goals. The good person is someone who achieves them.

Christian ethics seems at first to present a sharp contrast to this Aristotelian teleology. The teaching of Jesus seems deliberately to turn common ideas of happiness upside down. The one who is *makarios* is meek, merciful, peaceable, and persecuted (Matthew 5:3-12).[3] The *Epistle to Diognetus,* a Christian text from the second century, is even more clear about the contrast between the Christian life and the kind of happiness most people appear to be seeking:

> But happiness is not to be found in dominating one's fellows, or in wanting to have more than his weaker brethren, or in possessing riches and riding rough-shod over his inferiors. No one can become an imitator of God like that, for such things are wholly alien to His greatness. But if a man will shoulder another's burden; if he be ready to supply another's need from his own abundance; if, by sharing the blessings he has received from God with those who are in want, he himself becomes a god to those who receive his bounty—such a man is indeed an imitator of God.[4]

What the early Christian writings share that sets them apart from an Aristotelian understanding of happiness is the conviction that everything depends on relationship with God, or in the terminology of the Gospels, on "entering the kingdom of heaven." All other goods are less than this good, and a wise person will eagerly give up everything else to obtain it (Matthew 13:44-45).

Augustine makes this explicit when he discusses true happiness. Like other Christians who know philosophy, he assumes that happiness is what everyone is seeking. But he knows that happiness will have to be reinterpreted in light of Christian experience. As we have seen, he argues that the things we expect to make us happy actually make us anxious, because we are afraid that we might lose them. If we are really going to be happy, we must find a good that cannot be lost, even in death. Only one good fits that description. True happiness is relationship to God. "God alone, therefore, should be loved, but this whole world, that is, all sensible things, should be held in contempt. We must, however, use them for the needs of this life."[5]

What Augustine means by "things" are not only the material goods that are the object of so much of goal-setting and goal-seeking. Augustine's list of things to be used would include higher-level activities, like taking part in government and using your reason to discuss philosophy. Aristotle saw these as essential elements of the good life. Augustine had been an ambitious participant in the political world as a professor of rhetoric in Milan, and he never lost the sense that a good person should accept the duties of public office when called upon to do so. He continued to read philosophy, and he enjoyed discussing ideas with his friends, both in person and in correspondence with those who lived far away. But he did not regard either public life or philosophical reflection as a source of true happiness.[6] Such activities are things to be used. So, too, are the people who share these activities with us. If we start making decisions on the basis of our love for these people and activities, he warns, we will be misled by our anxieties about losing them, and we will lose them in the end, because they will distract us from the love for God on which everything else depends. Even those familiar virtues of prudence, courage, temperance, and justice have to be reinterpreted so that they are focused on God alone:

> Temperance is love preserving itself whole and entire for God. Fortitude [courage] is love readily enduring all things for God. Justice is love that serves only God and, for this reason, correctly governs other things that are subject to a human being. And prudence is love distinguishing correctly those things by which it is helped toward God from those things by which it can be impeded.[7]

Because Augustine views the world from the Christian stance, he cannot suppose that true happiness will be found in the disciplined life of the

Stoic philosophers, who acquire goods and virtues through steady habits and avoid commitments and desires that entangle them with events that they cannot control. Nor does he think that the Neoplatonists will be successful in their ascent through higher and higher levels of contemplation until they arrive at the idea of the Good itself. Augustine's understanding of sin gives him a more realistic picture of what happens when people go off in pursuit of goals they think will lead to true happiness. Because individual human beings are sinful and separated from God, their choice of which goods to pursue and how to pursue them will often be mistaken; and because we all live in a fallen world, any good we might happen to achieve after all will be subject to decay or destruction.

Augustine sees that someone who tries to live a good life on the philosophers' terms is not going to enjoy steady progress toward the goal of true happiness. More likely, that person will be found running from one project to the next, trying to undo the results of mistaken choices that were not really good at all and anxiously shoring up whatever good has been accomplished against real or imagined threats of destruction. This is not the picture of a truly happy life, but it is the likely result of trying to be happy according to the philosophers' directions.

For Augustine, true happiness begins with the ultimate goal, for unlike Aristotle's *eudaimonia*, which we come to understand by reflecting on the combination of activities and achievements that make it up, God is so different from everything that God has created that love for God is best understood when it is seen by itself alone, distinct from all the other loves that might be confused with it. When we love God, we will be able to put all other things to their appropriate uses, but we will never learn to love God by thinking first about other things.

Radical Monotheism

Augustine emphasizes the uniqueness of God's reality to explain why God alone is to be loved and why no other object of love can supply true happiness. This is a key theme in his work, especially as he tries to distinguish the creator God of Genesis from Manichean accounts of creation, in which the good creator must struggle against an opposite, evil power.[8] God stands apart from creation, and yet God is the source of all of it.

Unless we can see the world in those terms, our efforts to set goals for our life will lack direction and end in frustration and loss.

This idea runs through the history of Christian ethics from Augustine down to our own times. The theologian H. Richard Niebuhr (1894–1962) observed that many people, even in the modern world, are *polytheists* of a sort. That is not to say that they believe in many gods, the way an ancient Greek might have believed in the existence of Zeus, Athena, Apollo, and the rest. (Most of the Greek philosophers probably did not believe that literally, either.) But they seek many different, competing goods, and they have many different loyalties. They may sincerely say they believe in one God, but it would be hard to see what difference that makes in the shifting patterns of their goals and actions. Even more prevalent, Niebuhr suggested, is *henotheism*, in which people recognize the existence of many different goods, but give their loyalty to one of them, setting it against all the others. This may take the form of nationalism, ethnic loyalties, political ideologies, and even certain kinds of religious commitment, where competing values are unified in opposition to other, similar centers of unity: The United States against China, say, or conservative against liberal, or Christian against Muslim.

Against these ways of thinking about goods, whether in their modern forms or in the religions of the ancient world, Niebuhr argued that Christianity has throughout its history exemplified *radical monotheism*. That is, it has unified different and potentially competing goods by the claim that God is uniquely good and worthy of love, and the value of everything else must be known and measured in relation to God.[9] Against the egocentrism or ethnocentrism of polytheism and henotheism, radical monotheism is theocentric. Theocentrism does not suppose that it must defend God against rival sources of power and value, nor does it expect that God will defend the faithful against those rivals. The Christian God has no rivals. What theocentrism requires is a revaluation of all other things, including ourselves and our own aims and desires, in relation to God.[10]

To be sure, Augustine's theocentric ethics can give the appearance of defending God against the world. We have seen the sharp lines that he sometimes draws: There are two cities, one in which people love God and another in which they love themselves to the point of contempt for God. God alone is to be loved and all other things—objects, people, relationships, and institutions—are to be used. Nevertheless, Augustine the theologian is no longer a Manichean dualist, dividing reality into good and evil. His point is not so much a defense of God as it is an astute analysis of the limitations of human love as a way of understanding the world. People cannot help loving something. Efforts at Stoic detachment are bound to fail. But when people attach their love to particular things, it distorts their perception of the rest of reality.

For Augustine, everything is good because it is part of God's creation. What we call evil is not some alien reality opposed to God. It is the absence of a certain good that should be there. Disease is a body lacking the healthy functioning that is its natural good. War and social unrest are the absence of the peace that everyone naturally seeks. Sin and its evil consequences are the result of a will turned toward itself and away from God. These failures of good can be severe, resulting in natural and human evils in which little of the goodness of God's creation remains, but something totally lacking in good could not continue to exist.[11]

All things are good, because God made them. But they are good in different ways and in different degrees. God is the highest degree of every kind of goodness, while other things have more or less of one kind of goodness or another, as God has ordered them in creation. The point of ethics is to understand how things are good and how they are related to other goods. To put good things together into a good life, they have to be arranged in the proper relationships. Enjoyment of good friends and good conversation are worthwhile enjoyments, but these immediate goods must sometimes be subordinated to the demands of larger responsibilities that only bear their good results over a longer time. Succeeding in a career and being held in honor by your neighbors are good things, but if these goods become more important than devotion to God or contemplation of the truth, you will not have a good life. In this, Augustine has an understanding of how good things fit into the good life that was widely shared by reflective people in the ancient world. Aristotle himself might have concurred.

What Augustine adds from his insights into human psychology is that when we love something, we are apt to distort the real value that it has in this ordering of created goodness. To have the money you require to meet your needs in life is a good thing, but it is clearly a better thing to relieve the hunger of a person who is starving. When it is *my* money that is in question, however, my love of it is apt to lead me to misjudge the point at which it would be a better thing to feed the hungry than to save it for my own future or devote it to the wishes of my family. Rome is good, but it is not the center of God's purposes in human history. If I am a Roman, however, I am apt to forget that when the barbarians are in the streets. We might say that Augustine wrote his *City of God* to show that many of those who were lamenting the decline of Rome had let their love for country rearrange their ideas about the good in the wrong order.

To value things appropriately, God must be the "center of value," as H. Richard Niebuhr puts it.[12] It is not that God alone is good, or that things are good only because God says they are. Rather, the goodness of things can only be accurately determined by their relationship to this center from which all goodness ultimately comes. Our transitory projects and personal desires obviously make it difficult to see goods as they really are, but distortions also happen with great goods like love of country, devotion to learning, dedication to a profession, or even commitment to our own version of the Christian stance. Perhaps it is even more difficult to see goods clearly when we love things that are really important, because then we are apt to be surrounded by other people who share these loves with us—fellow citizens, teachers and students, professional colleagues, and people who worship with us.

So Augustine suggests that it would be wise, until our desires can be reshaped, not to love these things at all, but merely to use them as we have need of them, concentrating our love instead on God alone. This is not a purely emotional effort. A good deal of learning and reflection goes into it, too. *City of God* is Augustine's invitation to the learned people of his day to rethink human history, which they had learned from the poets, orators, and historians of Greek and Roman culture, in terms of God's purposes from creation through resurrection destiny. Augustine draws that plan out of scripture and relocates the events of human history in it, but he is not chiefly interested in predicting the future or explaining the disaster that has befallen Rome. Like the Hebrew prophets on whose texts he draws, he aims to show people how they might reorder their goals in the present so that their loves might more accurately reflect the real value of things in God's sight.

If we do that, Augustine told the readers of his books and the hearers of his sermons, we will see that some goods are worth the sacrifice of present happiness in order to secure a more lasting good. He told a congregation whose faith was shaken by reports of barbarian invasions that they should remember the Christian martyrs who, not so long ago in his time, had kept their faith and given up their lives.[13]

Likewise, by loving God and trying to see other things in relation to that love, we might see our neighbor's needs more accurately, as God sees them, and not only as they appear to us when we are preoccupied with our own plans and possessions. Certainly, we would see ourselves differently. We would not exactly become the object of our own contempt, except perhaps as we saw how limited our own self-centered loves had been. We would no longer be able to measure everything in terms of how it fit into our own idea of a good life. We might find ourselves unable to love some things about ourselves that had been sources of pride and self-satisfaction when we compared ourselves to the less gifted people around us, but we might also begin to love things in ourselves because God loves them, even though we had previously seen them as failures to be denied and faults to be concealed. At that point, knowing both the world around us and ourselves more accurately than before, we might even be able safely to begin loving our neighbors, as well as using them. "In these precepts, a man finds three things which he is to love: God, himself, and his neighbour; for a man who loves God does not err in loving himself."[14]

Augustine's theocentrism is thus a very different way of thinking about human goods and goals from Aristotle's eudaimonism. For Augustine, true happiness comes from knowing ourselves, the world, and other people in relation to God. We take the first step toward a good life when we begin to think about our relationship to God, and happiness is only secure as long as that relationship is maintained. For Aristotle, by contrast, we build up a good life piece by piece, as we master the skills and acquire the habits that reason makes possible for us. To be sure, we have to learn to be critical of our own desires in this process. We must come to understand that honor is better than simple pleasure and that true happiness encompasses more than both of them together. It is even true for Aristotle that the good life culminates in a kind of philosophical contemplation that might, in his view of the world, effect a change of values something like Augustine expects from religious devotion. Still, our own good remains the center of attention, and when we have our goods in the right order, that ensures that we will give other people what they deserve and demand for ourselves what we deserve from them. The objective is to do justice to others, not to love them.

Moral Realism

We would expect Augustine, who is primarily concerned to lead people into thinking and living as Christians, to focus on distinctive things that make the Christian's idea of a good life different from the happiness sought by other people. He emphasizes and perhaps even exaggerates his differences with the philosophers whose ideas can be traced back to Aristotle. To understand the possibilities and limitations of teleological ethics, however, it is important to see how much these two views have in common. For both, ethics begins with an effort to identify the goal of a good human life, and whether our actions are right or wrong depends on which goals we pursue.

Moreover, for both Augustine and Aristotle, when we make the right choices, the goodness of those goals is part of their reality. When a eudaimonist philosopher and a theocentric theologian say that something is good, they both mean that its goodness is part of what makes it what it is. The philosopher sees this goodness in relation to the good human life, and the theologian sees it in relation to God's ordering of creation. That makes for important differences in exactly what things each sees as good, but both would agree that when something is good, it has this goodness as part of what it is. It is not good because it is the goal of our plans and actions. It ought to be our goal because it is objectively good.

Likewise, different kinds of good are really different for Aristotle and Augustine. The good that comes from health is quite a different thing from the good that comes from close relationships with family and friends, and that in turn is different from the good of being held in honor by one's fellow citizens. All of these goods satisfy human desires in various ways, but they are not interchangeable parts that we can trade off so long as the sum total of satisfaction remains the same. The good life or the Christian life is made up of a variety of different goods. People have to learn what those goods are and how they are related.

To put the matter in the language of modern philosophy, both Aristotle and Augustine are *moral realists*. They both would argue that the goodness of things, people, and states of affairs is part of the reality of whatever it is that we accurately identify as good. Goodness exists independently of the ideas that we have about it, just as a real table in the next room is there whether we know that it is there or not. Whether there is a table there does not depend on our ideas about tables. Whether there is a table is something we have to find out by learning about how the world around us really is. Of course, our ideas about tables may help or hinder us in that effort to find out how the world really is. If we think that tables are the sort of thing we are apt to find in the refrigerator, we might just overlook the real table, but that does not make it any less real. A realist about tables, then, holds that we can make statements about tables that are true or false, depending on how things are with the real tables in the real world, not on how we think about tables. A moral realist holds the same thing about goodness.

MORAL REALISM

Realism in philosophy is the position that holds that things exist independently of our ideas about them. Our ideas about them may be true or false, and we may be able to discover whether they are true or false by investigating reality.

Most people are realists about objects in everyday experience, but they may have quite a different view of theoretical objects or abstract concepts. For example, is the Higgs Boson (a subatomic particle too small ever to be seen) real, or does it exist only in the theoretical models in which it explains other phenomena that we can observe? What about abstract ideas like beauty or the nation? Can statements about them be true or false, apart from the ideas that people have about them? Some philosophers are *realists* about these theoretical entities and abstract ideas, while others are *anti-realists* or *idealists*.

Moral realism holds that goodness or rightness exists independently of our ideas about what is good and what is right. It is a real property of the people, things, and states of affairs we call good, and statements we make about good may be true or false, depending on whether the people, things, and states of affairs they call good really are.

Both *realism* and *idealism* in the sense discussed here should be distinguished from more ordinary uses of the terms in which realism means having carefully limited expectations (as in Reinhold Niebuhr's *Christian realism*) and idealism means having high (and perhaps unrealistic) hopes for what other people will do.

We can contrast moral realism with what we might call an idealist, subjectivist, or simply an anti-realist understanding of the good. While most philosophers in the ancient world were moral realists, as Aristotle and Augustine were, an Epicurean materialist clearly thought about goodness in a different way. The world that exists independently of the mind consists only of atoms of matter moving in different ways, coming together and breaking apart, forming objects and decaying. Goodness is no part of that reality. If the Epicureans say that a person, an object, or a situation is good, that must be because of how those objects appear to them and not because of something they find in the objects. They would not have had the term, but we can contrast them to Aristotle and Augustine by saying that they were moral anti-realists. Before we can say that something is good, the anti-realist insists that we must specify *for whom* it is good. Since there is nothing in things themselves that makes them good or bad, we must look to the way that some person or group thinks about them to make that judgment. Anti-realists may make this point of reference wide or narrow. An ethical egoist will insist that each person has a unique set of values by which he or she judges things in moral terms. A moral relativist will say that groups, cultures, religions, or political ideologies all impose different moral values on the world, but no one set of goods works for everyone. An anti-realist might even argue that there are some things, like pain, that everyone considers evil and others things, like pleasure, that everyone seeks. But the anti-realist will insist that these things are good only because everyone seeks them. The realist will say that they ought to be sought because they are good.

The Persistence of Moral Realism

Aristotle and Augustine share both a teleological approach to ethics and a commitment to moral realism. Despite the many differences between them, they have this much in common, and the approach to ethics that they share still makes sense to many people today. We do not read the *Nicomachean Ethics* or Augustine's *City of God* the way we might read Aristotle's *Physics* or his texts about biology, just to find out what people once believed about subjects about which we now have much better knowledge. The works of Aristotle and Augustine seem appropriate places to start thinking about the good life or the Christian life, in part because many people share their assumption that when we ask what is good and what goals we ought to pursue, we are asking a question about how the world is, and not just about what we and other people happen to want. The human good seems to be something we can discover, something about which we can be right or wrong, something about which changing our minds is not simply a matter of changing what we want.

Moreover, the different kinds of good that make up the human good or the order of goods that God has created seem genuinely different. They are not just variations on human desire and aversion. We know that in our own lives, some of the most difficult decisions come when we have to choose between goals where both seem good, but we are not quite sure how to relate them. We can see pretty clearly, for example, that the good of feeding a starving child on another continent outweighs the good of another cup of gourmet coffee for ourselves, even if we do not always act on that knowledge. But how do we set our goals when we have to choose between family and career, between learning and service, between living a useful life and living a long one? There are no easy answers to those questions, but the very fact that the questions are so difficult seems like evidence that there are real goods to be chosen and real differences between them. We suspect that there is a real risk of getting the answers wrong, even if the results turn out to be satisfying.

That is to say that much of the time, we think as moral realists, just as Aristotle and Augustine did. The Christian stance, with its idea that God created all things as good and ordered them in relation to one another, supports this moral realism, but Christians are not the only people who have these ideas. Many people believe that things are good independently of our ideas about them. The goodness of a good person, a good habit, or a good situation is part of the reality of that thing, not just a feature of the way we think about it. Of course, it might turn out that moral realists are mistaken about this. Perhaps there is nothing about the goodness of a thing that is part of its own reality, and goodness is strictly the result of the way that people relate to it. Things are good because they satisfy our desires, and the idea that there are different kinds of good is an illusion that can be ignored as long as the results are equally satisfying. As we will see in the next chapter, many modern moral thinkers have sought to resolve our moral perplexities by adopting this kind of anti-realism, especially for choices that involve large institutions and many different people. Nevertheless, many of us persist in moral realism when we come to think about our own moral choices.

The Limitations of Teleology

Although the picture of a good life or a Christian life that people put together for themselves tends to resemble the teleology of Aristotle or Augustine, it is often quite difficult to make that teleology the place to start when you have a moral decision to make. There are several reasons why this is so.

First, it is hard to predict the future. This is a problem for all versions of teleological ethics, since doing the right thing, in teleological terms, requires getting good results. Making the right choice thus requires a judgment not only that the results will be good, but that they will likely be achieved. We can all think of occasions when we failed to achieve the large results we hoped for and as a result had to conclude that the right choice would have been to settle for lesser goods that would have been more easily achieved. What we want from moral reasoning, however, is a method that tells us the right thing to do before we have to do it. Because it is hard to predict the future, it is not clear that teleological ethics can provide this.

When teleology is linked to moral realism, another problem arises. Not only is it difficult to know the future; it is also difficult to know the good as thoroughly as we would need to in order to choose the best among a number of competing goods. Especially, as we have noted, it is difficult to choose between different kinds of goods when all of them seem to have a place in the life we are seeking: work *or* family, success *or* service, public honors *or* personal satisfaction. These are the dilemmas of which the moral life often seems to be made, and even if these goods have a reality in the world that could tell us which of them to choose, we often have to confess that we do not know what it is at the point that the choice has to be made.

The problem is multiplied when more people become involved. Teleological ethics seems to require that in order to agree on which good should become our goal, everyone must agree on what the real goods are and how they are related. If this is often difficult for one person to do alone, it seems nearly impossible to follow this way of making moral choices in large groups, or for a whole society. Teleological ethics might be useful when a few people with closely linked ideas and experiences need to make a choice together, but even spouses will tell you that it is not easy to come to a conclusion that is a genuine agreement on what the good is, as opposed to a compromise between two different ideas about the good.

Aristotle and Augustine would not have been surprised by this. Aristotle believed that accurate knowledge of the human good is built up piece by piece, out of many different choices, and he warned that those who lack experience are not likely to be very good students of ethics.[15] Augustine's idea that the true goodness of everything can be understood through its relation to God seems to offer a more complete picture, but he did not expect that God would reveal this picture to the inquiring theocentric theologian all at once. It is a knowledge built up through the slow acquisition of virtue, "the way of life through which we may merit to know what we believe."[16] It seems on this account that to know what belongs in the good life we are trying to choose, we must already be living it.

Perhaps what Augustine meant was something close to that. To truly love things as God loves them might take a lifetime, accompanied by a long apprenticeship in which it would be safe only to use them in ways that served our immediate necessities and try to reserve our love for God alone. In that case, the ability to answer our moral questions in teleological terms would itself be an important goal of the Christian life, but not a very effective starting point for it.

To use the kind of teleology Augustine had in mind as the starting point for Christian ethics, you would have to have a well-developed account of the goods that human beings might choose and how they are related to one another. You would need to know what to do and what to avoid in a comprehensive way in order to decide what to do and what to avoid in the specific choices faced in your own life. That is to say, you would need a strong authority or a strong tradition to instruct you, substituting the experience of the church and its leaders for the lifetime of experience that none of us has yet at the point when we have to make our choices about what kind of life we are going to live.

Augustine no doubt wanted to provide that authority and tradition in the unstable world where he and the Christians of Hippo lived at the beginning of the fifth Christian century. He did not quite achieve it in his lifetime, but in other places and other centuries, Christians have often been able to live with this shared understanding of the good, accumulated in tradition and taught with authority. They are rarely able to live that way today, nor has it been easy to do that anywhere since the modern world began. It is understandable, then, that the emphasis in Christian ethics has shifted from goals to rules. We will see more of how that shift happened in chapter 6, but before that, we need to see how some philosophers and theologians adapted a different understanding of the good to provide a starting point for teleology in modern times.

Additional Reading

Elshtain, Jean Bethke. *Augustine and the Limits of Politics.* Notre Dame, IN: University of Notre Dame Press, 1995.

Frankena, William K. *Ethics.* 2nd ed. Englewood Cliffs, NJ: Prentice-Hall, 1973.

Holmes, Arthur F. *Ethics: Approaching Moral Decisions.* 2nd ed. Downers Grove, IL: InterVarsity Press, 2007.

Meilaender, Gilbert. *The Way That Leads There: Augustinian Reflections on the Christian Life.* Grand Rapids: Eerdmans, 2006.

Niebuhr, H. Richard. *Faith on Earth: An Inquiry into the Structure of Human Faith.* Richard R. Niebuhr, ed. New Haven: Yale University Press, 1989.

Pinckaers, Servais. *Morality: The Catholic View.* South Bend, IN: Saint Augustine's Press, 2001.

Werpehowski, William. *American Protestant Ethics and the Legacy of H. Richard Niebuhr.* Washington, DC: Georgetown University Press, 2002.

CHAPTER FIVE

THE GREATEST GOOD FOR THE GREATEST NUMBER?

Teleological thinking is important in modern theology and ethics, just as it was for Aristotle and Augustine. Modern teleology, however, begins by identifying a single good by which all goods, personal and political, can be measured. Once all goods are commensurable, "the greatest good for the greatest number" provides the goal for all choices. For some, this modern teleology becomes a way to replace the stern judgments and confusing rules of religious ethics. For others, it represents the heart of the moral teaching of Jesus. Both points of view agree, however, that "the greatest good for the greatest number" sets a standard very different from previous systems of ethics.

Teleological thinking is very important in our personal lives. We all have goals, short and long term, that identify the goods we seek for ourselves, for the people around us, and for larger groups in which we participate. Most of the time, when we are making our own choices between various goods, we think like moral realists. It seems that the goodness of things and states of affairs is really part of them, something to be discovered about them and not just a way we have of thinking about them. The differences between goods seem real to us, too, so that we are often less concerned with *how much* good we have overall than with *which* goods we are pursuing and how they are related to other kinds of good that we may want to have alongside them, or that we may have to give up to reach the goals that are more important. When we are trying to choose between a summer school course that will help with career preparation and a summer service project that will help other people, the question "how much?" does not seem appropriate. These are just different goods. Either one might be better than lounging on the beach all summer—though there might be some good in that, too—but there does not seem to be any quantitative way to make the choices between the goods that compete for our attention. What we do instead is balance these different goods against one another and rank them in relation to other goods, seeking a combination that will enable us to live a good life.

As we saw in chapter 4, Aristotle and Augustine both thought of the goods people seek in this moral realist way, and each of them can give us some guidance about how to make our choices and set our goals. Sometimes, we try to understand goods the way Aristotle did, from the bottom up. That is, we consider the whole set of goods available to us, and we try to compare them and rank them to arrive at a comprehensive picture of the good life. Immediate pleasures may be worth pursuing, but upon reflection, they often take a back seat to goals like health, friendship, and accomplishment. Those are goods which sustain the kind of happiness that Aristotle said we seek over a lifetime. When we are doing teleology in the Aristotelian way, from the bottom up, the problem is to make sure that this hierarchy of goals rises high enough, so that in our pursuit of many different goods, we do not neglect something that is really important, something that ought to take priority over all of our other goals.

At other times, we look at goods the way Augustine did, from the top down. That is, we begin with that one good that is clearly better than all the rest, and we try to understand all other goods in relationship to it. For Augustine, it is clear that the greatest good is a relationship with God. When we think about ethics as Augustine did, it is easy to see what belongs at the top of the hierarchy of goals. The difficulty is to figure out how this hierarchy extends downward from the top, so that we see even our everyday choices about how to spend our time and what to do with our money in relationship to God.

Either way, when we are thinking about goods and goals in these personal terms, we find that there is no one scale on which all goods can be measured. There is no formula by which we could decide that this much health is worth that much achievement, so that we determine with mathematical certainty which choice is the right one when there are different goals that we could pursue. For all the differences between Aristotle and Augustine in their thinking about human goods, both would have agreed on this.

Modern Teleology

There is another way to think about competing goods and goals, however. It has developed more recently in moral philosophy, since the eighteenth century, and it seems particularly useful when the choices involve large groups and the results affect many people. When many different goals have to be brought together in a single decision, we struggle to find some common measure of the good that could be accepted by everyone. Perhaps this would not be so difficult if there were a shared tradition or a powerful authority that told everyone in society how to think about the different kinds of good, so that we all agreed on how they ought to be combined to make a good life or a good society.[1] Today, however, we do not have that tradition, and we probably would not want that kind of authority, so philosophers and theologians have devised various ways of thinking about goods on the larger scale that a modern, diverse society requires.

Consider, for example, a state legislator who has to choose between subsidizing a telecommunications company that will bring new jobs to the state and funding medical clinics in poor urban neighborhoods. Both economic opportunity and medical care seem to be good things, but in this case, limited resources require a choice between them. The legislator knows that some people will be unemployed if the telecommunications company goes elsewhere, and others may suffer illness if the clinics are not built. Over the long run, the citizens who vote for these legislators are involved in this moral decision, too.

The legislators could take a teleological approach to this decision, focusing their attention and the attention of the citizens on the goal at which their choice is directed. You have probably read or heard about this kind of thinking in politics, even if you did not know to call it "teleology" at the time. If a choice has to be made between telecommunications and clinics, the modern teleologist will insist that nothing is going to be gained by declaiming about the values of free enterprise or the importance of good health care. What we want to know is which choice leads to the best results overall. If there are more long-term economic and social benefits associated with subsidizing the telecommunications company, then that is the right action to take. Any other action is wrong, even though some good may come of it. Likewise, someone who wants the health clinics may have great concern for those who lack adequate medical care and feel deep sympathy for their suffering, but these altruistic motivations are not what make a good decision in teleological ethics. The right choice is the action that leads to the best results overall.

This modern kind of teleological thinking is widely used, not only in politics, but in business and in other organizations. Corporations use it to allocate resources, and legislatures use it to set budget priorities. Colleges and universities may use it in tough financial times to decide which programs get cut and which get spared. As in all teleological ethics, the assumption behind the explanation is that what makes this the right choice is the good that will be achieved. What is different about modern teleology is the way this good is recognized and measured. Aristotle and Augustine speak of goods in qualitative terms. What makes a situation good is a particular mix of distinct goods that, taken together in this particular combination, identify an action worth doing or a life worth living. Modern teleology, by contrast, speaks of good in quantitative terms. What makes an action worth doing is that it achieves the most good on the whole, or the greatest good for the greatest number. Although this way of thinking began with large groups and public choices, the modern teleologist readily extends it into personal life, too. What makes a life worth living is that its pleasures, of whatever sort, exceed its pains.

Utilitarianism

This quantitative way of talking about goods and goals developed along with the modern world, as democratic politics and market economics began to replace traditional patterns of life and customary ways of doing business. These ideas have become central in politics, economics, and policy studies, but they originated in ethics. Francis Hutcheson (1694–1746) was a moral philosopher in Scotland whose "moral sense" theory placed confidence in the judgments of ordinary people, even though they were not trained in the formal reasoning that belonged to the academic study of ethics. "Ask any honest farmer" was the way that Hutcheson sometimes began his moral inquiries, since the honest farmer knows as much as the moral philosopher about what makes for the greatest happiness over the long run. Adam Smith (1723–1790), author of *The Wealth of Nations*, is credited with beginning the modern study of economics, but he also had a career as a moral philosopher in Scotland. His system of open markets and free trade began as the answer to the moral problem of how to satisfy the needs of as many people as possible at the same time. Markets were the best way to organize an economy, Smith argued, because they would produce more wealth for more people than the systems of customary arrangements, regulations, and taxation that had governed trade in Europe up to that time.

MODERN TELEOLOGY

Francis Hutcheson (1694–1746) argued that ethics should rely on the "moral sense" shared by ordinary people, who know what makes for human happiness.

Adam Smith (1723–1790) wrote *The Wealth of Nations* and founded modern economics. He argued that social goals could be set by the goods people choose in markets.

Jeremy Bentham (1748–1832) argued that both personal and political choices should follow the "principle of utility."

John Stuart Mill (1806–1873) further developed utilitarianism as a philosophy for democracy and social reform.

Jeremy Bentham (1748–1832), an English philosopher and political reformer, devised a way of thinking that has been called "utilitarianism." According to Bentham, the "principle of utility" evaluates every action according to whether it increases or diminishes the happiness of the parties concerned. Given a range of possible actions, then, the right choice is the one that produces the greatest happiness for the greatest number of people. The principle of utility, Bentham argues, should guide us in every situation of choice, "and therefore not only of every action of a private individual, but of every measure of government."[2]

That is a sweeping claim, but Bentham thought it would simplify the moral life considerably if it were generally followed. Pleasure and pain are the only guides that human beings have in nature, and when we follow them without being distracted by rules, authorities, and traditions that tell us what to do, we will arrive at the course of action that leads to the greatest happiness. Knowing the right thing to do involves an intricate calculation of how much pleasure or pain a choice will produce, how long these pleasures and pains will last, how widely they will be spread, and whether they are likely to be followed by similar effects in the future. The calculation may be difficult, but the basic idea is simple: Once we know what produces the most happiness for the most people, we know what we ought to do. Rules, especially rules that claim to tell us what God commands, only keep people from thinking clearly about the results of their choices.

Bentham assumed that utilitarian reforms would eliminate the need for traditional moral teachers like the clergy and spell the end for aristocrats who claimed privileges that did not produce any good for the people as a whole. His ideas alarmed people who thought that he was telling people to do whatever would make them most happy and forget about self-discipline, sacrifice, and respect for authority. But Bentham's utilitarianism was not simple hedonism. The crucial requirement in utilitarianism is that we are to do what makes for the greatest happiness *for the greatest number*. If the expensive luxuries that give me momentary pleasure would pay for food that would relieve the suffering of dozens of starving people, then clearly the right thing to do is to forego those pleasures and give the money to the starving. If my child is a mediocre musician, I will be a good person by giving the lessons—and maybe the piano, too—to a poor child who has talent and who may in time share the pleasures of music with many others. Carried through consistently, utilitarianism is not simply about seeking our own happiness by going against the rules. Utilitarianism may require a great deal of self-discipline and sacrifice, especially if our awareness of how many people are affected by our choices is broad enough. Bentham thought that most Christians in his day had missed this simple truth, but his pupil, John Stuart Mill (1806-1873), believed that utilitarianism was exactly the kind of simplification of morality that Jesus had in mind. "In the golden rule of Jesus of Nazareth, we read the complete spirit of the ethics of utility. To do as one would be done by, and to love one's neighbour as oneself, constitute the ideal perfection of utilitarian morality."[3]

What a utilitarian teleology requires, then, is that we measure all of our choices by the happiness of the people who are affected, and not by any other ideas about what is or is not valuable. For Bentham, moreover, happiness is simply the balance of pleasure over pain in any situation. Parents must not be distracted by a special sense of responsibility for their own children's musical education. The art collector must not claim that the enjoyment of a great painting is somehow superior to the happiness that a hungry person gets from a good meal, though the utilitarian calculation may consider that the painting will be available to provide pleasure for far longer than the meal will. We make the best calculation we can of the consequences, measured in terms of happiness. When we have done that, we know the right thing to do. We are to choose the course of action that maximizes happiness, whatever mix of goods may be involved in that result.

To be sure, later utilitarians tried to correct the impression left by Bentham that to treat people as equals, we have to treat whatever gives them happiness as equal, too. John Stuart Mill insisted that people who have experienced both ordinary and more refined pleasures can tell the difference between them in their own experience, so that the happiness that comes from a brilliant performance of a Mozart aria does not have to count the same as a karaoke rendition of "My Way" when we are calculating the sum total of happiness.

Hutcheson, Smith, Bentham, and Mill together thus provided a new way of thinking about personal and public choices. They argued that utilitarianism was the clearest way of thinking about morality, and they changed the institutions of modern society in democratic, market-oriented ways that still influence ways we make our choices today. In a market economy, money gives us a convenient way of measuring how much pleasure we expect from the various possibilities that are open to us, so that what we are willing to pay for something becomes our way of signaling to other people how much happiness we think we will get from their products or services. One way this works can be seen in the economist's calculation of "marginal utility," in which each additional unit of a good acquired makes less of a contribution to our happiness, and as a result, the price we are willing to pay for it declines. When I am hungry, a cheeseburger contributes a great deal to my happiness, and I will pay for it accordingly. A second cheeseburger makes me pretty happy, too, though the restaurant quickly discovers that I will be more likely to buy it if the second cheeseburger comes at a discount when I buy two. By the time we get to the third cheeseburger, however, I am most likely full, and I would not pay enough for it to make it worth the proprietor's trouble. Someone will have to offer me something else to buy, and thus give me another way to participate in the market, increase my happiness, and continue my contributions to the happiness of others.

Of course, this model works best in simple transactions in small markets, especially where we can ignore the fact that some people have more money than others do. The rich can use money to signal their happiness a lot more effectively than the poor can. For that reason, we sometimes determine the greatest happiness of the greatest number by voting, rather than by market choices. In an election, we can arrive at a rough and ready calculation of what makes for the greatest happiness for the greatest number by seeing which policy, party, or candidate wins. This works best, of course, if everybody has a vote, and Bentham and Mill worked for political reforms that extended the vote to more men. Mill was also among the first philosophers to argue for extending the vote to women. These democratic reforms took over a century to complete, but they fit with the logic of utilitarian ethics from the beginning. When determining what makes for the greatest happiness for the greatest number, the principle must be "everybody to count for one, nobody for more than one."[4]

Measuring Good

We are all utilitarians at some points in our lives. We participate in elections where everyone has one vote, and we buy and sell in markets, where everyone's money has equal value, supposing that the best outcome will be achieved when we determine the results by these Benthamite methods. It is an attractive idea to think that we might settle our disputes efficiently and democratically, treating everyone equally, not bowing to customs, superstitions, or arbitrary authorities, and doing whatever leads to the greatest good for the greatest number of people. For this to work, however, we must be able to determine the most good with some precision.

That is not quite the same task as determining the "greatest good" or the "highest good" in the way that Aristotle and Augustine did. As we have seen, they thought that the goals people seek are really different from one another, and each good must be correctly ordered in relation to the others to make up a good life. If the highest good is to use your reason in a certain way, as Aristotle believed, then pleasures, honors, wealth, and personal characteristics like courage and generosity must be ordered toward that highest good. Augustine made the same comparisons between different goods, ordering all of them toward love for God as the highest good. Ancient philosophers, in fact, were constantly comparing goods, identifying them as higher and lower, greater or lesser. We do the same, when we decide that taking care of a friend is a greater good than studying for a test, or that two weeks volunteering on a service project is better than two weeks lying on the beach. But it does not quite make sense to say that there is "more" good in the service project and "less" of it in studying for the test. The goods can be compared, but they are not *commensurable*. There is no common measure by which we could determine that this much service is worth that much beach time. They are just different goods, and part of what sometimes makes it difficult to choose between different goods is precisely that we do not know how to measure them against one another.

For Bentham, the situation is quite different. His system depends on being able to say that there is more good, quantitatively, in one state of affairs than another. If two weeks of service are better than two weeks on the beach, this cannot be because someone tells us that service is better than self-indulgence. It has to be because more good is accomplished by this particular service than by the same time devoted to recreation. We cannot choose by comparing one good to another and deciding that service is qualitatively better. We need a standard of measurement that renders the goods commensurable, so that we can compare them quantitatively.

It is easy to see what that standard is for Bentham. Pleasure or happiness is what renders all goods commensurable. People take pleasure in all sorts of different situations, from being with people they love to completing a good job to enjoying a good meal. Different goods can be compared because each of them yields a quantity of pleasure that can be compared to the quantity yielded by other goods. We feel real satisfaction in doing something for others, and they, of course, take a different kind of pleasure in having their needs met. Taken together, the sum of that happiness is probably greater than the rather different pleasures I would enjoy in two weeks at the beach, so the right choice is the service project. On the other hand, I cannot do very much for very many people in three or four hours, so I might provide the greatest good for the greatest number by taking off early some day during the project and tending to my own happiness for an afternoon.

CONSEQUENTIALISM

Consequentialism is another name for teleology, a system of ethics that considers results to determine what actions are right.

Hedonism is consequentialism that measures those results in terms of pleasure and pain. An individualistic hedonism simply asks whether the choice results in more pleasure than pain for one individual, usually the person who is making the choice. Utilitarianism is sometimes called *universalistic hedonism*, because it considers the results in terms of pleasure and pain for everyone involved.

Consequentialism, then, can be *egocentric* or *universalistic*, depending on whether it considers results only for the person making the choice or for everyone involved.

Consequentialism can use other measures besides pleasure and pain to calculate the best results. Economic decisions are often made with a view toward maximizing wealth or profits. *Agapism* is a term sometimes used for Christian versions of consequentialism. Derived from the Greek word *agapē* (love), it measures consequences in terms of the kind of love that Jesus said should be given to God and the neighbor.

Like the Epicureans of old, Bentham and Mill find nothing in the world of things that makes any of them objectively good. Things are good only because there are persons who take pleasure in them, and they are evil only because there are persons who find them painful. For the utilitarian, we make our decisions between the various goals that we might pursue by asking not whether they are good in themselves, but whether they give people pleasure or pain. If so, how many people and how much pain or pleasure? Is the pleasure certain and immediate, or is it distant in time and likely to be changed by intervening events? Are these outcomes concentrated on a few people, or are they spread over many? Bentham even devised a formula by which the value of pleasure or pain could be calculated, based on these quantitative considerations. This process, he insisted, could be applied to pleasures in whatever forms they appear, and however they may be labeled. Good, profit, convenience, advantage, benefit, or happiness are simply names by which pleasure is known, as mischief, inconvenience, disadvantage, loss, or unhappiness name its opposite.[5] Where Aristotle or Augustine might see all lesser goods related in various ways to a highest good, Bentham finds all goods reducible to the one thing they have in common, which is the pleasure they provide. For him, there are no other goods that are higher than pleasure. That is what enables him to determine what the greatest good for the greatest number is.

Utilitarianism Today

Utilitarianism thus provides little guidance for the personal choices in which we very much want to know how to rank one good in relation to another. Despite Bentham's idea that the principle of utility is the best guide for individual choices and measures of government alike, utilitarianism seems to work best when it is used in large groups. It reminds individuals that they need to think for themselves about these questions, paying attention to their own pains and pleasures and not allowing moral or religious authorities to tell them that some pleasures are higher or better than others. It also offers the equality that comes from knowing that we are all involved in the same effort to secure happiness through the greatest balance of pleasure over pain.

These values continue to be important in moral thinking two centuries after Bentham and Mill. They shape the work of the contemporary utilitarian philosopher Peter Singer. Singer denies that there is any God who could create a variety of objective goods. Nor is there any teleological order in nature from which we could learn that one good is better than another. Besides the universal experience of happiness that follows when pleasure outweighs pain, there is no other basis for calling something "good." Singer carries this through consistently by noting that there is no reason to prefer *human* happiness to the happiness of other beings that are able to feel pleasure and pain, and thus he arrives at a version of utilitarianism in which the principle is to choose the action that leads to the greatest balance of pleasure over pain for all sentient beings. Indeed, Singer sometimes suggests that the amount of suffering in the world is such that calculating this maximized outcome is hardly necessary for most of our actions. We will have all we can do, and all we need to have a meaningful life, if we simply do as much as we can to reduce the amount of pain and suffering in the universe.[6]

Singer's teleology, consistently applied, leaves no room for preferring my own good, the good of my country, or even the good of our species, if I can instead do something that will produce a greater reduction in the suffering of other sentient beings. Because it is the reduction of suffering that counts, there is nothing obviously superior about reducing the suffering of my family or my fellow citizens, if I can relieve more suffering by directing my efforts elsewhere.[7] Because it is the quality of life, measured in terms of lack of suffering, that counts, rather than some objective good in life itself, we must face the sad fact that some lives will have such a surplus of pain over pleasure that they will not be worth living at all, and death by suicide or euthanasia may be an appropriate way to relieve suffering. Singer has been attacked for all of these positions, particularly by persons with disabilities who feel that his views threaten them with some authoritarian calculation that their lives add too much to the world's supply of suffering to allow them to continue. Singer denies that these conclusions follow from his position, and he tries to show clearly in his own life what he thinks it does mean. He is a vegetarian, and a vigorous advocate for animal rights. He works to protect the environment, for though nature itself cannot feel pain, environmental quality has enormous implications for the well-being or suffering of all forms of sentient life. He lives modestly and gives away a large percentage of his income, because it is clear—the old idea of marginal utility again—that after a certain point, his money will reduce the suffering of others living in the depths of poverty far more than it will increase his own happiness.

No one should think, then, that a teleology that maximizes good from a human point of view and bundles all kinds of goods together under a common measurement of pain and pleasure is a self-centered approach to ethics, or an undemanding one. Singer admits that it is difficult to treat all suffering as equal to one's own or to the suffering of those near to oneself. Nevertheless, for a consistently non-theological approach to ethics, in which the pleasures and pains felt by individual sentient beings provide the only measure of value, this kind of utilitarianism may be the most rational way to choose between alternative courses of action. In any case, Singer says, people who take his point of view "may be daunted by the immensity of the task that faces them; but they are not bored, and do not need psychotherapy to make their lives meaningful."[8] Christian ethics sees the world in quite a different way, but a Christian might well pray to be able to make the same claim.

Modern Teleology and Christian Ethics

Utilitarianism took shape as a reaction against religious rules and authorities, and even those who thought that utilitarianism reflected the ethics of Jesus had little use for the familiar forms of Christianity. Nevertheless, the idea that human happiness is somehow central to the moral life made its impact on Christian ethics, too. Ever since Isaac Newton (1643–1727) discovered the scientific laws that govern all motion, theologians had regarded the world as an intricate machine, designed by God and running with great precision to serve God's purposes. William Paley (1743–1805) was an Anglican clergyman who popularized this image of an orderly, mechanical universe by comparing our contemplation of the natural world to a hiker who discovers a watch along his path. Because of its intricate parts, the hiker knows at once that the watch is something different from the rock lying next to it. The watch shows that it has been designed for a purpose, and because of the design, the hiker concludes with equal certainty that somewhere there was a watchmaker who put those parts together according to that design. In the same way, Paley argued, the orderliness of the natural world suggests that it has a purpose, and if it has a purpose, it must have a maker. His "watchmaker" analogy became one of the best known versions of the *teleological argument* for the existence of God.[9]

For Paley, it was a short step from observing the order of nature to identifying its purpose or goal. The world is so wonderfully suited to human happiness that we must conclude that God designed it for that end. This, in turn, leads to an understanding of the will of God that would have sounded familiar to Bentham:

> We conclude, therefore, that God wishes and wills the happiness of his creatures. And this conclusion being once established, we are at liberty to go on with the rule built upon it, namely, "that the method of coming at the will of God, concerning any action, by the light of nature, is to inquire into the tendency of that action to promote or diminish the general happiness."[10]

Paley's commitment to general happiness, however, did not develop in quite the same way that Bentham's did. Paley argued that rules, far from being contrary to the principle of promoting general happiness, are essential to it. To render judgment fair and predictable, we must suppose that even God makes judgments in accordance with general rules, and not by determining the happiness that might result from any action viewed by itself apart from a system of rules.[11] If we believe that God has created an orderly world, we must use reason to look for laws that govern moral choices, just as Newton found the laws that govern the motions of natural objects.

Paley's teleological thinking remained important to Christian ethics long after his time, and his influence may have reached as far as another Anglican ethicist who did his most important work in the middle of the twentieth century. Joseph Fletcher (1905–1993) was a professor of Christian ethics at Episcopal Divinity School in Cambridge, Massachusetts. During the 1960s, he was deeply involved in the emerging discipline of medical ethics, and he saw rapid changes in society that accompanied the civil rights movement, the rise of feminism, and the use of new technologies in medicine. Traditional Christian ethics did not seem to offer much guidance for the new questions raised by reproductive medicine, genetic engineering, and end-of-life care, nor could it respond to the hard choices that people have to make under extreme conditions of war, imprisonment, or poverty. Conventional rules just were not formulated to provide guidance for these situations, and Christian teaching often left the people faced with these choices feeling guilty and rejected, no matter what they decided to do.

Fletcher's solution, like Paley's, was to return to the purpose served by moral action. His goal, however, was not "the greatest happiness for the greatest number," but "the most loving thing possible" in the situation.

> *Christian* situation ethics has only one norm or principle or law (call it what you will) that is binding and unexceptionable, always good and right regardless of circumstances. That is "love"—the *agapē* of the summary commandment to love God and the neighbor. Everything else without exception, all laws and rules and principles and ideals and norms, are only *contingent*, only valid *if they happen* to serve love in any situation.[12]

Fletcher argued for a more realistic and compassionate approach that would avoid *legalism*, which insists that for every situation of choice there is a moral rule that must be followed. Legalism reduces Christian ethics to a system of inflexible rules that may be impossible to apply under new and unusual conditions. But Christian ethics must also avoid *antinomianism*, which says that there is no purpose against which we can judge our individual choices and actions. For antinomianism, each choice is a new reality, which has to be decided entirely on its own terms.

In between these two extremes is what Fletcher called "situation ethics," which makes decisions by assessing the consequences in light of Jesus' teaching about love of God and neighbor. We are not left without guidance in a new or difficult situation. Rules and principles help us see what love might require, but we cannot determine what to do just by following the rules. Our aim must be to do the most loving thing for everyone in the situation. If following the rules helps to do that, then the rules should be followed. If not, they should be set aside without feelings of regret or guilt.

Suppose, for example, that I am an employer, and I discover that my office manager has been helping herself to small "loans" from the company's cash receipts. There are rules against theft. A legalist would no doubt remind me of them and warn me not to let such conduct go unpunished. The legalist might advise dismissing the office manager, or even calling in the police. In addition to the rules, though, I might also consider the real needs that led my trusted employee to take these risky actions. Since no one else is aware of the theft and the company and its other employees have not yet been harmed by it, I might decide to regularize the "loan" and allow the office manager to make a written agreement to pay the money back. If the office manager's needs are really pressing, I might even make a gift from my own funds to help with the situation. Finally, I would probably also put some new procedures in place to make sure that this does not happen again. After all that has been said and done, the wisdom behind the rule has been considered, even though the rule has not been followed. Care has been shown for the office manager, but also for the company and the other employees who depend on it, and because this seems to be the most loving solution for everyone involved, I can say—assuming that I am a follower of situation ethics—that I have done the right thing.

Fletcher's effort to avoid antinomianism requires some consideration of traditional moral rules, but in his attitude toward rules, he is probably closer to Bentham than to Paley. For Paley, once we have determined what the rules governing the greatest happiness are, we can expect that even God will follow them. For Fletcher, any rules we might devise are no more than general guidelines. They are no substitute for thinking seriously about how to be most loving in this particular situation. To put the distinction in philosophical terms, Fletcher follows an *act teleology*. He is concerned with the consequences of each possible action and believes that the right choice is the specific action that has the best results.[13] Paley, by contrast, suggests that when we calculate consequences, we should try to determine which rules would lead to the best results, if generally followed. When we know that, we know the will of God, or, as Paley sometimes puts it, the rule by which God judges human conduct. This is what contemporary moral philosophers would call a *rule teleology*. The rule is designed for the purpose of maximizing human happiness, but our obligation is to obey the rule, not to calculate the consequences. For Fletcher, rules that do not lead to the most loving consequences must be set aside. For Paley, the rule must still be obeyed.[14]

Fletcher received a great deal of criticism for his efforts to move beyond traditional moral rules. His opponents argued that situation ethics, with its effort to find the "most loving" solution, leaves people with no guidance except their own feelings. This was not helped by Fletcher's penchant for quoting a line from Augustine that he translated as "love with care and *then*, what you will, do."[15] The position the critics of situation ethics were attacking, however, was closer to what Fletcher himself called "antinomianism." Fletcher was trying to reject legalism. The traditional moral rules have a place in Fletcher's ethics. They are not to be discarded in advance, before we consider the situation. They may help us determine the most loving thing to do, but we should never follow the rules *instead* of doing the most loving thing.

> ACT TELEOLOGY determines the right action by calculating which action will produce the greatest good. We should do the action that produces the greatest good in this particular case. Joseph Fletcher provides an example.
>
> RULE TELEOLOGY determines the right action by a rule that generally leads to the greatest good. We should do the action that the rule requires, even if some other action would lead to better results in this case. William Paley provides an example.

Situation ethics is an appealing way to deal with a moral problem when the rules are unclear or when different rules conflict. As we will see, even deontological ethicists, who rely primarily on rules to determine right and wrong, will sometimes let the results be decisive in such cases. However, readers who appreciate Fletcher's rejection of legalism and antinomianism still find his middle way hard to pin down. Happiness may be difficult to measure precisely, but we know what it means for someone to be more happy or less happy in two different situations. What, exactly, does it mean for someone to be more loved, or more loving in those circumstances?

The Uses and Limits of Goals

Goals, as we said at the outset, are an important part of the moral life. We cannot describe a good human life without discussing some of the goods that are part of it and explaining how to go about acquiring them. When we set goals for a business or a social group or a volunteer organization, we are making decisions about how to use resources and estimating how much we will be able to accomplish. We want to increase sales by this amount, add a certain number of new members, or repair so many homes for needy families. But often our statements of goals become a statement about what a good human life is. Repairing homes reminds us that families need shelter and security to flourish. Putting our energy into that goal says something about how we think our own lives become meaningful. Setting goals and working to achieve them is closer than we might at first think to what Augustine had in mind when he told Christians to love God alone and use all things as this life requires.

The question which we set out to answer in these two chapters about teleological ethics, however, is where we should start when we need to make a decision about a specific moral problem.[16] Can the student who knows that a classmate is cheating or a family member waiting for the doctor outside the intensive care unit figure out the right thing to do by asking, "What is the most loving thing to do in this situation?" or "What makes for the greatest happiness of the greatest number of people?" Are the choices of the market and the voting booth the *right* choices, just because they tell us what the greatest number of people believe will make them happy?

There are some reasons to think not, and those reasons have to do with things that we often do not know when we try to decide the answers to those questions about maximizing a good: (1) We do not know how to measure the pleasures and pains of others. (2) We do not know what the ultimate outcome of our choices will be. (3) We do not know how the good we create will be distributed. Any of these problems might lead a person to hesitate before adopting a teleological approach as the primary starting point for moral decisions.

Interpersonal comparisons. We can estimate pleasures and pains by noting how people vote or how much they are willing to pay for something they want, but we really do not know what they are feeling. We know what they report about their feelings. Using the formula, "the greatest happiness for the greatest number," as a decision-making procedure runs into difficulties of interpersonal comparison as soon as the happiness of more than one person is involved. Participants have an incentive to exaggerate their own feelings and minimize the pains of others, because in a utilitarian calculus, those who feel the greatest pain or the greatest pleasure have the most influence on the choice. Applications of utilitarian ideas therefore frequently rely on a standardized model of preferences and aversions, based on how an "impartial spectator"[17] would react to a situation, or on a calculation of "welfare" in purely economic terms. The greatest happiness is determined by how the experts judge a rational person would feel, rather than by gathering up reports of people's actual feelings. This is necessary for practical reasons, but it backs away from Bentham's claim that a utilitarian teleology can dispense with tradition and authority because it is based on what people actually want. Tradition and authority, by contrast, allow us to assume a structure of shared goods and goals, but as we have seen, many moral problems arise precisely because people do not share traditions and authorities by which to resolve their disagreements.

Predictions. It is not only hard to know what other people are thinking. It is difficult to predict the future. As we noted in discussing Aristotle and Augustine, teleological systems of all sorts require us to choose the course of action that leads to good results,[18] but this leaves us with a problem when things do not turn out as we planned. Suppose that in the problem we discussed at the beginning of this chapter, a hypothetical legislator decides that subsidizing a telecommunications company to create new jobs will create more happiness for more people than providing health care by funding community clinics. The right choice, then, is clearly to vote for the telecommunications subsidy. But suppose now that the telecommunications company goes bankrupt shortly after spending the subsidy, so that there are no jobs and no health care. Shall we say that the legislator made a wrong choice because it did not result in the greatest good for the greatest number? Or shall we say that the legislator's choice was right since the legislator intended to produce the greatest good for the greatest number, even though that was not the result? If we move in the latter way, it becomes easier to claim that any choice is right, because we can just stipulate how we intended it to turn out. If we insist on seeing the actual outcome, there is no way to know what the right choice is before we make it.

The same problem arises for the Aristotelian or Augustinian who tries to make choices in terms not just of more, but of better goods. It would be a great good to resolve a conflict between two nations, so that their people could live in peace for the indefinite future. But if the attempts at peacemaking fail, should we say that was the wrong choice, and that the right choice would have been to secure the lesser good of a strong defense to minimize the risk of outright war? Or should we say that peacemaking is the right choice anyway, on grounds that lasting peace will never be achieved if peacemaking is not attempted? Political realists and peace advocates have this argument almost every time an international dispute approaches the boiling point, but there may be no way to settle it on teleological terms as long as the outcome remains unknown.

The problem is that our knowledge of the future is always limited. Our actions often produce results different from what we expect, and even when things do turn out according to plan, subsequent developments may lead us to conclude that what produced the most good immediately did not lead on to the most good on the whole. Human beings cannot know the future. As a result, they need an idea of right choices and moral goodness that is not completely dependent on outcomes. Otherwise, Aristotle's old saying that we should call no man happy until he is dead[19] becomes the odd statement that we can call no one good until all the results are in.

Distribution. The problems with interpersonal comparisons and predictions arise from what we cannot know. The problem with distribution, by contrast, arises from what a utilitarian calculation does not tell us. Knowing the arrangements that would result in the greatest happiness for the greatest number does not tell us how happiness would be distributed. We might suppose that a small group of people sharing goods with one another would most likely be happiest if their shares were more or less equal, but that assumption quickly comes into question in larger groups. More happiness overall might result if a large group of consumers were served by a smaller number of workers who toiled under miserable conditions to make things that the consumers would be happy to purchase at low prices, especially if the workers and the consumers were separated by enough distance that the consumers did not have to think about how they got their low-priced goods.

Most people are inclined to think that there is something morally wrong with this situation, but if we are guided strictly by the principle of utility, it is hard to say what that is. We want to say that the workers must have some rights in this situation, but the idea of rights may be another one of those traditional superstitions that disappears in the utilitarian simplification of ethics. Bentham called the idea of natural rights "simple nonsense" and natural rights that cannot be limited "nonsense upon stilts."[20] The right arrangement according to utilitarian principles, remember, is the one that produces the greatest happiness for the greatest number of people, not the one that produces roughly equal happiness for everyone.

This problem is easy to see, once you think about it, and utilitarians have tried to answer it. Most of their solutions involve arguments that find some minimal set of protections included in the idea of general happiness. They might argue that everyone would be less happy in a society in which people were at risk of falling into extreme poverty. Therefore, a society that provides some kind of protection for its poorest members will always be more likely to produce the greatest good for the greatest number than one which lets the differences fall out however they may. The resulting blueprint for society may not be very different from one which begins with a set of rights, but the exercise leaves us thinking that there are more questions to be asked in any moral evaluation than Bentham's one question about the greatest good for the greatest number.

It is all too easy to imagine a society that is on the whole happy and prosperous, yet distributes that prosperity very unevenly, creating a group that lives with lower expectations and finds what happiness they can when they succeed within those limits. We might explain to those left out that they should be grateful for the smaller share that they have, since it depends on the prosperity of those who have more. Such explanations were used to justify racial segregation in the United States and apartheid in South Africa. A utilitarian might well argue that such a system will never produce the greatest happiness for the greatest number, but before we redo that calculation, we might want to ask whether there are standards of justice, independent of the principle of utility, against which a society ought to be measured.

We can also imagine a person whose goals are good, someone whose art or learning or political skills create great things that enrich the lives of many people, who nevertheless pursues those goals so relentlessly that many other people along the way suffer for her genius or his power. Perhaps a utilitarian could convince us that these sufferings were necessary, but we might also want to ask whether there are some things that we should never do to other people, even to achieve a good goal.

What happens, then, to Bentham's appealing idea that general happiness is the whole point of the moral life? Joseph Butler (1692–1752) was an English bishop who explored that question at the beginning of the century that culminated in the work of Hutcheson, Smith, and Bentham. Already, moral philosophers were suggesting that general happiness was the only reliable guide to moral choice, but Butler made the acute observation that happiness is not something that we obtain by pursuing it directly. We set goals, practice skills, follow rules, build relationships, try to be a certain kind of person, and if we do these things well, then in the course of these complex, interconnected activities—as an accompaniment, and not as their goal—we find that we are happy. Butler thought that paying attention to this complex mix of duties, relationships, and virtues made more sense than the early teleological ethics, with its ideas about pursuing general happiness, precisely because we are not in a good position to know what will make for our own happiness, let alone the happiness of humanity as a whole.

> As we are not competent judges, what is upon the whole for the good of the world; there may be other immediate ends appointed us to pursue, besides that one of doing good, or producing happiness. Though the good of the creation be the only end of the Author of it, yet he may have laid us under particular obligations, which we may discern and feel ourselves under, quite distinct from a perception, that the observance or violation of them is for the happiness or misery of our fellow-creatures.[21]

For understanding the moral life, then, goals are necessary but not sufficient. We will want to remember the self-discipline and concern for suffering that a contemporary utilitarian like Peter Singer can draw from an ethics based on teleology alone, but our search for a starting point for Christian thinking about moral problems must move on to some of those "particular obligations" to which Butler directed our attention. We want to ask about duties.

Additional Reading

Fletcher, Joseph. *Moral Responsibility: Situation Ethics at Work.* Philadelphia: Westminster Press, 1967.

Irwin, Terence. *The Development of Ethics: Volume II. From Suarez to Rousseau.* Oxford: Oxford University Press, 2008.

Long, D. Stephen, and Nancy Ruth Fox. *Calculated Futures: Theology, Ethics, and Economics.* Waco, TX: Baylor University Press, 2007.

Ramsey, Paul. *Deeds and Rules in Christian Ethics.* New York: Charles Scribner's Sons, 1967.

Singer, Peter. *Practical Ethics.* 3rd ed. Cambridge: Cambridge University Press, 2011.

GOALS: A Test Case

In a part of the world that we may vaguely locate as lying in a mountainous region like those found in Eastern Europe, two rival nations face each other across the rugged terrain of a long border. Let us call them the Alpha Republic and the Beta Federation. Because the great cities of the Republic and the Federation are located so near this border and the border itself is so long and difficult to defend, each side feels itself vulnerable to attack by the other.

Like all sovereign states, the Alpha Republic and the Beta Federation have governments that believe they have a right to defend themselves against an actual attack by a foreign power. That right to self-defense is a settled principle of international law. Each government also understands that protecting the security of its people is one of the main reasons why governments exist. Security is one goal we can assume that every government has.

In recent years, however, tensions between these two countries have escalated. There have been terrorist attacks in the Alpha Republic's cities, attacks which may or may not have been instigated by the government of the Beta Federation. Border skirmishes between the armies of the two countries have happened on several occasions, with each side blaming the other for starting the incident.

The Alpha Republic has long been the dominant power in this pair, with a stronger economy and a larger, better equipped military. The Beta Federation, however, enjoys a rapidly growing economy and has invested much of this new wealth in military hardware, so that the Republic has come to realize that it cannot be sure that its military superiority or the deterrent strength of its armed forces will last into the future.

In the face of these developments, the leaders of the Alpha Republic formulated a strategic doctrine of pre-emptive defense. Without waiting for the actual threat of an imminent attack, they made plans to destroy any part of the Beta Federation's military resources that seemed designed primarily for use in offensive operations. They have recently executed such a "pre-emptive defense" operation, destroying a large part of the Federation's air force on the ground and effectively creating a situation in which the Federation does not have the capacity to wage outright war against the Republic any time in the near future.

The prime minister of the Alpha Republic has defended this move, arguing that it was essential to his nation's security. He also insists that it was a moral choice, because the sum total of the political, material, and human losses inflicted on the Beta Federation were far less than they would have been in a general war, and indeed, a general war is now impossible. Peace has been obtained, as well as security.

Questions

The story of the Alpha Republic and the Beta Federation bears many resemblances to actual situations in global politics. For present purposes, however, try to confine yourself to the situation as it is described here, and think about how you would answer the following questions:

1. If the prime minister of the Alpha Republic were to take time to construct a systematic moral argument for his claim that the destruction of the Beta Federation's air force was a moral goal, what might he say? Assume for the moment that his argument would be teleological. That is, he will be defending his government's action on the basis that the goal was a good one. What would that argument look like?

2. Having identified the goods at which the prime minister's teleological argument would aim, what are the goods that might be lost that would argue against his claim that the Alpha Republic's goal is a good one? Are all of these goods commensurable? If so, what provides the common measure?

3. If you were the archbishop of the Alpha Republic and well-versed, as archbishops ought to be, in Christian ethics, how might you respond to this crisis and to what your prime minister has to say about the morality of the government's action? What authors or elements of the Christian stance might provide you with some guidance?

4. If you were the outraged foreign minister of the Beta Federation, how would you respond to the moral claims of the prime minister of the Alpha Republic? Would you be able to construct a teleological argument against "pre-emptive defense"? Or would you have to rely on some other starting point for your moral argument?

Part 3
Duties

CHAPTER SIX

NATURAL LAW AND HUMAN LAW

Duty is an important part of the moral life. Obligations, responsibilities, rules, and rights often tell us what we ought to do, without calculating consequences. In this chapter, we will see how some theologians used reason to organize a unified system from many different sources of duty, and we will see how others, who had less confidence in reason, created systems that relied more heavily on scripture and rules that belong particularly to the Christian life. These different ways of thinking, in turn, shaped different ways of understanding how the laws that make social order possible are related to ethics, to human nature, and to God. These historic ways of thinking remain important in Christian ethics, and Synergy, Integrity, Realism, and Liberation draw on them in different ways today.

Although our thinking about choices often begins with goals, we have seen that it is difficult to build a complete system of ethics around goals alone. Goals conflict, and even in personal life it is difficult to know how to relate them to one another. Love for God may provide a way to give order to these competing goods in Christian ethics, as Augustine suggested, but he also warned us that it takes a lifetime to learn those relationships. Choices have to be made more quickly.

Utilitarianism provides another way to organize competing goods. Utilitarianism seeks to maximize the happiness of everyone concerned, and this sets the terms in which all other goods can be measured. But utilitarianism also has its problems. It is difficult to be sure what the results of a choice will be, and even if you think you know what the greatest good for the greatest number is, there is the question whether that result is fair to everyone. Consider again the case in which you learn that one of your classmates has submitted a term paper that she purchased on the Internet.[1] You can calculate the happiness of the people involved in this situation in many different ways, balancing your classmate's short term gains against the long-term consequences of making a habit of dishonesty, or weighing the heavy penalty she would face if caught against the satisfaction that other students might take in seeing her punishment as a recognition of their own honesty. If you conclude that the greatest good of the greatest number involves reporting your classmate, you have to ask whether the satisfaction the professor and the other students might feel is fair to her. If you decide that escaping the consequences of her dishonesty really makes for the greatest happiness on the whole, you have to ask whether that is fair to the other students who wrote their own term papers. After turning the problem over in your mind for a while, it might come as something of a relief to remember that your school has an honor code that requires you to report academic dishonesty. You may not know how to calculate the greatest happiness of the greatest number, but you know what your duty is.

And this is no small thing. It is one way to describe a good human life, the kind of flourishing that Aristotle had in mind when he talked about people who use their reason to make consistent choices over a whole lifetime.[2] People who know what their duty is, even when situations are confusing and it is difficult to do the right thing, live at peace with themselves. As the Stoics warned, such people may not be rich or successful. They may even be at the center of controversy or subjected to persecution. But we admire their integrity, and unless we have lost moral direction ourselves, we would rather be like them than like their persecutors.

Many of our moral decisions are made in search of this kind of integrity, especially when the decisions involve us with many other people and it is difficult to come to agreement on goals, or when our choices have long-term consequences that are difficult to predict. We turn to laws and rules, instead of guesses about results, and we say that we ought to obey the law or follow the student handbook or do what our conscience tells us is right. We may continue to hold on to our goals, but there are some things we should not do, even to achieve a good goal. Driving down the expressway at 105 miles per hour is the wrong thing to do, even if it gets us where we want to be without an accident. Buying a term paper off the Internet is the wrong thing to do, even if it gets us the grade we need and we tell ourselves that we will never do that sort of thing again.

Often, we recognize these duties because we have already agreed to them. You may have signed a statement that you have read the school's honor code and agree to follow its provisions. Much of daily life is regulated by agreements that commit us to make payments on schedule or deliver work by a deadline, following certain rules and restrictions as we go. We all do many things because of agreements we have made, and we try to meet those commitments, even if we rarely read the small print on our credit card statements or the back of the concert tickets we have bought.

Other duties are imposed on us. Governments have authority to make laws and regulations for anyone within their territory. If you disagree with the rules in your school's honor code, you can refuse to sign the statement and look for another school, but you have no choice about the traffic codes, health regulations, and criminal laws that apply in the place where you find yourself.

Some duties have an even more universal reach. Christians, Jews, and Muslims recognize some duties as commands of God. Buddhists and Hindus speak of *karma*, a law of cause and effect that connects what we do to what happens over the course of our lives, even when we do not see the connections immediately. Religious ethics often centers on these requirements that come from a source that makes them truly universal and inescapable.

Other duties seem to be self-imposed. We do some things not because we have been told we must do them, but because it would be irrational to do otherwise. We know, if we think about it, that we should tell the truth, because if we all told lies whenever it suited us, no one would believe anyone, and there would be no point in telling the truth or making promises in the first place. The German philosopher Immanuel Kant (1724–1804) argued that this *autonomy* or self-legislation is what distinguishes genuine moral duties from all the others which are imposed on us by something other than reason, whether that other power is an outside authority or simply the force of our own desires.[3]

Still other duties are self-imposed in the sense that they arise from an awareness of who we are and what we must do to live with integrity. There may be no logical contradiction in abandoning our friends when the going gets rough, or in settling for just enough to meet the assignment when we know how to produce excellent work, but we feel that behavior like that goes against something important in ourselves. We have duties that go with our abilities, relationships, and our human nature, and whether we think of these obligations as self-imposed, given to us by God, or expected of us by the people around us, they become part of who we are and what we know we ought to do.

What all these sources have in common is that they give us ways to think about moral choices in terms of what we ought to do, independent of the consequences. Consequences may be important, but for the deontologist, they cannot provide the primary moral reasons for our choices. The best evidence for the rightness of an action is that we have made this choice in a way that we would be willing to make future choices, too, and in a way that we would want others to follow in making choices of their own.

We may speak of the actions that we choose in this way as duties or as obligations. We may also say that other people have a right to have us do these things. If I have a duty to return the book that I borrowed from you, you have a right to receive the book back. If I have a right to a fair contest, my competitors have a duty not to cheat. Sometimes, of course, it is not so easy to say who has what duty. If we agree that a starving person has a right to food, there may still be a debate about who, exactly, has a duty to provide it. But it is clear that the debate rests on something different from the teleological claim that it would be a good outcome if the starving person received food. Rights and duties are the language of deontological ethics, in which right actions are identified by obligations, rather than by the goals we are pursuing. As the philosopher John Rawls (1921–2002) put it, right has priority over the good in deontological ethics.[4] Once we have done our duty, we can turn our attention to the good things we hope for in the outcome, but we must first do the right thing.

DEONTOLOGY

Moral thinking is about the use of reason to identify duties and apply them in particular situations.

What makes an action right is that it conforms to duty.

What makes a person good is that he or she does right actions.

Once we turn to deontological ethics, there is no shortage of duties we might consider. Christian ethics provides some of these out of its own resources, as when Jesus tells his disciples that the two commandments to love God and to love your neighbor as yourself sum up the Law and the Prophets; but Christian ethics also provides ways to organize and order all the other sources of duty encountered in everyday life. Sometimes, the different sources of duty can be brought together in a single system. Many duties set forth in the Bible are identified as God's commandments, but most Christian thinkers would agree that what God commands is rational and also consistent with the persons God has created us to be. Biblical sources also connect command and agreement, so that the duty to follow God's commandments does not rest on God's authority alone. It is part of a covenant in which God's people consent to the commandments and agree to obey them (Exodus 24:7). Other passages, especially in the New Testament, are addressed to God's people scattered in different places and remind them to respect the laws set down by the authorities where they happen to live (1 Peter 2:13-17). So reason, authority, agreement, and conscience all work together in some ways of thinking about deontology in Christian ethics. Other ways of thinking, however, emphasize the possibility of conflict between these different sources and give special attention to the distinctive features of Christian life that separate it from other ways of understanding duty. From this point of view, use of any other sources marks a compromise with non-Christian ethics, and the duties those sources suggest must be regarded with varying degrees of suspicion.

It is clear, then, that someone who wants to take a deontological approach to the questions of ethics will have no difficulty finding laws, rules, scriptures, contracts, proverbs, warning signs, sermons, syllabi, and self-help books that offer duties for consideration. The problem for ethics is not to find duties, but to decide which ones to follow and how to apply them to the specific questions that we face. Throughout the history of Christian ethics, the duties imposed by governments, laws, and rulers have posed a particular problem for this kind of critical thinking. The New Testament lumps these powers that impose duties together as "authorities" (Romans 13:1) or "the kings of the earth" (Matthew 17:25). Other writers, as we will see, speak of "secular authority" or "civil government," to distinguish the power that makes and enforces law from religious authorities or other voices who speak with the weight of custom, cultural sophistication, or social expectation behind them. However we identify these sources of legally binding duties, their rules pose special problems for integration into Christian deontological ethics, and we will use those problems in this chapter as a way of understanding the work of some important thinkers who have shaped Christian ethics since the Middle Ages. In the next chapter, we will complete our study of Christian deontology by looking at the ways some contemporary Christian ethicists relate these rules and principles to specific moral choices.

Thomas Aquinas

A comprehensive account of how all the various sources of duty are related in Christian ethics was given by Thomas Aquinas (ca. 1225–1274), a teacher of theology whose *Summa theologiae* brought the work of Augustine and other earlier Christian writers together with the best understandings of science, law, and logic available at the time. That body of knowledge was growing rapidly in Thomas's day. European cities were becoming centers of learning as well as commerce, as teachers and students moved from monasteries into the new universities in Paris, Bologna, Oxford, and Salamanca. New ideas about philosophy, medicine, and mathematics reached these universities through centers of Muslim and Jewish scholarship in Spain, and this sparked new ways of study among the Christian scholars, including the beginnings of modern scientific ideas about nature and a new, more systematic approach to the study of theology. The works of Aristotle, including his writings on ethics and poiltics, were particularly important to these developments, for although some of Aristotle's ideas had become part of the Greek philosophy that early Christian writers knew, his own writings had fallen out of use and were almost unknown in Western Europe until scholars rediscovered them in Arabic translations.

THOMAS AQUINAS (ca. 1225–1274)

Major developments in his time:

Rebirth of European cities and commerce
Growth of systems of law and government
Founding of major universities
Rediscovery of Aristotle

Major events of his life:

1244—Enters the Dominican order.
1256—Becomes professor of theology in Paris.
1266—Begins writing the *Summa theologiae.*
1273—Ceases writing after a religious experience.
1274—Dies while travelling to a church council in Lyon.

Thomas incorporated this learning into his own great *Summa* of Christian theology. Like Augustine's *City of God*, the *Summa theologiae* covers the whole story of God's relationship to humanity and history. Thomas's work, however, is more systematically organized, drawing on the pattern of medieval academic disputations. When he wants to defend an idea, he first states all the objections to it, backing them up with references to scripture, Christian writers, and other ancient authorities, especially Aristotle. Only after he has exhaustively made the case for the other side does he state his own position. Then he replies to each of the objections with another set of references to appropriate authorities, this time those who back up his side of the argument. This *Scholastic method* is confusing to modern readers, since Thomas seems at first to be arguing for a position exactly opposite to the one he wants to defend, but the method served the purposes of medieval scholars, who were mastering the techniques of argument at the same time that they were learning theology.

Duties and rules are important in Thomas Aquinas's ethics because reason uses them to direct us toward action. Drawing on Aristotle's ideas about nature and human nature,[5] Thomas argues that everything God has created has a purpose. To ensure the fulfillment of those purposes, God has implanted in each thing a nature that gives it an inclination to act as it should as part of creation. Plants and animals, and even rocks and rivers, follow these inclinations by nature, but human beings use reason to determine how they should act in order to fulfill their human nature.

Clearly, for Aristotle or Thomas, nature is teleological. The nature of a thing is the goal toward which it is developing, if events are unfolding as they should. We might expect, then, that Thomas would have a teleological ethics in which people use reason to think about these natural goals and direct their actions toward realizing them. But there is a distinction between *theoretical* reason, which allows us to understand the system of nature as a whole, and *practical* reason, which guides our inclinations toward the fulfillment of our own human nature. Theoretical reason is about distinguishing true from false. Practical reason, by contrast, tells us what is to be done and what is to be avoided. It enables us to formulate rules and general principles that can be applied to specific situations to guide choice and action: Theft is to be avoided. The poor should be helped. You should not injure another person, but injury may be done to defend against an attacker. Nature is teleological, but our way of knowing it for practical purposes comes in the form of rules and principles that enable us to identify what we should and should not do. Practical reason is deontological.

Four Kinds of Law

For Thomas Aquinas, then, duty is known by a rule of practical reason that tells us how our human nature requires us to act. We experience many other kinds of rules, however, from traffic laws and library fines to religious obligations and social expectations. One of the most important parts of the *Summa theologiae* is a series of questions that has become known as the *Treatise on Law*. Here, Thomas relates different kinds of laws or rules to one another and explains their origin in the plan of God.[6]

Three things identify a law, according to Thomas: (1) Law is a rule of reason directed toward the common good. A law cannot be an arbitrary command or a force that pushes against us without our understanding or cooperation. A law can be formulated into a proposition that we can understand and follow. One reason why we can understand it is that a law is always directed toward the common good. People can order us or force us to do what they want us to do, but a law is directed toward a good in which we all have a share. Like Aristotle's understanding of politics, to which Thomas specifically refers, law is about doing things that make a community in which it is possible to live a good human life. (2) Law is given by proper authority. While any reasonable person can think about how people ought to act, only the people as a whole or someone designated as their ruler can require them to act in that way, imposing penalties and punishments on them if they do not comply. (3) Law must be published and made known. This, too, is related to the requirement that the law must be rational. If people are to obey the law because they understand it, they have to know what it is.

These three necessary features of a law help to explain what we expect from the laws we have to live by in human society, but they also explain why Thomas thinks of reality itself as a kind of law. For Thomas, creation is the element in the Christian stance from which all the rest of God's dealings with humanity and history begin. Because creation as a whole is ordered by reason, the order of nature is reasonable and directed toward the common good of the whole creation. God as creator has proper authority to make these laws, and God has made them known to us in various ways, so that we can use our own reason to follow them.

The beginning of all law, then, is what Thomas calls *eternal law*, by which God calls things into being and gives them the nature that they have and their place in the larger order of creation. Once created, everything has a *natural law*, which is the way that the eternal law is present in it. Most created things follow this natural law automatically, having no choice in the matter and no need to think about it, but human beings, as we have seen, can formulate its requirements by reason and determine for themselves how and whether they will do what their nature requires. That makes possible a somewhat wider range of human responses to the natural law, which in turn requires *human law* to specify exactly which actions are required and which are forbidden. Also, because of sin, people do sometimes decide not to do what the natural law requires, and human law is therefore needed to back up the requirements of practical reason with a definite command and a threat of punishment. Finally, too, there is *divine law*, for though God has included a great deal of what should govern human life in the natural law, there are some points on which God acts directly to give commands to particular people or to make the eternal law known in ways that it could not be known through natural law. Such divine law includes both the Law of Moses, which was given particularly to the people of Israel, and the New Law, which inwardly transforms those who participate in Christ's work of redemption.

With this four-fold classification of laws, Thomas ties the idea of natural law that he inherits from Aristotle and Stoic philosophy more closely to his Christian stance, which centers on God's creation. At the same time, he integrates sin, incarnation, and redemption into his understanding of the created order in nature, and he provides for specific commandments that come to Christians through scripture and the teaching of the church, so that the requirements of Christian baptism, for example, can be understood as part of divine law. Thomas thus uses a synergistic version of the Christian stance to bring together all of the different kinds of duties that Christians recognize in their everyday experience into a unified system. The will of God, originating in the eternal law, is central to all of these other forms of law, and in some way, the eternal law is known through each of the other forms of law as well; but in Thomas Aquinas's deontological ethics, all the different sources of duty have a place.

Natural Law

Because the natural law is part of human nature, there are some duties that everyone knows. These include basic moral rules that prohibit murder or theft. But natural law encompasses a great deal more of life than this. According to Thomas Aquinas, the requirements of natural law include a duty of self-preservation and other duties that provide for reasoned guidance of those inclinations that we share with non-human animals: duties related to sexuality, for example, and duties to care for offspring. But there are also inclinations that are distinctive to human nature, and the natural law governs these, too. According to Thomas, natural law imposes a duty to recognize and worship God, and it provides rules that are essential to human societies, like an obligation to create governments, obey laws, and refrain from harming other people.[7]

This confidence that everyone shares knowledge of natural law leads to some important conclusions. Because all people know what natural law requires, we have an immediate moral relationship to everyone we meet. We are obliged to refrain from harming them or taking their possessions from them, and they have the same duties toward us. Everyone is accountable to natural law, but everyone is likewise entitled to its protection.

No framework of human law is required to create this moral relationship. It is part of our human nature. Strangers who encounter one another in distant places are required to follow natural law, just as we follow it closer to home in the more familiar settings governed by human law. Indeed, human law should be shaped by natural law. Thomas goes so far as to say that a human law that conflicts with the natural law really does not count as a law at all. "Hence every humanly made law has the character of law to the extent that it stems from the law of nature. On the other hand, if a humanly made law conflicts with the natural law, then it is no longer a law, but a corruption of law."[8] A law that singled out a certain group of people and declared that they could be assaulted and robbed without penalty would not be a law, even if it were made by the proper authorities and proclaimed in the usual manner. It conflicts with the more basic requirements of natural law, and people who understand their own human nature could not suppose that reason allows them to follow such a law. On the other hand, human laws against theft, which usually provide an important reinforcement of the natural law, do not apply in extreme cases where the natural law of self-preservation comes into effect. A starving person who takes the food that is necessary for bare survival does not commit theft.

Natural law thus provides a strong basis for individual moral accountability. The place where moral decisions are made is in the conscience of the individual, where moral principles are applied to individual situations. Thomas has a strong sense of the duty of obedience we owe to human authorities, and he is writing primarily for clergy and members of religious orders, who have specific obligations to obey their bishops and religious superiors. Nevertheless, he is clear that in a conflict between authority and conscience, it is conscience that we are to follow. Conscience may turn out to be mistaken. It may even turn out that our sin and stubbornness have distorted our conscience, so that it is our own fault when conscience gives us the wrong answer. Still, the right thing to do is what conscience tells us. Bad judgments will need to be corrected, and if we have contributed to them by our own sin, we may expect punishment for it at some later point, but we must not obey anyone who tells us to go against what conscience tells us now.[9]

Natural law also provides a basis for criticism of human laws that do not conform to the requirements of natural law or fail to support the common good. In natural law, human beings have a strong basis for cooperation and a framework in which they can discuss their differences, even when they have very different ideas about God and about the ultimate goals of human life. Augustine, as we have seen, raised a question about how much Christians could share in common with those whose lives are not directed toward love of God,[10] and Christians have argued ever since about whether Christian ethics reaches beyond the boundaries of the Christian community, or whether the best that can be hoped for is a temporary peace. Thomas's idea of natural law provides the strongest case for a close connection between the Christian life and a moral life in which all humanity shares.

Objections and Replies

Thomas makes a thorough case for natural law, drawing from scripture, logic, philosophy, and a whole range of theologians prior to his time. Many Christians today, however, find the argument a bit too confident. If there really are moral rules that everyone knows, why is there so much disagreement about what we ought to do? If these duties are part of our human nature, why do they seem to change over time or between different cultures? Perhaps the idea of universal rules that are part of human nature made sense in the thirteenth century, but it is more difficult to establish today, when we know so much more about the world and human history.

These questions need to be raised, but they are not as new as we might think. Thomas himself realized that people often disagree on what natural law requires and that moral rules seem to change over time. He addressed these concerns directly by asking, "Is there a single law of nature for everyone?" He begins, as we would expect with his Scholastic method, by pointing out all of the reasons why we might think that there are different natural laws for different people. We see differences in their circumstances, and different things seem to be good for different people.

Nevertheless—quoting an authority, which is also what we would expect with his method—Thomas asserts, "In *Etymologia* Isidore says, 'The natural law (*ius naturale*) is common to all nations.' "[11]

By quoting Isidore of Seville, a seventh-century theologian, Thomas establishes the position he wants to defend. Then he makes that defense by replying to all of the objections that seem to make the natural law different for different people. He points out that natural law thinking proceeds from general principles, through more specific rules, down to conclusions that establish our duty in particular cases: Promises should be kept. Receiving something for safekeeping is a kind of promise, so things received for safekeeping should be returned when requested by their owners. The owner who gave you this thing for safekeeping wants it back, so you should return it. But, says Thomas, if the thing in question is a weapon that its owner is going to use to harm someone, the general rule does not apply.

The problem with practical reasoning is that it is full of complex cases like this one, so that the closer we get to particular conclusions, the more likely we are to run into exceptions that lead to disagreements or create the impression that there are different rules for different people. The rules will apply to most cases, but there will sometimes be what Thomas calls "differences with respect to correctness," in which circumstances create exceptions to the general rule. Also, there will be "differences with respect to knowledge." Our reasoning simply is not always good enough, and we sometimes willfully refuse to see the truth. So it is hardly surprising that different observers arrive at different conclusions about particular cases, even though "one should claim that with respect to its first universal principles, the law of nature is the same for everyone both with respect to correctness and with respect to knowledge."[12]

Determining exactly what the natural law requires in any given situation is a difficult task. Indeed, many of the arguments in moral theology are about *casuistry*, the reasoning by which we move from general principles of morality to particular conclusions. What Thomas wants us to see is that our disagreements about what we ought to do in particular cases do not call the principles of morality into question. Indeed, disagreements about what we ought to do in particular cases make no sense unless there are general ideas of right and wrong on which we do agree.

Thomas offers a similar response to his critics when he considers the question "Can the law of nature be changed?"[13] The explanation here centers on the relationship between natural law and human law. Many important changes in ethics are the result of human laws that have been added to the natural law to give it specificity and effectiveness in particular situations. "For many things useful to human life have been added to the natural law, both by divine law and by human law."[14] It is important to understand that Thomas thought that many things that are virtually universal features of human life, such as rules about private property and rules governing business transactions, are the creation of human law. Property exists within the natural law framework of a duty of self-preservation that requires people to make good use of the resources provided in nature, and business transactions take place in the context of duties to tell the truth and avoid harm to others, but beyond these very general principles, right and wrong in particular settings are determined by the laws that a society has established to govern property and transactions. A thirteenth-century theo-logian could hardly have imagined the complexity and diversity of these arrangements in the modern world, but his understanding of natural law makes a place for them. More important, we could not argue about the details of property and finance if we did not share some ideas about fairness, needs, and the human good that establish a framework for the argument. That is what Thomas means when he argues that the natural law is the same for everyone and that it does not change.

The Importance of Natural Law

Thomas's explanations in the *Summa theologiae* do not answer all of the questions that might be raised about natural law, but he ensured its place in later developments in Christian ethics, especially in the Catholic tradition. Many of the most important uses of natural law were prompted by political and economic changes that happened in the centuries after his death, when Europe began to take its modern shape, with independent nations seeking wealth, making war, and establishing colonial empires. There was no central authority to govern the relationships between these new powers, and after the Protestant Reformation, there was no common religion, either. Natural law, however, provided a starting point for modern international law, as Catholic and Protestant scholars worked to establish rules for trade and commerce and limit the damages of war, drawing on ideas that went back to Thomas Aquinas and to sources in Roman law long before him. Francisco de Vitoria (d. 1546) and Francisco Suarez (1548–1617) led these developments in Catholic Spain, while Hugo Grotius (1583–1646) influenced the rulers, jurists, and diplomats of the Protestant countries of Northern Europe.

As the Spanish colonial empire grew, Bartholome de las Casas (1484–1556) and other priests from the Dominican order to which Thomas himself had belonged spoke out against the exploitation of the indigenous peoples of the Americas, drawing on natural law ideas to warn the Europeans that they could not simply take what they wanted from people who did not share their Christian religion or their European ideas about property. The Dominicans were not very effective at curbing the ambition of the conquerors, but they spoke a word of moral condemnation that still troubles the conscience of the descendants of the colonizers.

For the contemporary liberation theologian Gustavo Gutiérrez, las Casas's criticism of the Spanish conquistadors provides a historical starting point for the defense of the poor that is central to Christian ethics from a Liberation perspective.[15] Others find the tradition of natural law more ambiguous in its defense of freedom. Reformers and revolutionaries could refer to the "laws of nature and nature's God," as Thomas Jefferson did in the Declaration of Independence, to explain why the American colonies were entitled to independent status among the other nations of the world. But Jefferson was also a slave-owner, and his well-educated Virginia compatriots could easily find natural law arguments for slavery going all the way back to Aristotle. Considering the historical record as a whole, today's liberationists are generally cautious about natural law. While advocates of the poor from Bartholome de las Casas to Martin Luther King, Jr., have appealed to natural law against the injustices of conquest, slavery, and discrimination, liberationists see these as exceptions among the arguments that have generally provided a system of law that supports those who already hold the power.[16]

In any case, appeals to natural law became less frequent as modern nations developed more extensive systems of law and international relations were increasingly governed by written agreements between nations. There was simply less need for the idea of natural law to fill in the gaps in the legislation and treaties. In the twentieth century, however, natural law ideas became important once again, as the world responded to the attempted extermination of European Jews during the Second World War and to numerous incidents of genocide, mass murder, and violation of human rights around the globe. A new idea of "crimes against humanity" led to tribunals set up to prosecute political leaders, military and police personnel, and ordinary perpetrators, even in situations where their actions may have been protected by prevailing laws at the time their crimes were committed. Prohibitions of these crimes against humanity have been incorporated into written law by the United Nations and other international bodies, but these new legal arrangements depended heavily at their origins on the natural law idea that there are basic moral requirements that everyone should know and to which everyone should be held accountable.

Over the course of history, then, natural law has been an important element in the synergistic understanding of Christian ethics. Natural law provided Thomas Aquinas with a way to integrate the different forms of law that he knew into one system of deontological ethics, connecting eternal, natural, human, and divine laws, while still maintaining the important distinctions between them. From his time to the present, natural law has provided a starting point for important political ideas about the obligations of rulers, relations between nations, and the rights to which all persons are entitled, so that John Courtney Murray could rightly draw a connection between his Catholic natural law ethics and the presuppositions of modern democracy.[17] Wherever Christian ethics emphasizes what it has in common with other understandings of the moral life and enters into moral discussions about law and society, natural law provides a way to make the connections.

Reason, Sin, and Human Nature

The idea that some moral rules are universal because they are part of nature is older than Christianity,[18] but Christian and Jewish thinkers readily made use of it, because it allowed them to locate the origins of morality in the same act of creation in which God made human nature itself. Creation, however, is only the beginning of God's dealings with history and humanity. Sin is also an element of the Christian stance, and as theologians considered the idea of natural law taking shape in Christian thought, some questioned whether fallen human beings who were in need of redemption still had enough of the human nature that God had created to know what it required. Even Thomas Aquinas acknowledged that sin makes it difficult to reason correctly from the general premises of natural law to practical conclusions. But if sinful human beings really cannot figure out what the natural law requires, the whole idea of duties to which everyone can be held accountable begins to crumble.

Thomas himself insisted that only "secondary" principles of the natural law could be erased by sin. People might fail to grasp specific things that they ought to do, but "as far as the universal principles are concerned, the natural law cannot in any way be erased entirely from the hearts of men."[19] In the years that followed, however, this issue was a focus of continuing controversy. It became a particularly important point of contention for leaders of the Protestant Reformation, beginning with Martin Luther, who made his final break with the Catholic Church in 1521. For the Reformers, all aspects of human nature had been damaged by sin, and unaided reason lacked a secure knowledge of anything that nature requires. They rejected the Scholastic method, which employs logic and reason to arrive at its theological conclusions, and also the whole system of Aristotelian philosophy, which supplied much of the understanding of human nature with which earlier theologians like Thomas Aquinas had worked. With those resources gone, Thomas's way of thinking about natural law was lost as well. The idea that God had created humanity to live in a certain way remained, but without God's assistance, fallen human beings could not determine what that way of life is.

MARTIN LUTHER (1483–1546)

1505—Luther joins the Augustinian order in Erfurt, Germany.

1508—He begins teaching theology in Wittenberg.

1517—He writes a *Disputation against Scholastic Theology* and posts *Ninety-Five Theses* that begin the Protestant Reformation.

1521—Luther's final break with the Catholic Church at the Diet of Worms.

1523—He writes *On Secular Authority*.

1534—Translation of the Bible into German completed.

This theological controversy had a profound effect on Christian ethics, breaking the connection between the Christian life and the more general search for the human good that had set the main direction for Christian ethics since the time of Augustine. Without natural law to bridge the gap between divine law and human law and connect them both to the eternal law, Luther's ethics necessarily turned to the other possibility that Augustine had explored, the idea that there is a sharp difference between the good life and the Christian life, and no connection between the human city and the City of God.[20]

> Here we must divide Adam's children, all mankind, into two parts: the first belong to the kingdom of God, the second to the kingdom of the world. All those who truly believe in Christ belong to God's kingdom, for Christ is king and lord in God's kingdom...[21]

To know what God requires, these true Christians cannot follow reason or study human nature. Even the words of scripture serve primarily to awaken those who are not yet true Christians to their need for this transformation that God alone can work in their hearts. Those who are guided by love do what they should do without a written law and without the need for force to make them do it.

> And if all the world were true Christians, that is, if everyone truly believed, there would be neither need nor use for princes, kings, lords, the Sword or law. What would there be for them to do? Seeing that [true Christians] have the Holy Spirit in their hearts, which teaches and moves them to love everyone, wrong no one, and suffer wrongs gladly, even unto death. Where all wrongs are endured willingly and what is right is done freely, there is no place for quarrelling, disputes, courts, punishments, laws or the Sword. And therefore laws and the secular Sword cannot possibly find any work to do among Christians, especially since they of themselves do much more than any laws or teachings might demand.[22]

Clearly, the place of duty is radically changed in this approach to Christian ethics. There is little reason to discuss duties in the Christian life, since the Holy Spirit teaches them directly; but the meaning of human law is different, too. Human law is no longer a way for people who are seeking to live good lives to add new discoveries to the basic requirements of natural law. Rulers, courts, and laws now serve only to limit the damage that would otherwise be done by those who are not guided by love. Human law restrains evil; it cannot accomplish good.

This, in turn, changes the relationship of the people to the law and to their rulers. Thomas could say that a human law that goes against natural law is not really a law at all, but for Luther, there is no such critical principle by which people might tell the difference between good laws and bad ones. Anything the ruler commands with respect to life and property is law.[23] Christians do not need these laws, because they are already doing everything that justice requires without any external compulsion; but they willingly obey the law because they know that the wider society needs this restraint. More than that, they take on the task of enforcing the law and wielding what Luther calls "the sword" with all the resources and abilities they have at their disposal.

> For this is a work of which you yourself have no need, but your neighbour and the whole world most certainly do. And therefore if you see that there is a lack of hangmen, court officials, judges, lords or princes, and you find that you have the necessary skills, you should offer your services and seek office, so that authority, which is so greatly needed, will never come to be held in contempt, become powerless, or perish. The world cannot get by without it.[24]

Luther thus makes a strong distinction between the Christian community, where law is not needed and duties are known immediately, and the wider society, where most are not "true" Christians. In the wider society, as Augustine warned, force must be used if evil is to be restrained.[25] If evil were to be restrained, Christians would have to have a hand in it. They should not attempt to restrain evil with love, however, for that would bring chaos, probably with bad results for the true Christians. "And so to try to rule a whole country or the world by means of the Gospel is like herding together wolves, lions, eagles and sheep in the same pen.... The sheep would certainly keep the peace and let themselves be governed and pastured peaceably, but they would not live long."[26] There are important responsibilities for the Christian in this world where power holds sway, from the grim duties of the hangman to the more glorious callings of lords and princes. Luther only wants to be sure we see that there is little difference between the prince and the hangman, and neither has much to do with truly Christian life.

Integrity and Realism

Still, if true Christians do not need the law for themselves and take on its gruesome tasks only for the good of their neighbors, it is hard to avoid the question that some of Luther's critics asked: "Why not abandon the sword, since we do not need it? Let others take on that task, since there is never any shortage of people who want power. We will devote ourselves to living as true Christians."

In 1527, a group of Swiss reformers under the leadership of Michael Sattler met at Schleitheim and produced a statement of faith that repeated Augustine's and Luther's sharp division of humanity into two groups, multiplying the images for emphasis. "Now there is nothing else in the world and all creation than good or evil, believing and unbelieving, darkness and light, the world and those who are [come] out of the world, God's temple and idols, Christ and Belial, and none will have part with the other."[27] But the Swiss Brethren who issued this Schleitheim Confession of Faith came to a very different decision about Christian responsibility for the work of government, arguing that

> it does not befit a Christian to be a magistrate: the rule of the government is according to the flesh, that of the Christians according to the Spirit. Their houses and dwelling remain in this world, that of the Christians is in heaven. Their citizenship is in this world, that of the Christians is in heaven. The weapons of their battle and warfare are carnal and only against the flesh, but the weapons of Christians are spiritual, against the fortification of the devil. The worldly are armed with steel and iron, but Christians are armed with the armor of God, with truth, righteousness, peace, faith, salvation, and with the word of God.[28]

The Swiss Brethren and others who shared these convictions followed them to their logical conclusion. They became pacifists, and some of the historic "peace churches," like the Mennonites and the Church of the Brethren, owe their origins to this part of the Protestant Reformation. Beyond their rejection of military service, they sought to withdraw as far as possible from government and politics. Their worship emphasized community and simplicity, and these groups are known collectively as "Anabaptists" for their practice of receiving Christian baptism as adults, in distinction from both Lutheran and Catholic churches, where infants are baptized. Because the early Anabaptists sought to minimize their connections to the wider society, they often lived in self-sufficient farming communities, and because they refused taxation and military service, they were often persecuted. Over the centuries, many of them came to live in the Americas or in Russia, where they could spread out over vast new lands and build their communities in true isolation from the society that depended on the sword for its order.

Both Lutheran and Anabaptist understandings of political duty continue to be important in Christian ethics today, and these ideas are influential far beyond the churches that were founded around them during the Protestant Reformation. The Integrity version of the Christian stance draws on Anabaptist influences for its pacifism, but in the hands of a contemporary interpreter like Stanley Hauerwas, the position broadens to a more general critique of governments and political power. All of the activities of government rest on coercion and the threat of violence, not only the military and police forces. Christian duties largely involve keeping a distance from this use of force and reminding other people what the real nature of political power is. The separation is not so easy to maintain as it might have been for Anabaptist farming communities, and Hauerwas rejects the idea that his position is a withdrawal from society. Integrity in the modern world is always involved in political life and social institutions. What Hauerwas rejects is the idea that this minimal, necessary cooperation creates any kind of moral community. Not surprisingly, he rejects the use of natural law ethics to link specific policy choices to broader moral principles. Where the Synergy of Thomas Aquinas's ethics identifies duties that Christians should follow precisely because they are derived by reason from an understanding of human nature that anyone can follow, Hauerwas warns that natural law ideas tempt us to un-Christian uses of force. Those who do not see the requirements of reason as we do will have to be compelled to do what they ought to know is the right thing.[29]

Realism, by contrast, draws more heavily on Luther's idea that Christians have a duty to help maintain the social order that government supplies. For Luther, as we have seen, that requires unquestioning obedience to whatever the ruler commands with respect to our lives and material goods. Reinhold Niebuhr's contemporary Realism incorporates more of the critical assessment of laws and commands that Thomas derives from natural law. We need law and government because people tend to act in their own self-interest, while law directs their actions toward the common good.[30] But Niebuhr reminds us that governments and authorities also pursue their own interest. The value of modern democracy, which neither Thomas nor Luther could have anticipated, is that it allows the people as a whole to make the all-important judgment about whether a law is really directed toward the common good.[31]

Still, Niebuhr is skeptical of our ability to reason accurately from general principles to specific conclusions of natural law, and like Luther, he thinks it would be a mistake to apply the requirements of Christian love directly to the problems of society. What a society ordinarily calls justice is probably as close an approximation of love as we can get, given the reality of sin. But justice quickly deteriorates into a calculation of self-interest if it not enlarged by some measure of genuine love.[32] Realism requires a sharp distinction between the requirements of Christian love and the possibilities of ordinary social life, just as Luther said; but in the modern world, individual Christians must find their duty in this tension between love and justice, and not only in obedience to authority.

The Third Use of the Law

The Protestant Reformation gave rise to one more way of thinking about duty in Christian ethics. Jean Calvin (1509–1564) sided with Luther against the Anabaptists, but he gave rules and law a more important place in the lives of true Christians than Luther did. Like all of the Reformers, he believed that sin has changed human nature and limited the powers of human reason, so that nothing like the use of natural law that Thomas Aquinas taught is possible. Reason is unable to see clearly the path from our natural inclinations to the things we ought to do, and even if it could, our inclinations point us in the wrong direction. Under conditions of sin, our first impulse is to love ourselves and to use reason to figure out how to get what we want for ourselves. We have to be taught to love God and our neighbor. That is why Jesus emphasized that point so strongly that it became the center of his moral teaching.

Indeed, to express how profoundly we must be inclined to love our neighbors, the Lord measured it by the love of ourselves because he had at hand no more violent or stronger emotion than this. And we ought diligently to ponder the force of this expression. For he does not concede the first place to self-love as certain Sophists stupidly imagine, and assign the second place to love. Rather, he transfers to others the emotion of love that we naturally feel toward ourselves.[33]

CALVIN AND CALVINISM

Jean Calvin was a lawyer who turned his attention to theology as the Protestant Reformation spread from Germany into France and Switzerland. When the Swiss city of Geneva sought to reform its churches and its government, Calvin provided the new guidelines for both faith and civic order. His proposals were controversial, and at one point he was expelled from the city, but his work in Geneva was central to his life and thought from 1536 to his death in 1564.

Calvin wrote many volumes of sermons and essays, but his most important work was his *Institutes of the Christian Religion*, which grew as it went through several editions from 1536 to 1559. *Calvinism* is the name given to the theology derived from the *Institutes* and Calvin's other writings. Calvinism influenced the development of Reformed churches in continental Europe, Presbyterian and Congregational churches in Scotland and England, and Puritan colonies in New England that became part of the United States. From these starting points, churches that draw their theology from Calvin's writings and their organization from his Genevan model have spread around the world.

Calvin emphasizes the important role that Jesus' teaching and other parts of scripture play in the Christian life. Because fallen human beings cannot depend on natural inclinations to guide them, even true Christians must pay attention to the rules that are set out in the Bible as they try to determine the right thing to do. Law does serve the two limited functions that Luther assigned to it. It can convince fallen human beings of their sinfulness, and it restrains the evil that they would do if left to make their own choices. But for Calvin, there is a third use of the law that is the most important. It guides Christians to know what they ought to do and encourages them to do it. "And not one of us may escape from this necessity," he writes, perhaps with a sidelong glance at those who think that their faith alone is enough to ensure the rightness of their actions, "For no man has heretofore attained to such wisdom as to be unable, from the daily instruction of the law, to make fresh progress toward a purer knowledge of the divine will."[34]

The important role of biblical law in the Christian life led Calvin to think in a different way about human law, too. The laws made by rulers and governments are not only for the restraint of evil. They provide guidance for those who are already trying to do the right thing and live good lives. The result, for Calvinist theology, has been a continuing interest in the law and how law is made. Calvinists do not simply offer to help the ruler enforce the law on unruly subjects who are not true Christians. They are themselves ready to be guided by it, and ready to help make it. In Geneva, Calvin established a close working relationship between religious leaders and civil authorities, in which the church used scripture as a starting point for the requirements of Christian life and the magistrates translated those requirements into laws that supported the life of the church and the moral education of the citizens.

Calvinism thus created a different kind of Synergy between the good life and the Christian life. In place of natural law, which provided a framework of basic moral principles that could incorporate new discoveries about what contributes to the common good, Calvinists relied on the division of power and authority between clergy and magistrates to provide checks and balances. The clergy could insist on what the law of God required, as they understood it, but they needed the power of the magistrates to enforce it. The magistrates could make laws that everyone had to obey, but they needed the spiritual authority of the clergy if they expected most people to obey the law without being forced to do so. The idea was to produce a society in which law did more than restrain evil. It was supposed to help everyone to live a good life.

When the Reformation was in its early days and threatened by powerful external enemies, this collaboration between religious authority and government could be repressive. Calvin's theological opponents found little tolerance in Geneva, and some suffered exile or death under these new laws. Geneva during Calvin's Reformation is sometimes described as a "theocracy"—a government by religious law. But Calvin himself learned the hard way that his power over the magistrates was not absolute, and in theory, he always maintained that church and government were distinct centers of authority, each with its own responsibilities, both accountable to God, and neither subordinated to the other.

Covenant and Conscience

Over time, Calvinism developed this way of thinking about the church and its relationship to the magistrates into a comprehensive understanding of social organization. Calvin initially followed Luther in emphasizing the duty to obey those in authority. Magistrates and secular rulers are essential to society, and obedience to them is commanded in scripture. The conclusion follows that even when the authorities are in the wrong, the Christian's duty is to "obey and suffer."[35] However, Calvin noted an important exception to this requirement: If the law provides lower magistrates to restrain the authority of their superiors, these officials are not only allowed to oppose tyrants, but they have failed in their duty if they do not do so. Calvin notes that there are examples of such offices in history, and he adds that perhaps there is something similar to this in every kingdom.[36]

In the end, then, Calvin has an idea of secular authority that is distinct from the church. The society that human life requires works best when religious authority and civil authority cooperate to organize the community along the lines laid out in scripture. But where this ideal is impossible—where scripture is unknown, or the church is unreformed, or the civil authority is corrupt—there is a pattern built into the structures of society that provides the essential order that sustains human life. Later Calvinist theologians would expand this idea to include other basic elements of social life. Family, work, government, and religion are "orders of creation."[37] They are present everywhere, and what Christians learn about them from the third use of the law confirms and clarifies what people throughout history have discovered in their own experience. People are able to form families, earn a living, order society, and even, perhaps, worship God because they are already at least dimly aware of the duties that Christians learn from scripture.

This is not quite the idea of a natural law known to everyone by reason that we find in the Scholastic theologians. For the followers of Jean Calvin, sin distorts and dims moral knowledge far more severely than Thomas Aquinas supposed, and the moral order that results is only just adequate to the needs of human life. Some theologians call these institutions of family, work, government, and religion the "orders of preservation," to emphasize that what we get from this basic moral knowledge is not the human flourishing that philosophers since Aristotle's time have sought, but something more like what Luther thought we could get from human law: just enough restraint of sin to keep us from destroying ourselves, so that human life may continue until God's redemptive purposes can be worked out. The Calvinist understanding of the Christian stance thus stands poised between Thomist Synergy and Lutheran Realism, in a balancing act that has proved remarkably fruitful for Christian thinking about ethics and society.

One idea that has helped maintain this balance is the idea of *covenant*, an agreement that makes explicit the terms of a fundamental and enduring relationship between those who are parties to it. The covenant appears first in the relationship between God and the people of Israel, made explicit in the Law of Moses and in the people's commitment to follow it (Exodus 19:1–24:8), but for Calvinist theologians specific covenants are also made among God's people, setting out the way they intend to live on the basis of their relationship to God and to one another. Calvinists have drawn up covenants to begin new religious movements and organize new congregations. English Calvinists joined in covenants to journey to the New World and to establish their towns and settlements there, and some of the Presbyterians and New England Congregationalists who joined the convention in Philadelphia to draft the Constitution of the United States no doubt understood that gathering in covenantal terms, too.

The terms *covenant, compact,* or *contract* were used interchangeably in these early writings, but a covenant is not quite the same thing as the later modern idea of a contract, which suggests parties who are free to make an agreement on any terms that all of them accept. Covenants are set in the larger context of the rules and duties that maintain society and preserve human life. Scripture and human experience do not spell out their terms in detail, but they do set limits on what the parties to a covenant can agree. Covenant-making thus functions something like the process of practical reasoning, in which a general principle takes on more and more specific form as it is applied to a particular case.[38] As the questions become more detailed and the possibilities for error and disagreement multiply, coming to a covenantal agreement in advance is one way to reduce uncertainty and provide reliable guides for action, especially among people who are not so confident that they could all come to the same conclusions by using their reason individually.

The history that runs from Thomas Aquinas through Jean Calvin thus provides a rich resource for dealing with questions of duty in Christian ethics. Natural law and the orders of creation provide ways of thinking about the similarities that unite different systems of morality and ways of organizing the multiple sources of duty. Practical reason becomes the proving ground in which we work out what we can know, and what we can expect others to know, about moral rules. Conscience and covenant test the limits of authority in the moral life and provide ways of anticipating what we may not be able to see clearly under the pressure of the moment. With this history in mind, we can now turn to the uses of duty in contemporary Christian ethics.

Additional Reading

Biéler, André. *The Social Humanism of Calvin.* Richmond, VA: John Knox Press, 1964.

Davies, Brian. *The Thought of Thomas Aquinas.* Oxford: Clarendon Press, 1992.

Gutiérrez, Gustavo. *Las Casas: In Search of the Poor of Jesus Christ.* Maryknoll, NY: Orbis Books, 1993.

Kerr, Fergus. *After Aquinas: Versions of Thomism.* Oxford: Blackwell Publishing, 2002.

May, William F. *Testing the National Covenant: Fears and Appetites in American Politics.* Washington, DC: Georgetown University Press, 2011.

Niebuhr, Reinhold. *Moral Man and Immoral Society.* Louisville: Westminster John Knox Press, 2001.

Porter, Jean. *Nature as Reason: A Thomistic Theory of the Natural Law.* Grand Rapids: Eerdmans, 2005.

Rubenstein, Richard E. *Aristotle's Children.* Orlando: Harcourt, 2003.

Weisheipl, James A. *Friar Thomas D'Aquino: His Life, Thought, and Work.* Washington, DC: Catholic University of America Press, 1983.

Yoder, John Howard. *The Politics of Jesus.* 2nd ed. Grand Rapids: Eerdmans, 1994.

CHAPTER SEVEN

PRINCIPLES, CASUISTRY, AND COMMANDMENTS

Doing the right thing requires using reason to make consistent decisions about our duties under many different circumstances. Modern moral thought has emphasized that it is important for people to make these decisions for themselves, without relying on other powers and authorities to do their reasoning for them. Christian ethics has two main paths to this autonomy. One builds on consistent use of general rules and critical understanding of the circumstances of our choices. The other begins with the command of God, independent of any general rules or critical theories.

For most of us, there is no shortage of duties. We are surrounded by laws, rules, and warning signs. Alongside whatever subjects we are studying, we learn what we ought to do as students or as teachers, just as we master the rules of friendship, intimacy, and family life outside of the classroom. Then there is the whole world of modern democracy, which is full of duties that go with citizenship, political participation, and respect for others. For Christians, there are also duties that go with faith—moral standards that reflect the love of God and neighbor, times set apart for prayer and worship, and duties to fulfill in the life of the church.

Nor is the problem just that there are lots of duties making demands, one after another. They seem to converge on us, several at a time. I have a duty to help my friends and a duty to be honest in my academic work, but if my friend needs help with the answers during an exam, I cannot fulfill both duties at once. A physician has a duty to prolong life and a duty to relieve suffering, but if the patient is in intense pain during a terminal illness, someone may have to decide which duty takes priority. A citizen has a duty to obey the law and a Christian has a duty to worship, but if the law forbids gatherings for public prayer, the Christian citizen will have to decide which rule to follow.

These things happen all the time, in big and little ways. Duties converge on us from multiple directions, and most often we are left to sort out the conflicts on our own. There simply is no authority so omnipresent and no source of advice so reliable as to give us all the answers exactly when we need them. More important, we have a sense that answering these questions for ourselves is an essential part of the moral life. Doing our duty is not simply doing what someone has told us we must do. A right action is something we do because we think it is the right thing to do, not because we are obeying the authorities or because we have handed the decision over to other people who are giving us advice. In that sense, right actions are self-chosen or self-legislated. Moral philosophers say that they are *autonomous*. That does not mean that the right action is what we really want to do or that deciding to do it is what makes it right. What autonomy does mean is that we have thought through the reasons for the action, and we have determined for ourselves that this is the right thing to do.

The problem about doing the right thing, then, is not that we have no idea what to do. The problem is usually that when we face a moral choice, we can immediately think of two or three things that might be the right thing to do, and before we can sort those out, we are surrounded by people giving us advice or orders that add to the possibilities. The problem about doing the right thing is thinking for yourself. What guidance is relevant? Which of these several duties that seem to apply should I follow? The philosopher W. D. Ross (1877–1971) distinguished what he called a *prima facie* duty from an actual duty. A *prima facie* duty is a duty "at first appearance." An actual duty is the duty we are obliged to perform once the other *prima facie* contenders have been eliminated.[1] That kind of distinction between *prima facie* and actual duty seems required for almost every decision in deontological ethics.

AUTONOMY

Autonomy is a term used in ethics to indicate that persons have decided for themselves what course of action to follow. The word comes from two Greek terms, *auto* for *self* and *nomos*, which is the Greek word for *rule* or *law*. So autonomy is self-rule or self-legislation.

Autonomous actions are self-chosen, unlike *heteronomous* actions, which are dictated by someone else who issues orders. (*Heteros* is a Greek work for *other*.) For modern moral philosophers, however, an action is also heteronomous if it is dictated by our own desires or fears. For an action to be right, it must not only be the right thing to do. It must be done because we have chosen it as the right action. A right action must be autonomous.

Just how we go about making the distinction is extremely important to the moral life. In deontological ethics, the consistency and independence of our moral choices vouches for the rightness of our actions. A deontologist cannot appeal to the goodness of the results as a teleologist can. The evidence for the rightness of an action is that we would be willing to make future choices in the same way, and that we would want others to make choices in this way, too. If we know that we are just lining up the reasons to get the results we want, or if it appears to others that we are picking the *prima facie* duty that happens to match what we want to do at the moment, we have not really made a moral choice at all. Thus we should not expect to enjoy the kind of good life that goes with moral autonomy, nor are others likely to view us as someone who has achieved it.

The Importance of Rules

A person who faces these questions about how to determine her duty at the beginning of the twenty-first century has a lot of history behind her, especially in Christian ethics. From the end of the Middle Ages, through the Reformation, and well into modern times, Christian ethics gave more and more attention to duty in the Christian life. There were different ways of understanding this deontological emphasis in relation to the Christian stance. A Catholic synergist following Thomas Aquinas might focus on how the requirements of natural law direct people toward the ends for which they were created, while a Calvinist would be more likely to refer to rules learned from scripture that enable people to form communities, preserve the orders of creation, and restrain their sinful inclinations. A Lutheran realist, by contrast, might put restraint of sin in first place, emphasizing that Christians follow these duties freely, but requiring a strong authority to enforce them on unruly people who would otherwise wreck the prospects for a peaceful life for Christians and non-Christians alike. These differences were important, and they were sharp enough to divide Western Christianity into Catholics and different groups of Protestants following different kinds of Christian ethics, but what they shared in spite of their disagreements was that their thinking about ethics became more and more deontological.

In light of the virtues that were so important to Greek and Roman ethics and the goals which Augustine ordered by the love of God, this growing emphasis on duty that takes us from medieval Scholastic ethics into the modern world is somewhat surprising, but it reflects changes in the world in which the Christian life was lived. After years of plague and declining population, European cities had begun to grow again. Commerce expanded, and European explorers found lands previously unknown to them and established new routes for global trade. The idea of a universal Holy Roman Empire gave way to new nations that built their own empires. The customary ways of doing things could no longer cope with these new realities, and people with competing goals and uncertain lines of authority had to identify rules that would govern the transactions between individuals and even the relation between nations. We have already seen how this contributed to the development of international law and democratic politics.[2]

As the modern world took shape, thinking about personal moral choices changed, too. The idea of autonomy developed along with the new emphasis on duty. Merely following a rule because you are forced to do it is not enough to make your action right, nor is it enough to make a good law. You must use your own reason to determine what your duty is and apply the conclusion to your society as well as to yourself.

The most important of these modern deontological thinkers was the philosopher Immanuel Kant (1724–1804). Although he spent nearly his entire life in a German seaport town located in what is now Russia, Kant was deeply interested in the scientific discoveries, economic changes, and political revolutions that were spreading across Europe and America during his lifetime. People were thinking for themselves, throwing off their "self-incurred immaturity," and refusing to rely on traditional answers. That consistent application of reason to every problem was what Kant meant by "Enlightenment."

> Enlightenment is the human being's emancipation from its self-incurred immaturity. Immaturity is the inability to make use of one's intellect without the direction of another. This immaturity is self-incurred when it does not lie in a lack of intellect, but rather in a lack of resolve and courage to make use of one's intellect without direction of another.[3]

In ethics, Kant argued that a moral rule must be a "categorical imperative," formulated so that everyone can test it by the use of reason. Everyone is then required to follow it, not because it is required by the law, taught by the church, or advised by those who know how to succeed in business, but because to do otherwise would be irrational. Kant's favorite examples are rules like "Tell the truth." We know the rule applies to us, because it is addressed to anyone who is rational enough to understand it, and we know that it is a requirement of reason, because no matter how much we may want to tell a lie to achieve our own goals, no matter how much we struggle to convince ourselves that there are "noble" lies and "white" lies that contribute to the greater good, we cannot conceive a world in which rational people all follow a rule that says, "Lie when it seems good to you to do so."

Knowing the moral rules thus requires no special knowledge of human nature and no ability to sort out good and bad goals. We simply have to understand the basic logical form that all rules take: Act so that the rule you are following could be made into a universal law that everyone would follow.[4] This he calls a "categorical imperative," distinguishing it from a "hypothetical imperative," which commands us *only if* we have accepted some particular goal to which it is a means. "Complete your assignments on time, if you want a good grade in your ethics class" is a hypothetical imperative. So is "Exercise regularly, if you want to stay healthy." A hypothetical imperative may be based on goals that are very widely shared among the people we know, but it cannot be a universal law that applies to all rational beings. A categorical imperative, likewise, cannot be reduced to good advice for people who happen to want some particular goal.

What Kant understood himself to be doing was seeking out the underlying rational form of our ordinary ways of thinking. The way we express our moral ideas does not always show their rational form. We need critical thinking to see why these moral rules are requirements of reason, and Kant's way of thinking is sometimes called "critical philosophy." Critical thinking in this sense does not mean that Kant rejects ordinary ideas about morality. Kant in fact thought that most people know pretty well what their duties are, and he never suggested that he had discovered some new set of moral rules that nobody had ever thought of before. Critical philosophy is more like the critical reflection on a way of life that has been central to ethics from the very beginning.[5] What critical philosophy does, however, is not merely to ask what is really important in the moral life. Critical philosophy seeks the logic that holds our various duties together. It gets beneath the appearances and discerns what is really going on. In this way, Kant's moral philosophy keeps our thinking focused strictly on doing the right thing. Asking what a rational person would do and insisting that we impose that requirement on ourselves is one way to make sure that we are not distracted by what we desire, nor even by what we think is good for us. That is why moral rules must be autonomous. Any other kind of rule is heteronomous, imposed from outside by some force other than our own reason. The outside force may be an authority telling us what we are supposed to do, or it may be the power of our own desires.

Freedom, which is the goal of Enlightenment, thus cannot be equated with using your reason to justify whatever you want to do. That is simply another kind of heteronomy. Having to follow your desires, whims, and crazy ideas is no better than having to follow the orders of some powerful supervisor who never takes a day off. Only acting according to what your reason tells you puts you in charge of your own life. For Kant, that is what ethics is all about, and it is the only life that is worth living.

Here, Kant introduces a sharp distinction between moral and non-moral goods. In the beginning, as we saw with Aristotle, there was little distinction in ethics between the things that made for genuine happiness—health, possessions, honors, good relationships, and the like—and the personal qualities that we would think of as distinctly moral goods. A virtuous person would be courageous in misfortune, of course, and Aristotle insisted that one of the advantages of a good character is that even in the worst of circumstances, the noble person would not be completely miserable. Still, for Aristotle a good life had to include *both* those personal qualities and the excellences and achievements that made for lasting satisfaction. The Stoics warned that it might be more difficult than Aristotle thought to keep those two kinds of goodness together, and early Christians insisted that a relationship to God secured a happiness that could survive the loss of everything else. Nearly everyone continued to think, however, that a morally good life would also be a good life in the sense that it would be a happy life, the sort of life that a wise person would genuinely desire to live. For Kant, by contrast, the only thing good in itself is the good will, which acts out of respect for the moral law. Happiness, even the comprehensive and long-lasting happiness that Aristotle called *eudaimonia*, cannot make a good person. Nor does moral goodness make us happy, according to Kant. The most we can say is that moral goodness makes us worthy to be happy.[6]

Given this understanding of ethics, Kant himself was unsure whether Christian ethics is possible. Certainly it would not be morally good to do your duty because you expect a heavenly reward. Reliance on a moral law found in scripture also looks suspiciously heteronomous, and Kant's own early experience left him with little confidence in the strict Protestant moral training of his day. Nevertheless, his characteristically modern emphasis on the freedom to do your own moral thinking has deep roots in the traditions of Christian ethics that we have followed through this book. From the beginning, Christians had a critical perspective on the way the law of Moses was used by the religious authorities in the world where Jesus lived and taught, and they extended this criticism to all of the different ways of life they encountered as their new faith spread through the cities of the Roman Empire. When Paul urged Christians,

"Do not be conformed to this world," he did not simply tell them, "Be conformed to what I say instead." He said, "Be transformed by the renewing of your minds, so that you may discern what is the will of God—what is good and acceptable and perfect" (Romans 12:2). A measure of discernment and mental transformation is required, a kind of thinking on your own, in order to know what the will of God is. And while some Enlightenment thinkers might regard following the will of God as the ultimate form of "self-incurred immaturity," it is clear that from the perspective of the Christian stance, this is not simply an external authority, issuing commands from afar like a king or an emperor. God's will is present in the creation of human beings and of human reason. Given the realities of human sin, human beings know themselves more reliably through the will of God than they do through consulting their own desires. Nevertheless, to know the will of God, they must rely on their own discernment, rather than on the commands of others. Even when people are set up in positions of authority, they are no less susceptible to being misled by sin than the people they rule. That is why Thomas Aquinas said that conscience is binding at the point of decision, even if conscience turns out in the end to be mistaken.[7]

Over the two centuries since Kant reshaped modern thinking about ethics, Christian writers have often been critical of his work, because he seems to have made human reason into the standard by which God's will must be measured. But it would be more accurate to say that Kant makes it clear that reason is the standard by which Christians must decide between all the sources from which God's will might be known, including those authorities who say they speak for God and those texts which Christians believe to be a record of God's revelation. Dietrich Bonhoeffer (1906–1945), the German theologian who was executed for his resistance to Hitler's regime shortly before the end of the Second World War, offered a more balanced appraisal of what the Enlightenment emphasis on *ratio* (reason) means for Christian ethics.

> Liberated ratio achieved an unanticipated importance. Its free use created an atmosphere of truthfulness, light, and clarity. A fresh wind of bright intelligence cleared up prejudices, social conceits, hypocritical proprieties, and stifling sentimentality. Intellectual honesty in all things, including questions of faith, was the great good of liberated ratio. It has belonged ever since to the essential moral requirements of Western

humanity. Contempt for the age of rationalism is a suspicious sign of a deficient desire for truthfulness. Just because intellectual honesty does not have the last word on things and rational clarity often comes at the cost of the depth of reality, we are not absolved from our inner duty to make honest and clean use of ratio.[8]

In some of his last writings, Bonhoeffer spoke of a "world come of age." In the postwar era he anticipated, the "self-imposed immaturity" that Kant rejected 160 years before might finally disappear, and the obedience to authority that was bringing Germany to destruction would no longer be possible. The church and Christian faith might have a very different place in such a world, but Bonhoeffer had no doubt that this world, with the new kind of self-disciplined freedom it requires, is where Christian ethics now has to be done.[9] The problem of ethics in the modern world is to explain how people can determine their duty for themselves, independent of their desires, illusions, and wishful thinking, and apart from any "self-incurred immaturity" that would keep them from doing their own thinking. That kind of freedom is essential to Christian ethics, too. The question is how to achieve it.

Autonomy and the Christian Stance

Living without parental constraints usually comes easily at the end of immaturity, but the ability to think for yourself takes more work. This is also true for the achievement of autonomy after the end of "self-incurred immaturity." The most basic requirement is a way of thinking that will eliminate the commands of external authorities and internal compulsions and point you to your actual duty. Christian ethics offers several ways to do this kind of moral reasoning, and as we might expect, the different versions of the Christian stance that we have reviewed take different approaches to the problem.

We begin with the method of practical reasoning we found in Thomas Aquinas, in which secure general principles yield more specific rules as they are applied to more specific cases. People who can rigorously apply these rules without making exceptions for themselves or distorting the rules to serve their own interests will know what they ought to do in each case. Many Christian ethicists think that this *casuistry*, with its reliance on carefully formulated rules, is still the best way to ensure the independence of moral reasoning. Others argue that the old model of exceptionless rules and deductive reasoning too quickly becomes a rigid system that can only be applied by experts. That kind of thinking works against autonomy, instead of leading to it. The alternative is to follow more closely the ways that reason actually moves between principles and cases, seeking a way of independent moral reasoning that is available in the experience of people who are not trained as specialists in casuistry. Many authors, Protestant and Catholic, have contributed to these ways of reasoning about cases, and they argue vigorously among themselves. As a group, however, they use Synergy in their thinking about Christian ethics. Their ways of reasoning are accessible to many people with many different beliefs, and their shared judgments about issues can be used as the starting point for further moral discussions.

Still others suggest that the most important limits on the freedom of our moral thinking are the assumptions about ourselves and our neighbors that we absorb without thinking from the society around us. It is not poor reasoning that keeps us from discerning the right thing to do. Social patterns of wealth and power keep us from seeing the real possibilities. The most basic forms of heteronomous authority are so familiar that they have become part of our thinking. What the powerful do is accepted as right, both by the powerful and by the people whom they control. To determine what our duty really is, we need more than a critical philosophy of moral reasoning. We need a critical theory of society that will bring to light the structures of power that we do not see. In recent Christian ethics, both Realism and Liberation have made important contributions to this kind of critical thinking.

Integrity takes a different approach from all of these others. For this version of the Christian stance, duty cannot be understood apart from the command of God. Because we are created by God and make our choices in a world that is already constituted by God's choice, God's command can never be heteronomous, but any attempt to conceive autonomy apart from the command of God will eventually trade this real freedom for the heteronomy of some abstract moral rule or some movement of history that absorbs all of our decisions and choices into itself.

PATHWAYS TO AUTONOMY

1. Autonomous moral reasoning is primarily a matter of properly connecting principles and general moral rules to particular cases. This may be done through:

    A. Traditional *casuistry*, or

    B. New models of *practical reason*.

2. Autonomous moral reasoning is primarily a matter of thinking critically about the assumptions by which a society connects power and right. This may be done through:

    A. Realist analysis of structures of power and self-interest, or

    B. Liberation of specific groups of oppressed people.

3. Obedience to the command of God in a specific, concrete choice is the real path to moral autonomy. Moral reasoning independent of this command deteriorates into a form of heteronomy.

Each of these pathways to autonomy has been important in recent Christian ethics, and each has been articulated by writers who draw on important resources in the Christian tradition to define the position. Our task for the remainder of this chapter will be to review these approaches to deontological ethics and introduce the authors who have made them important.

Casuistry

Thomas Aquinas had suggested one way to keep moral reasoning independent, long before Kant introduced his critical philosophy. Reason allows us to formulate moral ideas, which seem upon reflection both to be true and to be shared by other rational minds. These moral ideas range from the very general to the specific. "Promises ought to be kept" is general. It encompasses things as various as meeting a friend when and where you said you would to upholding the vows you take at your wedding. More specific moral ideas can be formulated as rules that govern a limited range of situations: "All books must be checked out before leaving the library." The general ideas provide principles from which a number of rules could be derived: "Theft is wrong" covers the library rule and the criminal statutes against grand theft auto. The most general of these principles, says Thomas, is the first principle of practical reason, which is that good ought to be done and evil ought to be avoided.[10] Reason suggests many of these moral ideas to people in the course of their ordinary experience. It would not be difficult to come up with a long list of them, arranged from the more general to the more specific, with which nearly everyone would agree.

If we know these rules and principles because we have thought them through for ourselves, rather than because someone has told us they are true, and if we decide what to do by applying them to our own situation, rather than because someone has told us what to do, then we have given the rule to ourselves. We are autonomous, not exactly in the way that Kant had in mind, but in the more general sense that our choices have been guided by our moral ideas, and we have not traded what we know we ought to do for what we want or for what others tell us.

The problem is to identify the ways of thinking that maintain this independence in complex situations where it is not clear exactly which rules apply, and where the line between what we want and what we ought to do is not easily drawn. Is it theft to take a newspaper that belongs to someone else if they have accidentally left it behind on a bus? How about if what they left is an envelope that has five dollars in it? How about if the envelope contains five thousand dollars?

As Thomas Aquinas noted, the more specific the question, the more difficult practical reason becomes, and the more likely we are to need adjustments and exceptions to the general rule.[11] Promises are to be kept, he said, but not if what you promised was to return a weapon to someone who has become a homicidal maniac. That seems like a reasonable specification of the rule, but how do you keep from watering down your duty with exceptions that are actually nothing more than ways to satisfy your own desires? Promises are to be kept, but how about an exception if it turns out that keeping the promise will cost you more than it is worth? Truth should be told, but does that also apply when telling the truth gets you into real trouble? Debts should be paid, but suppose the lender has so much money that he or she has forgotten about the loan? Once desire has done its work, there may be very little left of duty.

Strictly speaking, this is not a problem for Kant, since his categorical imperative is not a general rule that has to be applied to particular cases, but a logical test that each moral decision has to pass. If your rule of action could be followed by everyone, as though it were a universal law, then that is the right course of action. "Tell the truth" seems straightforward enough and ought to be universalizable in most cases. If we want to build certain exceptions into the rule, they too would have to be universalizable, and so they would be available to everybody. Should you tell the truth to a would-be murderer who asks you where to find his intended victim? It seems easy enough to devise a universal law that covers that situation: Everyone should lie to save the life of an innocent person. But if your rule really could be a universal law, there would be no circumstances that would allow an exception just for yourself. "Everyone should tell the truth except me" does not get very far as a universal law.

Kant's idea makes sense, but when we get down to specific questions, it is harder than we might think to formulate a universal rule on which everyone could agree. Kant's own sense of duty was extremely demanding, and he himself argued, against the universal law we just proposed, that if the intended murder victim happens to be hiding in your closet, you have a duty not to lie to the would-be murderer, even to protect the intended victim.[12] (After all, Kant asks, how do you know that the intended victim has not escaped from the closet and run out into the street, where he will meet the murderer whom your lie has sent that way, too?)

Aquinas was perhaps wiser than Kant on this point. It is difficult to formulate universal rules for particular cases. Our moral thinking more often proceeds from general rules, on which it is relatively easy to agree, to their application in particular cases, where the probability of disagreements, mistakes, and self-serving exceptions is much higher. It does seem that we often have to make exceptions to general rules in order to do the right thing in particular cases. But the problem is to figure out how to justify the exception without simply saying that we like the result better than we like doing our duty in this case. For those who admit that exceptions are possible, the way we argue from rules to cases becomes an important part of the reasoned moral life. This kind of reasoning is called *casuistry*. The idea is to begin with the general rule, then stick strictly to sound reasoning and good evidence, so that when you arrive at your conclusion, you can be sure that it really is an application of the rule and not an excuse for doing whatever you like.

Casuistry became an important part of Christian ethics, especially when priests and pastors had to apply the rules their churches taught to the lives of individual Christians. This was especially true in the Catholic Church as it developed a more duty-centered ethics and the practice of individual confession became an expected part of Catholic life. But Calvinist and Anglican theologians wrote about casuistry, too. The objective for all of them was, much as Thomas Aquinas had explained it centuries earlier, to think about when it was important to follow the general rules of truth-telling, promise-keeping, and responsibility toward spouses and children strictly and when it was appropriate to apply those rules with some flexibility in particular circumstances. A wife might have a duty to be truthful to her husband, but did she violate that duty by concealing the truth when telling the truth might arouse his anger and lead to violence against her and her children? In the work of a thoughtful priest or pastor, casuistry could make deontological ethics more humane and more realistic, or adjust the traditional requirements of the church to new social conditions.

Of course, casuistry could be abused, as well as wisely used. It sometimes provided religious excuses for people who wanted to evade their duties, and it was easy enough to find someone who could supply a line of moral reasoning to support the desired results. Although the best of the casuists used their elaborate moral reasoning to help people think through their own situations, it is difficult to maintain autonomy when you are surrounded by experts, and many Christians came to rely on those experts instead of thinking for themselves. In turn, many philosophers and theologians became suspicious of casuistry, and a dictionary definition of it often includes something like "a quibbling or evasive way of dealing with difficult cases of duty."[13] But something like casuistry is nonetheless necessary for deontological ethics. Deontologists must reason about particular questions in a way that preserves the independence of moral ideas, even if they choose to abandon the term *casuistry* as outdated or discredited.

From Principles to Cases

Some writers advise us to stay very close to the basic pattern laid down by Aquinas, which moves by careful, reasoned steps from principles to cases. This is particularly advisable when the violation of important general rules will result in serious moral problems: An innocent person must not be deliberately killed, for example; people who engage in sexual relations must be open to the possibility that a new life will result; property must not be taken from its owners against their reasonable objections. Rules of this sort raise many difficult questions when they are applied to particular cases. What about the bystander who is killed when the police open fire to stop a terrorist suicide bomber? Can a married couple take steps to prevent conception if they are afraid that they cannot support another child? What kind of objections are "reasonable" when private property is needed for public purposes?

To get from principles and general rules to cases, we may have to look very closely to determine whether this particular case falls under the rule. The bystander who falls victim to a stray bullet when the police open fire has not been deliberately killed. Objections from the property owner who does not want to pay taxes to provide services to the homeless may not be reasonable, even though they are strongly felt. But if the rule does apply, no explanations about the benefits that might result from breaking it are relevant. Rules like these are exceptionless moral rules.

Pope John Paul II (1920–2005), in his encyclical *Veritatis splendor*, explained how natural law leads to the formulation of such rules. Human actions have an objective structure. They are designed by nature to reach a particular end, which we can understand and evaluate independently of the intentions and goals of the particular person who does the action. Acts which in their structure violate the purposes of God's creation and reduce the person to a level below the distinctive rational nature that belongs to humanity can have no place in the ordering of goods toward God that is the goal of the moral life. Hence those actions are "always and in every case" in conflict with the human good, and a rule that prohibits them cannot possibly interfere with someone's good intentions. An exceptionless moral rule "not only does not prohibit a good intention, but actually represents its basic expression."[14]

John Paul II follows Thomas Aquinas very closely in his understanding of exceptionless moral rules, but recent Protestant ethics has found reasons to emphasize them, too. Paul Ramsey (1913–1988) did a great deal to reintroduce natural law ideas into Protestant thinking about medical care, war, and legal rights.[15] Ramsey emphasized respect for the people with whom we are dealing as an essential feature of all moral action. Since some actions are incompatible with that respect, there are exceptionless moral rules that must be observed, even when we are dealing with complex situations that involve serious conflicts.[16] Innocent persons must not be directly killed. That rule holds even when we are dealing with a terminally ill patient whose death may be the indirect result of medical actions taken to relieve pain and suffering. It holds even in the case of war, where the death of innocent civilians may be the indirect result of legitimate military action taken against enemy combatants. Killing the patient to end suffering or deliberately targeting civilians to achieve a military goal is always wrong, and the rules of medical practice or of military engagement must be carefully formulated so that they do not permit such exceptions.

For Protestant and Catholic writers alike, the emphasis on exceptionless moral rules reflects an understanding of why duty is important in the moral life. It is rules that keep us from sacrificing the happiness, well-being, or perhaps even the life of an individual person to produce the greatest good for the greatest number. Rules also remind us of objective requirements of our own human nature, even when what we want is different from what we ought to do. Precisely because our duties make such strong demands on us, they can become unworkable or oppressive if they are not applied thoughtfully. Careful distinctions between direct and indirect effects or between reasonable and unreasonable burdens are not a clever way to evade our duties. They are the kind of thinking that is required if an ethics of duty is to be preserved. Nevertheless, the distinction between applying the rule carefully and creating an exception to it must be maintained.

Exceptions, Experience, and Relationships

Other recent Christian ethicists, however, suggest a different approach to principles and cases. The familiar forms of casuistry that proceed step by step from general rules to specific duties have an appearance of objectivity and logical rigor, but they are distant from the ways that most people make their moral decisions. Maintaining the importance of rules in the moral life requires more attention to the ways that rules are used and understood in ordinary moral experience.

As a starting point, we might note that most people, even those who are very concerned about doing their duty, do consider the consequences of their actions when trying to determine actual duties. Consequences become important especially when duties conflict. A physician who is called to a medical emergency as she leaves the office to meet a friend for coffee cannot both do her duty to the patient and keep her promise to her friend. Weighing the suffering that a delay might cause for the patient against the momentary annoyance and disappointment her friend might feel, the physician would probably decide to break her promise on consideration of the consequences, without going through elaborate reasoning about whether the general rule about keeping promises really applies in this case. Richard McCormick (1922–2000) and other Catholic moral theologians developed the idea of *proportionalism* to explain how people might reasonably include this kind of consideration of consequences in an ethics that remains basically deontological. Like other deontologists, the proportionalist agrees that we must not directly choose an action that is morally wrong in order to achieve good results. But when duties conflict, the proportionalist argues that it is reasonable to weigh the consequences in making a decision. It is wrong to kill an aggressor if innocent bystanders are likely to be killed or injured in the event. But if the aggressor is a suicide bomber who is about to set off an explosion in the midst of a large crowd, the right choice may be to save as many of those people as possible by using deadly force against the terrorist. No neatly defined rule tells us that this is the right choice. The decision follows from a judgment that harm done is proportional to the good achieved.

Proportionalism is just one of the ways that recent authors have tried to bring formal accounts of moral reasoning closer to the way that people actually think. Traditional casuistry leads to conclusions that are logically certain, but the way we really think about our choices rarely moves with such precision. When we say that it is a physician's duty to care for a particular patient, we are incorporating certain facts into that claim, along with moral rules. Exactly what the patient's needs are and the scope of this particular physician's competence come into consideration, along with the rules of medical ethics that establish a physician's duty to provide care, and moral and legal rules that prohibit discrimination on the basis of race, gender, religion, or other differences between people who might need medical care. The way we actually think about decisions like this takes account of different kinds of evidence about the facts and different degrees of certainty in our moral conclusions.

The philosopher Stephen Toulmin (1922–2009) developed an account of practical argumentation that takes account of ambiguity, incomplete knowledge, and degrees of certainty in stating its conclusions, and together with Albert Jonsen, he applied it to a reappraisal of casuistry that focused on the details of particular situations.[17] Moral conclusions in this approach arise from a detailed analysis of cases, rather than from the application of rules. The terrorist with a bomb in the middle of a crowd of innocent bystanders has to be seen in relation to the unarmed, would-be terrorist who is passing down a crowded street on the way to pick up a weapon. Stopping him with deadly force might be the right thing for the police to do in the first case. It is more questionable in the second. A third case, in which the police are not quite sure that the terrorist has a bomb, probably falls somewhere in between the first two. Exceptionless rules do not easily adjust to being pretty sure, but not quite certain, that a terrorist is about to set off a bomb, but decisions sometimes have to be made under those conditions.

In this sort of casuistry, our thinking moves in several directions at once. Like the familiar moral reasoning of Thomas Aquinas, it moves from principles to cases, seeking to determine what kind of moral problem is at issue. Should I keep my promise to this man who wants his sword back, or is it unreasonable to do that when he seems intent on treason? Is it my duty to aid a friend who needs help with an ethics paper by writing several pages for him about Thomas Aquinas and the return of deposits, or is that academic dishonesty, which it is my duty to avoid? But in real life, our thinking also moves from case to case, comparing the case in which my friend and I discuss Thomas Aquinas together and I write up the results with the case in which we merely talk about Thomas Aquinas together and he takes responsibility for writing up our conclusions, and comparing both with the case in which my friend saves me the trouble by downloading several pages on Thomas Aquinas from the Internet and inserting them in his term paper. The comparison is instructive, and each new case refines our understanding of what it means to help someone and what is and is not academic dishonesty. Perhaps most important, a casuistry that follows the ways that people really think moves from cases to principles, as well as from principles to cases. It is not just a question of which cases can be brought under an unchanging principle. The principle itself may change in light of the experience of the cases. As information technology makes collaboration on documents easier and more important, the understanding of what it means to represent something honestly as your own work may change. On the other hand, the increased flow of reliable and unreliable information may make it more important than ever to identify the one individual who is responsible for this particular combination of information and judgment. However that works out for particular rules and principles, it seems clear that the principles we apply in making moral judgments are not static conclusions that follow only from other moral principles. They are the product of what John Rawls calls a "reflective equilibrium" between our judgments about particular cases and the principles by which we account for those judgments.[18] Sometimes, when we think about the rules, we decide that our initial feeling about the case was mistaken. Sometimes, however, we decide to revise the rule so that it more clearly represents what we think is the right thing to do. This is not an easy process, nor does it ever come to a definitive end, as though there were some point, after we have thought about it long enough, when we can just use the rules, unchanged and unchanging. Like balance on a tightrope, reflective equilibrium is something that we have to maintain at all times.

A third point in recent thinking about how we maintain the independence of our moral reasoning is that when we make moral decisions, we make them about human actions taken as a whole. Our decisions about right and wrong are not about physical descriptions of writing term papers, financial transactions, sexual encounters, or military engagements. They involve motivations and intentions as well. To understand an action, we have to include those dimensions in its description, and we have to understand that other people respond to our actions in those terms, too. In various ways, then, recent writers in Christian ethics have sought to modify the deontological ethics that moves deductively from principles to rules to decisions about specific cases. They allow limited consideration of consequences in determining whether an act is wrong. They try to provide an account of moral reasoning that better represents the ways that people actually think about their moral decisions. They insist that what we evaluate in moral terms is not just an action in isolation, but something that is done by a responsible person, with motives, intentions, and multiple relationships. For the philosophers and theologians who have taken these steps to change the ways we think about deontological ethics, the idea is not to abandon duty as the starting point for moral thinking in favor of teleology, utilitarianism, or situation ethics. They believe that these changes are essential for the independent moral reasoning on which deontological ethics depends.

PRINCIPLES AND CASES

One pathway to moral autonomy is through rigorous moral reasoning that connects principles and general moral rules to particular cases, undistracted by desire for particular results or deference to the reasoning of other authorities.

For some, this independence is best secured by a casuistry that reasons from principles to cases, emphasizing the importance of exceptionless moral rules.

Others argue for a less rigid form of practical reason, closer to ordinary experience, in which conflicts between rules may be resolved by consideration of the consequences (*proportionalism*), reason sometimes revises principles in light of cases (*reflective equilibrium*), and actions are understood in terms of motives, intentions, and relationships, as well as physical descriptions.

Reason and Power

Poor reasoning is not the only thing that makes moral autonomy difficult, however. Thinking about what is right can be distorted by the social context, too. Prejudices against a racial minority, a religious group, or anybody who is "different" become part of daily life, and discrimination, subtle or obvious, becomes expected behavior. Those who are rich and powerful, by contrast, receive a deference that makes their privileged position seem right and even necessary. Both the powerful and the powerless learn to expect the treatment they receive, and these patterns of privilege and discrimination become part of how people decide what they ought to do. The threat to moral autonomy does not have to be a dictator telling you what to do or a demagogue telling you how to think. Autonomy can be undermined by assumptions about right and wrong that everybody shares, assumptions that are so much a part of a way of life that no one thinks to challenge them.

During the nineteenth century, finding ways to expose these socially imposed ways of thinking became central to the study of ethics and society. Observing the growth of industrial production and market economies, Karl Marx (1818–1883) developed a theory that the capitalist system was sustained by ideas about property, law, and justice that made the power of the owners seem right and concealed the ways that they gained their wealth at the expense of their workers. Marx argued that the kind of critical thinking that Kant applied to understanding reason[19] had to be applied to understanding society, too. In both cases, what we learn is that the way things really work is seldom what it seems to be on the surface. Marx's search for critical explanations of how societies create and maintain the ideas that they share was enormously influential. In the long run, it may prove far more important than his better known economic theory that provided inspiration for communist revolutions in Russia and China. Writers in sociology, psychology, and political philosophy have all built on these insights to provide critical thinking about moral and religious ideas.

Like Kant's critical philosophy, these theories were difficult to incorporate into Christian ethics. From a critical perspective, religion can appear as a prime example of the kind of ideas that become embedded in a society, conferring power and authority that have no basis in reality. Over time, however, some critical theorists have formulated more positive accounts of religion, and theologians have seen the connection between prophetic criticisms of religious authorities in the Hebrew Bible and the critical unmasking of the ways that religion sustains social power. Just as Kant's critical thinking about moral autonomy has become part of all contemporary ethics, critical thinking about social power is becoming an important first step in many ways of thinking about social justice in Christian ethics.

Reinhold Niebuhr's Christian Realism played a significant role in this transition.[20] When he published *Moral Man and Immoral Society* in 1932, it seemed to many of his contemporaries that he had almost abandoned Christian ethics in favor of a Marxist analysis of political and economic power. Niebuhr's Realism gained acceptance, however, as it became apparent that Christian ideals alone would not solve the economic issues between managers and factory workers or the growing racial divide in industrial cities like Detroit. Niebuhr also provided a more even-handed critical analysis than some other theorists. Having observed the Marxist-inspired revolution in Russia, he warned that the powerless were as susceptible to exaggerated estimates of their own virtue as the powerful. Critical thinking about society is not a task that will be finished when better people come to power. Realists whose criticism is rooted in an understanding of human sin as well as an understanding of society know that every group believes they are wiser, more just, and better suited to rule than they really are.

Realists seldom draw conclusions about actual duties from this critical analysis of social power. Realism may, indeed, be paralyzing, resulting in the disillusioning awareness that every program of action is distorted by self-interest and none can deliver the autonomy and justice that all of them promise. That is why Niebuhr generally insisted that realists must take their critical insights and rejoin the discussion about what to do in particular cases. Understanding how social forces affect moral judgments makes us aware that no compromise between labor and management achieves complete fairness, and no side in a war is completely innocent of aggression. But the fact that there is no perfect justice does not mean that the strike has to continue forever or that we should not resist the invaders. After critically surveying the ambiguities in every way of thinking about our duties and identifying the ways that every social context distorts our moral reasoning, we must still decide what we ought to do.

Martin Luther King, Jr. (1929–1968) continued this critical thinking as he led the struggle for racial justice that Niebuhr had anticipated. He was influenced by Niebuhr's analysis of social power, but he also drew on the relationship between natural law and human law. As he campaigned for new laws that would guarantee equal access to voting, housing, education, and public accommodations, he also led protests that violated the existing laws that enforced racial segregation. His opponents charged that he lacked respect for law and order, because he was ready to use the law when he could to gain equality and ready to break it when he did not like its requirements. Writing from the city jail in Birmingham, Alabama, King explained to his critics that he was not being inconsistent. He was employing Thomas Aquinas's principle that human law must not conflict with the natural law. "A just law is a man-made code that squares with the moral law or the law of God. An unjust law is a code that is out of harmony with the moral law. To put it in terms of Saint Thomas Aquinas, an unjust law is a human law that is not rooted in eternal law and natural law."[21]

The question, of course, is how we are to know which laws are which, since those who have power in society can make their prejudices seem natural and necessary, and King knew well enough that natural law arguments had been used in history to justify the enslavement of African Americans. His answer was to introduce a critical principle of his own, in an effort to distinguish the purposes of a law that reason could support from one that merely reflects the interests of the powerful. "Any law that uplifts human personality is just. Any law that degrades human personality is unjust," King wrote. "All segregation statutes are unjust because segregation distorts the soul and damages the personality. It gives the segregator a false sense of superiority and the segregated a false sense of inferiority."[22] King's critical argument aimed to preclude the strategy of many segregationists who wanted to "improve" the system of racial separation, making it more humane and more truly "separate but equal." He did not develop a casuistry that eliminated the segregation laws one by one. He had a critical argument that disposed of all of them as manifestations of a false sense of social superiority.

The Liberation understanding of the Christian stance employs a similar kind of critical thinking against the social assumptions of power and privilege. Theologians have employed various methods to identify the structures that keep power in the hands of social elites. Some have relied on economic analysis of the systems that deprive workers of control over their labor and trap them in cycles of dependence and poverty. Others have emphasized cultural expectations that keep indigenous peoples and racial minorities in subordinate positions where they have little control over the direction of their lives. The various methods of analysis converge on a common critical principle: the "preferential option for the poor." The phrase comes primarily from Catholic social ethics,[23] but the idea is widely shared in Liberation ethics. Given what we know about social realities, an even-handed ethics that treats all groups alike will not produce justice, nor will relieving the needs of the poor without changing the conditions under which they live. The poor must be empowered, and no way of moral reasoning that neglects this can tell us what our actual duty is.

Thinking Critically about Scripture

Liberationists emphasize the importance of bringing people who have been deprived of autonomy to a point where they can make their own decisions. As Kant understood long ago, this is not something that an ethicist or a religious leader or a political figure can do for them. Liberationists, however, find that reflection on the story of Jesus in light of their own experience can be a uniquely empowering experience for the poor and oppressed. This Liberation *hermeneutics*, or method of interpreting scripture, provides a distinctive theological approach to the critical task of identifying the social structures that must be understood before autonomous moral decisions are possible. As James Cone put it, the task of Black Theology is "to analyze the nature of the gospel of Jesus Christ in the light of oppressed blacks so they will see the gospel as inseparable from their humiliated condition, and as bestowing on them the necessary power to break the chains of oppression." Latin American theologians have likewise encouraged poor people to read and interpret the Bible for themselves, in light of their own situation. As a result, they often come to a clearer understanding of the forces that shape their lives. They no longer see these as inevitable and necessary realities, and seeing that things might be different becomes the first step toward making their own choices about the changes that should be made.[24]

The use of Liberation hermeneutics to guide autonomous moral decisions is particularly difficult, however, when Christianity itself is part of the structures of oppression that need to be understood. Churches and religious leaders can be part of powerful groups that maintain existing social patterns, and the poor can find liberation in a hermeneutics that realigns Jesus in the Gospels with the powerless and locates his enemies among the righteous, rather than the sinners. It is possible to use the Bible to reinterpret the church. More difficult problems begin when the Bible itself reflects the structures of a patriarchal society that sees dependence and obedience as appropriate for women. To bring them to a position where autonomy is possible, it may be necessary to use the Bible to reinterpret itself. Rosemary Radford Ruether has found three starting points for this feminist hermeneutic in the biblical text: (1) The prophets consistently insist that kings and common people stand equal before God. Distinctions of all sorts are condemned, and that condemnation must extend to distinctions between men and women as well. (2) Although the Bible draws analogies between God and human kings and fathers, it does so to set God above even these readily recognizable examples of human power. Because God is the real authority, kings and fathers never have the last word in human affairs. (3) Just as the Bible places all authority under God, it forbids people to represent God in idols made in human form. The commandment not to worship other gods implies that we must not treat social distinctions of our own making as though they were part of God's creation.[25] This applies to the social distinctions between men and women, but like all of Ruether's starting points for an internal criticism of the biblical text, it also suggests ways that biblical interpretation can serve, as other forms of social analysis do, to reveal structures of society that ordinarily go unnoticed or unchallenged.

CRITICAL THINKING ABOUT SOCIETY

Critical social theories seek to understand the structures of power on which ordinary assumptions about what is good and right depend.

Christian Realism uses these theories to show that self-interest and power are involved in every movement for justice, but it seeks to make responsible choices between these imperfect alternatives.

Liberation theology uses these theories for the liberation of oppressed people and for interpretations of the Bible that work against patterns of oppression built on religious ideas.

Conflict and Agreement

No single method emerges for thinking about duty in contemporary Christian ethics. Each way of describing moral reasoning has its own path to an independent way of thinking by which to determine what we ought to do. Advocates of the different methods do not agree, and often they are sharply critical of one another. Those who base their decisions on exceptionless moral rules charge proportionalists with trying to reach good ends by evil means. Proportionalists respond that their critics are inflexible and out of touch with the way that moral choices are actually made. Those who seek neutral moral principles often accuse liberation theology of distorting justice with its preferential option for the poor. Liberationists respond that an even-handed theory of justice distorts reality by treating the existing patterns of wealth and power as though they were necessary features of social life. The arguments have been with us for a while, and they are likely to continue far into the future.

Despite these conflicts over methods of moral reasoning in contemporary Christian ethics, there are nonetheless large areas of agreement on the way to approach particular moral problems. Thinking about war and peace provides an example. In recent years, ethicists have converged on the principles of "just war" theory as the right framework for thinking about decisions about war and peace. The idea of a just war is that a nation has a duty to use force only in self-defense, only in proportion to the danger posed by an aggressor, and only as a last resort, after other ways of settling the dispute have failed. Even after a war is underway, not everything is permissible, since the warring parties still have duties to limit the damage and protect civilian populations from harm. As Thomas Aquinas might warn us, agreement on these principles does not ensure agreement on more specific decisions about whether a particular war is just or whether a particular strategy meets the obligations to limit damage and protect civilians, but the just war idea does provide a framework within which those specific decisions can be discussed. Even with rapidly changing conditions of global politics and new kinds of threats from terrorist groups that are capable of international action, ethicists, politicians, military strategists, and religious groups have all used just war ideas to lead public thinking about the wars in Iraq and Afghanistan and about appropriate strategies to combat the threat of international terrorism.

Similar agreements are emerging in economic justice and in medical ethics. However they think about moral reasoning, Christian ethicists increasingly share the realist perspective that there is no one economic system, free market or socialist, that satisfies all of the requirements of economic justice. Duty in this area is a matter of carefully selecting the right combination of incentives and regulations to allow growth and opportunity while still protecting the individual persons who depend on the economic system for their well-being. In medical ethics, attention now focuses on decisions that carefully identify the fine line that separates unnecessarily prolonging the natural process of dying from actively using medical interventions to bring about death. Both prolonged death and active killing are evils to be avoided, and agreement on that provides a framework in which to ask the more difficult questions about exactly which acts constitute which of the two evils. In these discussions, there is also a new emphasis on the patient's autonomy, the right to make decisions about your own medical care and to have those decisions respected, even if you are not in a position to participate actively in the decision-making at the moment.

Among the major areas of moral concern in contemporary society, only sexual ethics falls outside of this growing agreement on the frameworks for discussion. In this area, the controversy between those who rely on exceptionless rules and those who seek a more personal, relational understanding of sexual relationships is sharp, and it seems likely to continue. Each side believes that the other has chosen a way of looking at choices in this most intimate area of life that loses what is most important. Rules, some say, keep us mindful of objective evils where we are most likely to be led astray by our own feelings. Personal relationships, others reply, are more important in moral decision-making than objective descriptions of sexual acts, and duties must be stated in terms of persons in relationship with other persons.

From what we have seen so far in this chapter, the conflict over how to think about duty in contemporary Christian ethics is important, but it should not obscure these substantial areas of agreement that also exist. The methodological differences that once predictably divided Protestant and Catholic ethics have been reduced, and Protestants and Catholics now appear on both sides of all of the contemporary arguments we have reviewed. Christian ethics has become a truly ecumenical field of study, not because it has resolved all of its controversies, but because all sides of every argument are now open to all participants.

The arguments continue, with all versions of the Christian stance involved, but the trajectory of the discussion as a whole moves toward Synergy. Broad agreements on the principles of just war, economic justice, and medical ethics provide starting points for discussions in which many other groups can join, including many different religious perspectives. Based on the current state of the discipline, we might expect a future in which discussions in Christian ethics are increasingly interwoven with discussions in political philosophy, jurisprudence, philosophical ethics, and the ethics of other religious traditions. Christian participants will not be identified with any one approach to the questions. They may find themselves on different sides of the issues, and at times, at least, they will find that they are more closely aligned with Muslims, Buddhists, or utilitarian moral philosophers than with others who share their Christian stance.

This is a new thing, and to the synergist, it must seem a good thing. It suggests that the Christian effort to understand the conditions under which all persons seek to live a good life has penetrated that reality deeply enough to identify common ground which can be discussed without the need for a common framework of Christian theology to set the limits. But it is just at that point that another version of the Christian stance raises a different question. Such a discussion may achieve autonomy, but does it have integrity?

The Command of God

During the twentieth century, these questions about Integrity in the Christian stance came most persistently from Karl Barth (1886–1968). This was no doubt in part a response to the particular time and place in which he lived. Barth was a German-speaking Swiss citizen who watched as the nations of Europe destroyed each other in the First World War. As a young pastor and theologian, he also observed that European churches were for the most part caught up in the war fever and offered no alternative to the loyalties that sent the armies into the trenches. In fact, the German theologians to whom he looked for theological insight and leadership literally stood beside the Kaiser as the troops marched by at the beginning of the war in 1914.

Two decades later, when he saw the same forces building with even greater intensity in the years before the Second World War, Barth was in a better position to resist. He had become a leading theologian, and he was then teaching in a German university. Barth became a driving force in the Confessing Church movement, which rejected the Nazification of the German churches that followed Hitler's rise to power. Barth was expelled from Germany before the Second World War, but he continued his teaching and his support of the Confessing Church from Switzerland. More important for the future significance of his work, he devoted himself to

Church Dogmatics, a massive work that eventually grew to thirteen volumes and articulated a theology that set the integrity of the church against the distractions, confusions, and false gods of culture.

For Barth, duty begins with undistracted attention to the command of God. "The task of theological ethics is to understand the Word of God as the command of God. Its fundamental, simple, and comprehensive answer to the ethical problem is that man's action is good in so far as it is sanctified by the Word of God which as such is also the command of God."[26] In contrast to any ethics that focuses on human decisions, Barth's theological ethics centers attention on God's decision. God has spoken the Word by which humanity was created and redeemed. In that Word is also contained what humanity should be and do. Ethics thus originates in the Word of God, and human decisions and actions can only be good or evil in relation to this first, decisive choice.

If that general statement about theological ethics is fundamental, simple, and comprehensive, its meaning for particular moral decisions, what Barth calls the problem of "special ethics," is anything but clear. At what point and in what way does the command of God tell me to do this or that particular thing? How does hearing that command relate to all of the other ways of determining my duty, from casuistry to liberation theology, that we have already considered? Of course, nearly all of those theologians would say that when we truly know our duty, we also know God's law or what God commands us to do. That is implicit in James Cone's statement that when oppressed people hear the gospel, they also obtain the power to end their own oppression. It is also implied in the way that Thomas Aquinas connects natural law to the eternal law, and thus to the will of God. But those connections are precisely what Barth wants to undo. We cannot possess the command of God in its concrete reality for us by making general statements about breaking the chains of oppression, or by applying a general rule drawn from natural law to the specific details of our own situation. Next to the real choices of particular individuals, shaped by their own place and time and acting on their own unique possibilities, moral rules are hopeless abstractions. The command of God is known only by the one who hears it, a unique Word to a particular situation.

Clearly, then, the whole structure of casuistry by which general rules and moral principles are connected to specific situations is something foreign to theological ethics as Barth understands it. Contemporary understandings of practical reason have attempted to revise traditional casuistry to bring it closer to the realities of actual moral experience, and critical social theories enable us to take more accurate aim at the particular structures of oppression that are at work in our own situation, but for Barth, even these revisions remain too general. They cannot possibly deal with the innumerable conditions and possibilities that surround every real human choice, and moral systems that turn principles and theories into universal rules that can be equated with the command of God offer only the illusion of certainty. They cannot possibly provide real guidance.

Nor should we suppose that Barth is simply another Protestant theologian turning our attention away from systems of ethics administered by the professional casuists and toward passages of scripture that offer more immediate guidance that people can read for themselves. The Word of God is God's own decisive choice and action, which is always the same and always effective, but the Word of God is not captured in scripture, any more than it can be captured in an ethics textbook or any other writing. The words of scripture may become the Word of God, so that in a moment of particular choice we hear the command of God in the words of the text. But there is no way to guarantee that this will happen, and no way to be sure that the word we have heard is, in fact, the Word of God. We can hold the Bible in our hands, buy it in a store, and put it on the shelf until we need it. We cannot possess the Word of God in that way.

What Barth leaves us with, then, is the Word of God in its eternal certainty and the human choice in all its particularity, complexity, and immediacy. Any system, theory, advisor, authority, or institution that builds a permanent structure to connect the Word and the choice must be rejected, so that the command of God may be heard. Here, Barth comes surprisingly close to Kant's idea of moral autonomy, which aims to ensure that our moral choices are genuinely free, uncoerced by authority or our own desires. His aim, like Kant's, is to eliminate every attraction or authority that might distract us from an immediate encounter with our real duty. The difference is that Barth recognizes that moral philosophy may be one of those distractions.

Even with all this clearing away of intermediaries and all this readiness to listen, certainty is elusive. Final judgment belongs to God.

> To this extent there is a practical casuistry, an active casuistry, the casu-
> istry of the prophetic *ethos*. It consists in the unavoidable venture—the
> final judgment upon this venture rests with God—of understanding
> God's concrete specific command here and now in this particular way,
> of making a corresponding decision in this particular way, and of sum-
> moning others to such a concrete and specific decision.[27]

Barth is not encouraging hesitation or timidity with these warnings against
casuistry and Bible-thumping. He does not mean to leave us wringing our
hands and wondering what our duty is. One way or another, we have to
come to a decision about that. Barth had in mind the kind of responsible
action that Bonhoeffer called a "free venture, not justified by any law,"
which a Christian undertakes without knowing what the results will be
and with full knowledge of the moral risks involved.[28] These ventures are
not small things. For Bonhoeffer, they included participation in a plot to
kill Hitler and bring the war to an end. You cannot go only part way with
such a decision, or leave yourself an easy way out in case you change your
mind. You have to take the decision, act on it, and summon others to join
you in it. You have full responsibility. What you do not have is certainty.

What kind of ethics is possible when our thinking about moral choice
begins in this way with the command of God? We recognize Bonhoeffer's
venture of responsibility readily enough, but once it is identified, Barth
seems determined to keep us from trying to say anything about it that
would carry us from one venture to the next.

Before we answer the question whether ethics is still possible for Barth,
however, we need to understand what Barth is trying to make impossible.
He wants to make sure that there is no place in Christian ethics for the
identification of duty with patriotism, obedience to a leader, or belief in a
national destiny. The German churches had proved themselves all too
eager to adopt that kind of ethics in the First War and even more disas-
trously in their enthusiasm for Hitler's programs and personality in the
years before the Second. As Barth understood the problem, this was not
an aberrant condition unique to the German personality. It was the result
of a theology that too readily identified the will of God with facts of nature
or forces of history and so too easily transferred the trust that belongs to
God alone to human powers and authorities. It was a mistake that any
Christian might make who had been taught to see the order of things as a

reflection of the will of God, and Barth intended to eliminate from theology all forms of thinking that might lead in that direction. He began with a famous attack on natural law published with the simple title "No!" and he continued with the first article of the Barmen Declaration, which he authored for the Confessing Church in 1934: "We reject the false doctrine, as though the church could and would have to acknowledge as a source of its proclamation, apart from and besides this one Word of God, still other events and powers, figures and truths, as God's revelation."[29] The later statement in the *Church Dogmatics* that the task of theological ethics is "to understand the Word of God as the command of God" follows in that same trajectory.

One might, of course, try to solve Barth's problem by making a list of the forbidden identifications: God's Word is not to be confused with Hitler's Reich, or with the values of Western democracy, or with the defeat of terrorism. With that strategy, a little casuistry might even help us to identify similar mistakes and avoid them, too. But Barth saw that the problem runs deeper than that. It lies in the certainty that the Word of God is in our hands, and we are called to execute vengeance on God's enemies. What Barth sought to do was to make that kind of certainty impossible, even for those who do hear the Word of God and obey. The certainty of possession must be replaced by the venture which always stands under God's judgment, as well as God's command.

"Special ethics" is still possible under these conditions, but the generalizations it permits will be about God's Word, not about our conclusions. "If we accept this information about God and man as given in the Word of God, the possibility and necessity of a special ethics confront us with a basic clarity. Comprehensively understood, its task will be to accompany this history of God and man from creation to reconciliation and redemption, indicating the mystery of the encounter at each point on the path according to its own distinctive character."[30] For Barth, the Christian stance itself becomes the content of Christian ethics. To go beyond that risks saying more than we can know, and saying more than we can know inevitably leads to obeying some other voice besides the one Word of God. The other voice may be the voice of a dictator or a demagogue, or it may be the voice of an authoritative casuist, making us just a little too certain of the rightness of our own moral conclusions.

Barth's emphasis on the freedom and uncertainty of our moral choices remains distinctive among the many ways that deontology has devised to say something specific about what our duty is. Barth has drawn criticism from many ethicists for making his judgments without adequate attention to the facts and, especially from Reinhold Niebuhr, for refusing to make moral choices between the greater and lesser evils that we encounter all the time in real moral experience.[31] Barth clearly gives us a theological criticism of ethics. Measured against the standard set by the other theologians we have considered, however, there is little in his work of the critical reflection on a way of life that we ordinarily think of as ethics. What there is instead is the "prophetic ethos" that makes possible a different kind of responsible action. As we will see, that ethos became particularly important for later theologians who were most concerned with the integrity of the Christian stance.

THE COMMAND OF GOD

Duty originates with the Word of God by which humanity is created and redeemed in Jesus Christ. General ethics is the theological understanding of the Word of God as the command of God.

Special ethics must not attempt to limit and measure the command of God through casuistry or other methods of moral reasoning, but it can provide a certain general understanding of ethics as this interaction of God and humanity.

Moral action can never be justified in advance of God's judgment, but it is necessary nonetheless to venture an understanding of God's commandment and to summon others to that same decision.

Synergy and Integrity

Duty is central to Christian ethics, as we have seen throughout this book. Jesus' summary of his moral teaching in Matthew's Gospel takes the form of two commandments, and although goals are important to our moral lives as individuals, whenever we find ourselves in larger groups with different goals, our moral thinking quickly refocuses on the need to specify our duties to one another, the rights that we have in relation to each other and to the society as a whole, and the rules by which we will live together. Duties are central to the integration of the four kinds of law that Thomas Aquinas traces in his *Summa theologiae*, and from the beginning of the modern world, different ways of specifying how we can use reason to determine what our duty is have become more and more important in Christian ethics, and in other kinds of moral thinking, too.

We are reminded of something else, however, by the contrast between Karl Barth's way of thinking about duty and all the other forms of casuistry and social criticism that took us from Kant to liberation theology. Even more basic than the effort to understand our duties is the tension between Synergy and Integrity that has been part of Christian moral thinking at least since Augustine. Are Christians, with their distinctive stance, nonetheless bound to the rest of humanity by a common search for the good life? Or does that stance mark the Christians off as part of a different, heavenly city that has nothing in common with the earthly city and its love of self? Augustine never quite resolved that tension in his own life and work, and it has been part of the Western Christian tradition ever since.

Karl Barth's ethics raises again the question whether Christian ethics is primarily, or perhaps entirely, about choosing between these two alternative ways that Christians live in the world and with their neighbors. On the one hand lie all the various paths that lead toward Synergy, by which Christians might build with their neighbors a wider understanding of their common duties and together take responsibility for society as a whole. On the other is the prophetic ethos of Integrity, which nurtures a distinct vision in which action is always a risk, and responsibility before God takes precedence over any responsibilities for society. Realism and Liberation look on society with critical eyes, and the oppressed, in particular, have reason to be wary of society's embrace; but Realism and Liberation generally choose the path of Synergy, at least as the path they would like to follow. Integrity maintains a solitary witness to the alternative.

But is the choice necessary, and if it is necessary, is it necessarily final? One thing we have learned in this long exploration through two chapters about duty is that Synergy and Integrity make sense in particular contexts, at particular moments in history. Augustine seems to have wavered between the two because he had lived both as a Christian convert in a pluralistic society that was still largely pagan and as a Christian bishop in a society that increasingly looked to him for order as well as for spiritual insight. Eight hundred years later, Aquinas had no difficulty imagining a human law that followed the requirements of eternal law, refracted through a natural law that everyone could understand. The Reformation and its conflicts brought a new opportunity for the Swiss Brethren and other Anabaptists to ask whether taking responsibility for society was worth the trouble it involved. Even Barth's effort to think about the Word of God quite apart from all historical events and empirical facts seems dictated by the clear dangers posed by others in his own time who were making those connections entirely too eagerly.

So perhaps the choice is not a final judgment between the various ways of doing Christian ethics, but also involves a judgment about what is going on in the world to which Christian ethics has to relate now. The authors we have considered all tend to write as if their particular form of casuistry, critical realism, liberation hermeneutics, or theological ethics were the only way to think about what Christian duty requires. But it may be that all of these systems are appropriate tools that may be useful in particular circumstances, depending on the particular balance between Synergy and Integrity needed to take a Christian stance toward the problems of the time. In that case, the question is not so much about which of these authors is right as it is about the wisdom to choose between them to find the right method for the present moment. Asking the question that way will take us from questions of duty to questions about virtue.

Additional Reading

Biggar, Nigel. *The Hastening That Waits: Karl Barth's Ethics.* Oxford: Clarendon Press, 1993.

Brady, Bernard. *Essential Catholic Social Thought.* Maryknoll, NY: Orbis Books, 2008.

Busch, Eberhard. *Barth.* Nashville: Abingdon Press, 2008.

Curran, Charles. *The Moral Theology of Pope John Paul II.* Washington, DC: Georgetown University Press, 2005.

Gustafson, James. *Protestant and Roman Catholic Ethics: Prospects for Rapprochement.* Chicago: University of Chicago Press, 1978.

Hare, John E. *God's Call: Moral Realism, God's Commands, and Human Autonomy.* Grand Rapids: Eerdmans, 2001.

Irwin, Terence. *The Development of Ethics: Volume III. From Kant to Rawls.* Oxford: Oxford University Press, 2009.

McKenny, Gerald. *The Analogy of Grace: Karl Barth's Moral Theology.* Oxford: Oxford University Press, 2010.

Miller, Richard B. *Casuistry and Modern Ethics: A Poetics of Practical Reasoning.* Chicago: University of Chicago Press, 1996.

O'Brien, David J., and Thomas A. Shannon. *Catholic Social Thought: The Documentary Heritage.* Maryknoll, NY: Orbis Books, 1992.

Ramsey, Paul. *The Essential Paul Ramsey.* Ed. William Werpehowski and Stephen D. Crocco. New Haven: Yale University Press, 1994.

Schneewind, Jerome. *The Invention of Autonomy.* Cambridge: Cambridge University Press, 1998.

Schuck, Michael. *That They Be One: The Social Teaching of the Papal Encyclicals, 1780–1989.* Washington, DC: Georgetown University Press, 1991.

DUTIES: A Test Case

Both religion and law provide rules by which people live, and these deontological systems are related in complex ways. When the European Union recently attempted to write a constitution for Europe, there was controversy over whether this constitution should mention God or take note of the fact that Europe has a Christian heritage that shapes its law and ethics. The U.S. Constitution does not mention God, but the First Amendment provides for freedom of religion.

In Christian ethics, theologians have taken very different positions on whether law should recognize God, or natural law, or the moral authority of scripture. For some, it is important that these be explicitly mentioned and recognized. For others, it is sufficient if the law conforms to the requirements of religious morality, without acknowledging religious authority. Still others argue that civil law cannot impose the kind of duties that are appropriate to the Christian moral life. They argue that Christians should keep their distance from law and politics.

Suppose for a moment that you, as a newly qualified expert on Christian deontological ethics, have been invited to address a symposium on law and religion that will be attended by legislators and government officials from a number of countries in Europe, North and South America, Asia, and Africa. Obviously, you cannot speak to them from the standpoint of a history or a legal system that they all share. You cannot assume that they all share a common religion or that they will agree with your religious beliefs. What you can do is to tell them what Christian ethics expects and requires law to do. It will be up to them to decide whether what you say is politically possible or compatible with their own religious beliefs.

The symposium panel is crowded. (There are a lot of religions, after all.) You will only have about eight minutes to make your case. You may want to suggest a couple of different Christian possibilities, but to get any-thing said in that time, you will have to decide which among the many Christian theological approaches you want to use and run with it. What is the most important thing these political leaders need to know, if they are to shape legal systems that are acceptable to Christian ethics?

Questions

To formulate your statement on the relationship between law and Christian ethics, you will want to consider questions like the following:

1. What part or parts of the Christian stance are most important for an appropriate understanding of law? Creation, as in the natural law of Thomas Aquinas? Sin, as in the coercive power of law emphasized by Luther? Other themes from the Christian stance, or some combination of them?

2. How important is it, if at all, that the legal system recognize God, or recognize that citizens who are subject to the law also have religious duties, or recognize that the laws made by governments can be judged by a "higher law," such as the natural law? These three ways that law might recognize religious authority are not the same, and different theologians would emphasize different possibilities. What would you see as most important?

3. What is the primary purpose of law in the Christian life? Do Christians see it mostly as coercive, restraining people who would do evil (Luther), as a guide to moral living (Calvin), or as a way of creating an approximation of a commonwealth that all people can share (Augustine)?

4. Martin Luther King, Jr., said that a just law uplifts human personality. What does this imply about the rights that a system of law must protect or the duties that it must impose on all citizens? If there are different rights and duties that law can recognize, which of these, or what combination of them, is important for Christian ethics?

5. How should people who make laws expect churches and other communities of Christians to relate to the legal and political system? Will Christians be active participants, or will they mostly try to remain separate from the political process and concentrate on the virtues they can develop in their own communities?

Part 4

Virtues

CHAPTER EIGHT

VIRTUES, NATURAL AND THEOLOGICAL

Sometimes, the best way to resolve a moral problem is to think about what makes a good person. Ideas of virtue have been part of the study of ethics since Plato and Aristotle, alongside the discussions of duty that have been more prominent in modern times. Nearly all writers discussed four important virtues— prudence, courage, justice, and self-control—but Augustine explained these virtues in Christian terms that differed from the philosophical understanding. Thomas Aquinas later combined ideas from Greek philosophy and from Augustine in a Christian ethics of virtue that connected relationship to God and the moral virtues required for human community.

It is easy to see why rules became more and more important in Christian ethics after the Reformation. Goals are the focus of many of our personal moral choices, but when goals conflict and many people are involved, rules allow us to set expectations, come to agreements, and hold one another accountable. Many of the decisions we make involve using moral reasoning to decide which rule to apply to a specific case. This is especially true in social ethics, where the decisions involve large groups of people or set the directions for a whole society. Courts, administrators, and executives all work from systems of rules, and legislators are typically involved in deciding what those rules ought to be.

That kind of deontological ethics is essential, even in a relatively small society like a campus, or in a single classroom. Recall again the case of a student who knows that a classmate has submitted a term paper that someone else wrote. In a tangle of conflicting goals and confusing loyalties, the rules embodied in an honor code can provide clarity about what your duty is, even if you still find it difficult to do what the rules require.[1]

Now consider a slightly different case of conflicting goals and confusing loyalties. Late at night, while you are studying for an important exam, a friend calls to tell you that she has just learned of a family emergency and needs to get home as soon as possible. The drive will take several hours, and it is clearly impossible for you to make the trip and get back to campus in time for the exam. There are rules about this, of course. Missing a major exam usually requires advance notice or a medical excuse. There are, however, other rules that are no less important just because they are not written in the student handbook. One of these rules tells you that you should not abandon a friend who is in real distress. The goals in this case seem to be similarly conflicted. Keeping a relationship with a friend is balanced against your academic goals, and the demands of immediate need are weighed against plans that reach farther into the future.

In this situation, you worry about the rules for a while, but you probably also ask yourself what sort of person you want to be. You want to be compassionate, of course. You would not want to be someone who is so focused on yourself that you cannot respond to other people's needs. But you also want to be known as steady and persistent, not the sort of person who is apt to drop everything and rush off with anybody who comes up with something urgent that needs to be done. You might like most to be the kind of person who is able to balance these demands and make the tough decisions, someone who just seems to know how to make the right choice. Then it occurs to you that if you were that kind of person, you would already know what you ought to do.

Virtue Ethics

Thinking about moral decisions in this way, people discover in everyday experience what ethicists have been saying for some years now: The emphasis on finding the right rule, which has dominated ethics since Kant, may not be telling us what we really want to know. Perhaps we cannot know what we ought to do unless we know what kind of people we want to be. The answer to that question is usually stated in terms of personal characteristics that we associate with a good person—compassion and persistence, for example, and also a capacity for balanced and appropriate decisions that is usually called prudence. These characteristics are virtues, and their place in ethics goes back well before the beginnings of Christianity.

Most contemporary ethicists now see an ethics based on virtue as a third way of determining right actions, alongside teleology and deontology. Borrowing another Greek word, *arete*, which is Greek for virtue, the ethicists have labeled this approach to ethics areteology, though it is also widely known simply as virtue ethics. In this way of thinking, it is the good person who provides direction in selecting the right actions, in contrast to teleology and deontology, which suggest that a good person is someone who achieves the goals or performs the duties that moral reasoning picks out as the right actions.

ARETEOLOGY

Moral thinking is about the use of reason to understand and develop the habits that make you a good person.
What makes an action right is that it is the sort of action that a good person would do.

While discussions of deontology and teleology often begin with modern philosophers like Kant and Bentham, virtue ethics takes us back to Aristotle's *Nicomachean Ethics*, since some key ideas about virtues and how we acquire them have remained largely unchanged since Aristotle first gave a systematic account of this field of study.

Back to Aristotle

For Aristotle, *arete* did not have the strong link with moral evaluation that it does for us. When we think of a virtue, we are generally thinking of a quality that we find in people who are morally good, apart from whatever other abilities they might have. In the Greek of Aristotle's time, *arete* was simply any kind of human excellence, the virtue of a great musician, for example, or the virtue of a champion athlete. Ethics, however, is concerned with the highest and best of these excellences, the ones that have to do with being a good person generally, rather than with being a good poet, a good ship captain, or a good physician.[2] Such excellence requires two things, according to Aristotle. We have to know what the human good is, so that we are able to identify it and figure out the actions that will lead us to it. But we also have to control our desires, so that the things we do will actually lead us to that good. Practical reason gives us those directions about what is to be done and what is to be avoided, and the skills that go into good practical reasoning are sometimes classified as *intellectual* virtues. Practical reason tells us what we ought to do, but it will not perform that job well unless we have developed the habits that turn our desires in the direction that practical reason dictates. That is the work of the *moral* virtues, which have a meaning closer to the narrow idea of virtue as we use the term today.

We see this need for control of our desires easily enough in ordinary experience. People want to be generous, but desires lead them into extravagant gifts that embarrass the recipient and make the giver feel foolish, rather than generous. Or they want to be generous, but they do not want it enough, and they end up giving cheap token gifts that leave the recipient feeling slighted and gain them only a reputation for stinginess. People want to be courageous, so they leap into danger so easily that onlookers are astounded by their recklessness. Or they want to be courageous, but when the test comes, their desires fall short and they end up being timid or cowardly instead.

Aristotle concluded from these observations of human behavior that what unites all of the moral virtues is that a virtue is the mean between two extremes, the mid-point between an excess and a defect. We see that clearly with generosity, which occupies the mid-point between extravagance and stinginess, and with courage, which is the mean between recklessness and cowardice. For each virtue, then, there are two corresponding vices, one for the excess and one for the defect, though sometimes one of the vices is so much more familiar that we may not even have a name for its opposite. (We have all kinds of names for people who overdo the search for various kinds of pleasure, but we are not quite sure what to call someone who doesn't seem to care enough about it.)

Having a virtue is more than just hitting the mark when we have to choose between too much and too little. That could be the result of a lucky accident, when someone does the right thing without really intending it. Or it could be the result of so much agonizing struggle with the requirements of practical reason that a person does not actually try to do anything until the moment for action has passed. To be a virtue, this ability to find the mid-point between excess and defect must be practiced to the point that we can do it whenever the occasion calls for it, without thinking about it. Aristotle says it must be a *hexis*, a word that is usually translated as "habit." But we must not think of this as one of those annoying habits that people do absent-mindedly, like biting their nails. Virtue is a habit in the sense that the right choices have become practiced until they are part of who we are. This is where the connection between moral virtue and other kinds of human excellence is helpful for understanding. An excellent musician can pick up an instrument and play a familiar piece without effort. We might say that she plays "by habit" in Aristotle's sense, but certainly not that she does it without thinking about it.

MORAL VIRTUE FOR ARISTOTLE

Virtue is a form of excellence that has to do with being a good person generally, as opposed to being good at some particular art or skill.
Virtue is a mean between two extremes, the excess and the defect.
Virtue is acquired by practice, so that acting virtuously becomes a habit.

In many cases, Aristotle's virtues seem quite familiar, despite the great distance in time between us. Courage and generosity are easily recognized today, along with their characteristic vices of excess and defect. Sometimes, however, his ideas of virtue seem quite strange. Aristotle writes about developing human excellences in a culture where it was very important to get what you have coming to you. So virtuous people will not want to seem ridiculous by demanding too much, but they will not let people get away with giving them too little, either. An honest self-estimate lies midway between boastfulness and self-deprecation, but the emphasis is always on estimating yourself accurately. By contrast, modern Western culture is deeply influenced by a Christian understanding of humility, so that understating your achievements is itself a virtue, rather than a vice. We are usually slightly amused and occasionally deeply annoyed by people who are eager to publicize their own achievements, but humble people who wait to be recognized would probably be thought slightly dishonest by Aristotle. By contrast, when Aristotle speaks of the virtue of magnanimity or "greatness of soul" in a man who speaks slowly, never hurries, and takes nothing too seriously, we are apt to find such a person pompous and self-important.[3] Virtue ethics often reflects these cultural differences, but it can also show us lines of continuity between thinkers who live in different times or seem quite opposed in their values.

Cardinal Virtues

Sometimes these different ideas of virtue are reflected in a different vocabulary that alerts us to the change. In other cases, the words remain the same, but the familiar terms mask a very different understanding of the moral life. That seems to be the case in Augustine's writings on the subject. He emphasized four key virtues that had long been important to Greek and Roman philosophers, but he insisted that these virtues take on a different meaning in the Christian way of life.

The four virtues were temperance, courage, prudence, and justice. Temperance, or self-control, is the ability to control your desires, so that you enjoy food and drink, recreation, music, sexual relations, sleep, and all sorts of other pleasures in moderate and healthy ways.[4] It was generally agreed that this virtue varies somewhat from person to person, so that temperance for an athlete in training might be very different from temperance for one of the spectators, and a young person might require different forms of self-control than an older one. In all cases, however, temperance would be a matter of finding the right amount of indulgence in the pleasures that are part of a good life, avoiding both obvious excess and unnecessary self-deprivation. Courage had to do with controlling a different set of urges. Courage was about the habitual, practiced ability to make good use of natural inclinations to defend yourself, to run risks to achieve your goals, and to protect those who are close to you. As we have seen, this requires striking a balance between the urges to aggressive recklessness and timid withdrawal. Courageous people are ready to stand up against the odds, resist aggression, and continue the struggle despite fear and failure. They do not give up easily, but neither are they quickly provoked into a fight. Courage, too, takes different forms. It requires very different things from a soldier in battle and a diplomat who is negotiating a peace agreement, but both learn it through practice, and much depends on people who have developed this virtue and keep their emotions under control in difficult situations.

Justice and prudence are closely related, since they are not virtues for keeping various kinds of desire under control, but habits of mind developed for making the right kind of judgments. Justice knows how to give each person what he or she is due, and also how to distribute burdens and benefits among groups in a community. We tend to think of justice as a virtue needed by judges or political leaders, but Greek and Roman philosophers saw a need for justice in an individual life, too. The same virtue that distributes things fairly in a group also sees to it that work and leisure, temperance and courage, enjoyment and effort each has its place in a balanced life as a whole. Without justice, a person may struggle courageously all the time, with no rest or enjoyment; or a person may pass life in temperate pleasures, never really striving for anything. Justice is having the habit of being courageous when courage is required and temperate when temperance is required, rather than devoting your moral energies to controlling passions that are not really relevant at the moment. Prudence, by contrast, seems to be more about how other virtues are put into practice. A courageous person may carry on a persistent struggle for an important goal but waste a great deal of effort in the process. We still admire the courage, and we do not think of people like this as reckless, exactly, but we reflect that they could accomplish a good deal more if they made a plan before striking out on their courageous course of action. They do not lack courage, but they need prudence, too. In extreme cases, courageous people who lack prudence actually undo the good they might accomplish and undermine their causes by failing to think about the effects of their actions or to anticipate things that might go wrong. The need for practiced judgments about how to act is overwhelmed by the habit of courageous action.

Temperance, courage, justice, and prudence are not the only virtues. We could easily list more, including generosity, patience, and compassion. We could add humility or magnanimity, depending on whether your list of virtues leans in a Christian or an Aristotelian direction. But the four virtues of temperance, courage, justice, and prudence have particular importance, going all the way back to the works of Plato. They are often singled out by later writers for special attention, and as we have seen, this set of four also appears in Jewish writings before Christianity began its own encounter with the traditions of Greek philosophy.[5] Part of this is no doubt because these four virtues had wide appeal in the ancient world and crossed cultural and religious boundaries more easily than some other ideas about the good life. But these four virtues also seemed to provide a comprehensive picture of virtuous use of human desires and abilities. People who are temperate, courageous, just, and prudent have disciplined both mind and body, and they have acquired the habit of making choices that work together to create the good life as a whole. By contrast, as the case of the courageous person who is nonetheless imprudent shows us, when any one of these virtues is missing, it becomes difficult or impossible to sustain the rest of them. For that reason, these four became known as the "cardinal" virtues, from the Latin word *cardo*, for "hinge." Temperance, courage, justice, and prudence are the hinges on which all the other virtues turn.

THE FOUR CARDINAL VIRTUES

The four cardinal virtues may appear in different order or under slightly different names, but the basic idea is always a set of closely connected virtues that cover all aspects of human life and make it possible to acquire and maintain other virtues.

TEMPERANCE controls the desires for pleasures that go with food, drink, and enjoyment of the senses, so that we enjoy all of them in a balanced way that contributes to a healthy life.

COURAGE controls desires for security, achievement, and honor, so that we make the effort required to attain these goods, but do not recklessly endanger ourselves or others in the process.

JUSTICE maintains a balance between temperance, prudence, and the other virtues, so we give each part of life the place it deserves and we give each person what is due to him or her in our relations with others.

PRUDENCE guides the other virtues, so that we both control our desires and obtain the results we seek.

Of course, a virtuous life could look very different, depending on exactly which philosophical stance was drawing the picture. For Epicureans, temperance and prudence provided a life of moderate enjoyments, while courage prevented too much nervous speculation about divine judgment and life after death. Stoics emphasized a courageous indifference to misfortune, while justice provided an ordered life that mirrored the balance and harmony of the universe. Platonists might connect these virtues to knowledge of the unchanging ideas that give shape to the transient realities of our experience, enabling rulers to guide nations and individuals to organize their own lives. All of them could agree, however, that these virtues were essential for a happy life, however happiness was understood, and virtuous citizens made for prosperous and stable communities.

Augustine on Virtue

Augustine shared this language of the virtues, but as we have seen, he emphasized the way that the Christian stance led to a very different idea of happiness. Philosophers might argue that everyone seeks happiness, but Augustine added that even those who have found happiness are unhappy, because they fear they might lose it. In an uncertain world, true happiness can only be found in something that cannot be lost. For Augustine, it is obvious that the only thing that satisfies that condition is a relationship with God, which cannot be ended by any misfortune and does not end, even in death. The goal of true happiness is a love for God that culminates in eternal life with God.[6]

That, in turn, changed the way Augustine thought about all the virtues. For the philosophers, different virtues were directed toward different objects. Temperance led to genuine pleasure, as courage led to honor. Happiness might sum up all those objects, as justice held them all in balance, but the differences between the objects of the virtues were important. For Augustine, they all come together in love of God, so all four of the virtues point us to a single goal:

> Temperance is love preserving itself whole and entire for God. Fortitude [courage] is love readily enduring all things for God. Justice is love that serves only God and, for this reason, correctly governs other things that

are subject to a human being. And prudence is love distinguishing correctly those things by which it is helped toward God from those things by which it can be impeded.[7]

Temperance, courage, prudence, and justice may take quite different forms for a Christian preparing for eternal life with God from the forms they would take for an Epicurean enjoying the pleasures of this life in moderation, or for a Platonist living in harmony with an impersonal justice. For Augustine, moreover, the models of these Christian virtues were drawn from the church's experiences of persecution and the early saints who had struggled against the distractions of the world. Courage is most clearly seen in the lives of martyrs who endured torture and death rather than deny their faith. Temperance is seen not in moderation, but in the zeal of those who leave ordinary life for the monasteries and hermitages where they can devote themselves wholly to God. Justice means knowing that God alone deserves worship and service. There is no balance to be struck between God and other authorities. Prudence requires "watchfulness and most diligent vigilance so that we are not deceived by an evil idea that gradually sneaks up on us."[8] There is no prudent use of the world's goods here. The best strategy is to seek silence and isolation, where the stealthy motions of any evil will be more easily noticed.

For Augustine, the martyrs who had suffered for their faith and the saints who withdrew from the cities to live lives of self-denial were not distant history. When he wrote his definitions of the four virtues, the great persecution of the emperor Diocletian was less than a century in the past, and Saint Anthony of Egypt, who led the ascetic movement in the Egyptian desert, had been dead only about thirty years. Although Christians were becoming used to the recognition and acceptance that followed the emperor Constantine's conversion to Christianity, they had formed their first ideas of virtue by turning away from the world and the society around them. Augustine did not want them to forget that, and he warned those who listened to his sermons that the disorders of their own times might mean that they would experience the same sorts of trials.[9] True happiness involves a single-minded devotion to God that may look unhappy or unbalanced to those who follow other versions of the four virtues, but a relationship with God is a happiness that cannot be lost.

For Augustine, virtue is firmly located in the Christian stance by its focus on redemption and resurrection destiny. This goal is higher than any happiness that is tied to the changing realities of present life. But Augustine's low estimate of the possibilities for happiness in this life is not based only on the hard times in which he happened to live. Barbarian invasions and political chaos were symptoms of the sinful conditions that began when the first human beings turned away from God to follow their own desires. Since then, no one is inclined by nature toward a relationship with God in the way that Aristotle thought that everyone naturally seeks happiness.

While Augustine sees relationship with God as a higher goal than Aristotle's happiness, he thought that our starting point toward that goal is lower. Aristotle said that everyone always seeks happiness, but Augustine knew from his own experience that people sometimes actively avoid God.[10] Augustine does not expect that they will be able to bridge this gap between the starting point and the goal unaided. This leads to one of the most important differences between Augustine's account of virtue and the idea of virtue that had prevailed since Aristotle. For Aristotle, virtues are acquired by practice. We work at them until they become habitual. For Augustine, God provides the starting point for virtue by turning people from self-love toward love of God. It is impossible for them to do this on their own.

Augustine seems uncertain, and his interpreters are divided, over whether humanity contributes anything at all to this transformation. What is quite clear, however, is that virtue in the sense that Augustine has in mind cannot be a human accomplishment, in the way that Aristotle compares moral virtues to other human excellences. In their fallen condition, human beings lack the first thing that is essential to an eternal relationship with God. They do not desire that relationship. They cannot take even the first step toward the goal unless God forgives their sin and restores that capacity for relationship with God that was lost in the Fall. If all true virtues are forms of love for God, then it must be God who makes them all possible.

VIRTUE FOR AUGUSTINE

All virtues are forms of love for God. Any human excellence that is not directed toward relationship with God is not really a virtue.

In their true forms, prudence, courage, temperance, justice, and other virtues known to philosophy direct human desires and abilities toward relationship with God.

Virtues are acquired by God's gift.

Because Christian virtues are so different in both origin and goal, it is understandable that Augustine would find little to praise in the moral life of those who did not share his faith. It is often said that he called the virtues of non-Christians "splendid vices." Actually, the works we have from him never say exactly that, and when he is writing to pagan correspondents, he can be quite eloquent about how Christian faith agrees with authors like Cicero about the sort of civic pride, personal honesty, and faithfulness in marriage that a flourishing city requires.[11] Nevertheless, he sticks to his main point, which is that admirable personal qualities that are not directed toward love of God cannot properly be called virtues.[12] In a world where Christianity was recently persecuted, still suspect, internally divided, and threatened by political chaos, Augustine would take no chances that it might be confused with anything else.

Natural and Supernatural Ends

Augustine and Thomas Aquinas were two of the greatest thinkers in Christian history. Between them, they set the direction for Western Christian ethics, and their influence remains important today. Thomas frequently draws on Augustine as an authority as he sets up his arguments, and he is obviously familiar with the works of his famous predecessor. In the timeless world of Scholastic theology, it can seem like the two were regular conversation partners. It is important for us to remember, however, that they are separated by considerable distance in time and circumstances. Eight hundred years passed between Augustine and Thomas, slightly more than the time that separates Thomas from us. Augustine lived in the waning days of the Roman Empire. He wrote his *City of God* in response to an invasion of Rome itself, and when he died, other invaders were just outside the gates of his city. Thomas Aquinas lived when European commerce and culture were expanding, and he was at the intellectual center of these stimulating new developments in Paris. Christian crusaders and Muslim armies might clash far away, but Thomas read Muslim and Jewish authors as collaborators in the great tasks of understanding the natural world and recovering the learning of ancient authors. Making distinctions between Christians and everyone else was no longer the most important thing, as it had become for Augustine.

Christians had inherited the whole intellectual wealth of the ancient world, and the task was to put that knowledge to work in the reawakened Europe for which they were now responsible.

FROM AUGUSTINE TO THOMAS AQUINAS	
430	Death of Augustine.
ca. 480	End of the Western Roman Empire.
610	Beginnings of Islam.
ca. 750–1200	Muslim and Jewish philosophers revive the study of ancient Greek sources, including Aristotle.
ca. 1150–1350	Rapid growth of European cities, commerce, and learning. Beginnings of the first European universities.
ca. 1250	Thomas Aquinas begins his theological writings.

For this task, Thomas Aquinas drew especially on the works of Aristotle, which had been largely forgotten even by those early Christian writers who knew the works of other Greek philosophers. In Thomas's capable hands, Aristotle's logic supported the structures of Scholastic argument. Aristotle's metaphysics organized ways of thinking about the world as God's creation. Aristotle's ethics provided a framework for understanding the Christian moral life. Of course, Aristotle did not understand the goal of the moral life in the same way that Augustine and other Christian writers had done, but for Thomas this posed no obstacle for Christian theology. The task was simply to show systematically how the two ways of thinking were related.

To begin, Thomas sorted out the problem of competing ends or goals. Aristotle believed we all aim at our own happiness. Augustine insisted that all true virtue is a form of love for God. But for Thomas, this did not lead to the simple opposition between love for self and love for God that Augustine sometimes saw. People have many different ends or goals, and they pursue them in different ways, at different times. The elements of happiness that Aristotle enumerated were important to many of the Christians Thomas saw around him in Paris. They, too, wanted a life that would be healthy and prosperous, marked by real achievements and sustained over time, just as Aristotle said that *eudaimonia* should be.[13] Nor were these just things that ancient Athenians and medieval Parisians happened both to enjoy. These are objective goods. Human beings are constituted by nature to seek them, and as we have seen, the pursuit of those natural goals is guided by principles of practical reason that provide the duties that are laid out for us in the natural law.[14] So human beings have a natural end, and that end can be understood more or less in the same terms that Aristotle set it out for us. People seek happiness.

The problem was that Augustine had insisted that this Aristotelian happiness is an illusion. Lasting happiness is found in loving God. Thomas Aquinas would not have wanted to deny that, but he would not learn much about loving God from Aristotle. To be sure, the *Nicomachean Ethics* suggests at one point that the best human life might be a life spent contemplating philosophical truths, rather than a life of action and achievement.[15] But a relationship to God is more than moments of contemplation. It shapes the whole of life. Nor is it available only to philosophers. Everyone is invited into it.

Instead of being the achievement of a few who choose the philosophical way of life, relationship with God is what human life is created for. Yet we can hardly call eternal life with God natural in the way that the search for happiness is natural. Naturally speaking, human life ends in death, and the virtuous pursuit of happiness goes on within that limit. We can acquire habits that may make our lives longer and healthier, but we cannot develop habits that will make them eternal.

If an eternal relationship with God is the goal of human life, Thomas Aquinas realized it must be a *supernatural* end, rather than a natural one. Aristotle and his understanding of virtue will not tell us very much about it, but scripture and the Christian understanding of God might. "Supernatural" means something quite specific in Thomas's terms here. The supernatural is not something weird or inexplicable. It is, literally, what is *super*-natural, above the natural, a different goal of a different sort that stands above and apart from the natural, not in opposition to it. What marks it out as supernatural is that it is not built into our ordinary goals and the ordinary ways of acquiring them in the way that Aristotle thought that natural goals and virtues are. People find their supernatural end only by God's gift, just as Augustine said.

Once the distinction between natural and supernatural ends is clear, we can see the possibility of different kinds of virtues by which people might be prepared to reach their different ends. The key to a good life is not choosing between natural and supernatural ends, but holding them in proper relationship to one another. To do that, we need habits that enable us to make the right choices, especially when our desires may incline us to short-term satisfactions that run counter to the lasting happiness of relationship with God.

Different Kinds of Virtue

Thomas thus proceeds to organize the virtues, just as he organized the four kinds of law that we encounter in God, in nature, in scripture, and in the commands of human rulers.[16] Some virtues are natural, and they equip us for the right use of human capacities that everyone shares. Some virtues concern supernatural ends, and they transform natural inclinations in ways that prepare human beings for eternal life with God. These Thomas calls *theological virtues*, and as we will see, they are acquired in a different way from the natural virtues, and they function quite differently in human life.

Natural virtues include both intellectual and moral virtues. Intellectual virtues enable us to grasp truths about the world and to distinguish true ideas from false ones. They also include the various arts by which we make the judgments necessary to produce things like useful objects, successful military strategies, or effective medical treatments. Memory, intelligence, and foresight are intellectual virtues, too, and prudence has a special place among the intellectual virtues, because it includes those skills in deliberation that allow us to apply rules correctly or to identify a fair and workable solution when the rules do not exactly fit.[17]

While intellectual virtues direct the mind toward right judgments, moral virtues direct the will to right action. The four cardinal virtues are paradigm examples. Without courage, we are unlikely to accomplish anything, since the timid person retreats at the first sign of opposition, and the reckless person may well perish before the job is done. Temperance allows us to control our desires, so that justice can select the ones we really need to act on. Notably, prudence belongs on this list, too, because prudence is both an intellectual and a moral virtue. We need prudence both to judge rightly what we ought to do, especially when we are dealing with difficult questions about specific moral choices, and to direct the will toward that course of action, so that we are not swayed by a desire for recognition when the situation requires a humble person who is willing to work in the background and let others take credit for the success. Of course, in another situation, prudence might require courageous action, stepping up and taking leadership so that a good plan does not fail. That is why prudence is a virtue. We cannot say in advance that the prudent person is always humble or that the prudent person is always courageous. You have to be a prudent person to know what a prudent person would do.

The list of moral virtues is long, and it includes gentleness, patience, piety, gratitude, and friendliness, as well as the cardinal virtues of temperance, courage, prudence, and justice.[18] All of this would have seemed familiar to Aristotle, whom Thomas repeatedly cites as his authority, telling his readers, "The Philosopher maintains that science and virtue are habits," or "The Philosopher says that virtue is 'of two kinds, intellectual and moral.'"[19] Thomas even includes in his list of moral virtues one that Aristotle supplies that we might call "quick-wittedness," the habit of a Greek gentleman who always knows how to say the right thing at just the right moment at a party.[20] Thomas also follows Aristotle's explanation of how we identify these natural virtues and how we come to have them. Both moral and intellectual virtues fit Aristotle's definition as the mean between two extremes, and they are habits which can be acquired by practice of the right kind of actions.[21]

What, then, becomes of Augustine's idea that the true virtues are those that prepare us for relationship with God? While some might like the idea of a heaven populated by people who know how to tell a good joke, "quick-wittedness" and some of the other moral virtues seem somewhat distant from the goal of "love preserving itself whole and entire for God...love readily enduring all things for God...love that serves only God."[22] For this purpose, Thomas introduces a new class of virtues alongside those that serve our natural ends. These are the theological virtues of faith, hope, and love.[23]

> What is above the nature of man should be distinguished from what is according to the nature of man. But the theological virtues are above the nature of man, whereas the intellectual and moral virtues belong to the

nature of man, as we have explained. Therefore the theological virtues should be distinguished from them.[24]

The Theological Virtues

To identify the theological virtues, Thomas looks not to Aristotle, but to the New Testament, where he finds these words at the end of the well-known passage on love: "And now faith, hope, and love abide, these three; and the greatest of these is love."[25] For Thomas, these virtues direct us toward happiness with God the same way that the intellectual and moral virtues direct us toward happiness in the fulfillment of our natural inclinations. Faith provides knowledge of God that is not available through the natural abilities by which we learn things about the world around us. This is obviously a special kind of knowledge that goes beyond simply knowing that God exists, since Thomas elsewhere argues that we can know that God exists by using our natural reason. Through the knowledge that faith provides, we also understand ourselves in relation to God. We see that this relationship completes the human search for happiness in a way that no ordinary satisfactions could do, because this is a happiness that once gained can never be lost, precisely as Augustine said.

As faith transforms the intellect, this in turn re-directs the will. Once we know what a relationship with God is, we hope to have it. Just as the virtues of temperance and courage direct our actions so that we attain our natural ends, hope leads us to do the things that make us ready for happiness with God. Hope also inspires love, for even when we are thinking of natural goods, we love the thing for which we hope, and we grow to love the one from whom we hope to receive it.

> As we have said earlier when treating of the passions, hope refers to two things. The first is its principal object, the good hoped for. With respect to this, love always precedes hope, for a good is never hoped for unless it is desired and loved. Secondly, hope also refers to the person from whom one hopes to be able to obtain a good. And in respect to this, hope precedes love at first, although afterward hope is increased by love. For when a man reflects on the fact that he can obtain something good through someone, he begins to love him, and by reason of loving him he hopes all the more in him.[26]

Through faith, hope, and love, then, we are directed to a goal that is different from any idea of happiness we might construct out of the Aristotelian building blocks that Thomas uses so freely. Relationship with God is not simply a different thing to want. Wanting it belongs to a different nature from the one that leads us through the world of common human experience.

For that reason, the theological virtues are different from their natural counterparts in two important ways. First, the virtues of faith, hope, and love cannot be acquired by practice the way the moral and intellectual virtues can. We cannot decide we want to have faith and then go to work on it, the way we might decide we want to be courageous, generous, or friendly. That capacity simply is not in us, and if we are ever to have it, God must take the first step, to which we have nothing to contribute. "God works in us, without us," says Thomas, quoting approvingly in this connection a definition of virtue that was understood by the Scholastic theologians to come from Augustine.[27] To use Thomas's technical term, the theological virtues are "infused" in us, placed in us by God, rather than built into habits by our own repeated actions. Second, the theological virtues cannot be defined by locating each of them as the midpoint between two vices.[28] While it is possible not to have enough faith, hope, or love, we cannot have too much of them, particularly since these theological virtues are always directed toward God. Despair, for example, stands in relation to hope as timidity stands in relation to courage, but with respect to hope in God, there can be nothing like reckless excess.

Thomas thus seems neatly to have both Augustine's virtues and Aristotle's, both the love of God and the pursuit of happiness. But what happens to Augustine's claim—at least the claim that Augustine sometimes seems to make—that these two ends are not simply different, but in conflict with one another? For Augustine, prudence, courage, temperance, and justice in their ordinary forms were not adequate preparation for life with God, and life with God required a different way of having those virtues.[29] Temperance, for example, provides sufficient control of human appetites to allow healthy moderation, but this natural virtue may not be adequate for a committed Christian whose religious life includes rigorous fasting and celibacy. Courage allows people to risk themselves in moments of danger, but it may not be sufficient to sustain a whole life of resisting temptation. Thomas understood Augustine's doubts on this point, but he supposed, too, that if God supplies faith, hope, and love, God will also enable a way of life that sustains them. So he posited special, infused forms of the moral virtues, along with the infused theological virtues, to make possible the special kinds of prudence, temperance, courage, and justice that would be required by someone who intended to live a life devoted solely to God.

VIRTUE FOR THOMAS AQUINAS

Moral and intellectual virtues
  Direct us toward our natural ends
  Are acquired by practice
  Aim at a midpoint between excess and defect
  Include temperance, courage, prudence, justice, and others
Theological virtues
  Include faith, hope, and love
  Direct us toward our supernatural end
  Must be given to us by God (infused)
  Can be deficient, but not excessive
  Are accompanied by infused forms of the moral virtues

Faith, hope, and love redirect lives in important ways. Those who live by them are working toward different ends, which are neither so quickly gained nor so easily lost as most of the things that people hope for. We should not be surprised if their wants and fears seem to be different from those of other people around them. The idea of infused virtues may be difficult to explain, but it is easy to see why the kinds of self-discipline these people of faith need could not be acquired in the pursuit of other kinds of goals.

Still, these are recognizably human virtues. People who place their hopes in a relationship with God do not become angels, unaffected by human passions and impervious to the pains and losses that other people feel. If they react differently to events, it will be because faith, hope, and love have become habits with them, just as courage, prudence, temperance, and justice become habits with people who practice finding that midpoint between too much and too little that guides action rightly. People who have the theological virtues not only *feel* hopeful and loving, they *act* in hopeful and loving ways. That is how all virtues work in us, no matter how they have been acquired.

Because people of faith do not lose their human nature, they continue to need moral virtues, and not only in the infused forms of those virtues that prepare them for relationship with God. This is especially true in their dealings with other people in the human communities in which even Christians are by nature intended to live. Thomas borrows from Neoplatonism a distinction between "political" and "purifying" virtues and adapts it to his own purposes here. While the cardinal virtues—in their infused forms, Thomas might add—have an important role in trans-forming human lives so that they are fully prepared for life in relationship with God, these virtues also exist in us in accordance with our human nature. In this form, they are appropriately called "political" virtues, "since man comports himself rightly in human affairs by these virtues."[30] We should expect those who live by faith, hope, and love to have some virtues that other people lack, but they should not lack any of the virtues we expect from ordinary people who live their lives in human community.

Thomistic Synergy

This ability to link natural and supernatural ends, moral and theologi-cal virtues, and political and perfecting forms of the moral virtues is characteristic of Thomas Aquinas's intellectual achievements. Just as he developed a fourfold structure of law that incorporated God's will, natu-ral order, human law, and biblical commandments in a single system, he now provides a way of thinking about virtue that reconciles Augustine and the philosophers.

This is more than the solution to a theoretical problem. It provides the basis for integrating responsible participation in social and political life with the life of faith. Thomas argues for the unity of the virtues, which means that it is difficult or impossible to sustain any one of them without acquiring all the rest, but it also means that acquiring the theological virtues assures your possession of the moral virtues as well. Here again, it is not a matter of choosing the supernatural end *instead* of a natural one. It is not really possible to live in relationship with God without acting rightly in every kind of relationship. "Now it is clear that charity [love], inasmuch as it directs man to his ultimate end, is the principle of all the good works that are referable to his ultimate end. Hence it is necessary that along with charity there be infused at the same time all the moral virtues by which man can perform each kind of good work."[31]

For Thomas, the infused virtues do not merely add a supernatural end with its accompanying theological virtues on top of human nature. As faith, hope, and love become habits that shape action, they supply whatever is lacking in the natural virtues, too.

This completion of nature is the basis for the Synergy that has characterized Thomist ethics in most of its forms through the seven centuries that separate us from the *Summa theologiae*. Just as natural law, divine law, and human law can serve the same purposes, the meaning of human goods is not exhausted by their natural ends. Especially for the most important and lasting human goods—goods like knowledge, political community, and culture—the ways that these goods enhance human life is also a preparation for relationship with God. They, too, are "referable to his ultimate end," at least for those who have been set on the way toward that end by the theological virtues. These goods do not need to be rejected. They need not even be regarded as things to be used, but not enjoyed, as Augustine sometimes dismisses them.[32] People of faith can participate fully in the pursuit of knowledge, the building of institutions, and the education of the next generation. A close reading of Thomas Aquinas suggests that they do this no worse than those who are acquainted only with natural virtues. We might expect them to do it better.

At the same time, the ultimate end of humanity lies beyond these natural goods. To say that natural goods come to fulfillment only in relationship with God implies that they cannot be completed by any program that tries to make an institution, a political party, a nation, or a mission into the ultimate goal of action. Any of these can be good, but they always remain limited goods. The integrity of faith is not compromised by political virtue. In fact, the integrity of faith requires it. But politics loses its virtue when political goals become the ultimate ones. People of faith need to remember that, even when politicians do not.

Virtue after Thomas Aquinas

The Synergy in Thomas Aquinas's account of the Christian moral life is not always easy to maintain in practice. Devotion to God that reshapes life according to the theological virtues can overshadow concern for human neighbors and the cultivation of ordinary goods, so that work becomes disconnected from its ultimate ends. The unity of the Christian life suggested by the unity of the virtues can fragment into a life of practical achievements that refer their goods to nothing higher than self-interest and a life of religious devotion that pays no attention to lesser goods. Thomas himself gave up writing theology after a mystical experience several months before his death in 1274.

Nevertheless, as the center of Christian life continued to shift from the monasteries to the growing commercial cities and their new universities, remarkable men and women were inspired to combine prayer and active public life by the idea that love for God gives rise to human virtues. One of these was Catherine of Siena (1347–1380). Catherine was born into a family of merchants and local political leaders in the Italian city of Siena, but she withdrew at an early age into a life of prayer and contemplation. After she emerged in her late teens to care for the sick and the poor, she became the leader of a spiritual community and a prominent mediator in the fractious politics that pitted the independent-minded Italian cities against the authority of the Pope, who lived at this time in Avignon, in France. Eventually, it was Catherine who persuaded Pope Gregory XI to return to Rome, reform the church leadership, and reconcile with the Italian cities.

Catherine also had her own idea of the unity of the virtues. While women could not participate in the Scholastic disputations that shaped theological writings like Thomas's *Summa*, Catherine devised a form of dialogue between the soul and God that gave her her own way to formulate theological concepts. Central to her idea of the virtues is that each person has one primary virtue. This implies different good works and different ways of life for different people, and yet when these diverse virtues are exercised with love for God, that love brings all the other virtues into being alongside the particular virtue with which the soul began. So in Catherine's *Dialogue*, God addresses her:

So to one person I give charity as the primary virtue, to another justice, to another humility, to another a lively faith or prudence or temperance or patience, and to still another courage. These and many other virtues I give differently to different souls, and the soul is most at ease with that virtue which has been made primary for her. But through her love of that virtue, she attracts all the other virtues to herself, since they are all bound together in loving charity.[33]

In both Catherine's *Dialogue* and Thomas's *Summa theologiae*, then, we see an idea of virtue that unifies moral and religious life, social and spiritual attitudes, and moral and theological virtues. Where Aristotle and other early philosophers focused on the particularity of the virtues, describing the distinctive excellences that belong to courage, justice, magnanimity, and the like, Catherine emphasizes that love draws all of them together. Augustine wrote that the virtues that arise from love for God serve different ends, even when the Christian virtues have the same names, but Thomas argues that the theological virtues require the moral virtues, too, and can supply them when the moral experience is lacking. This understanding of the virtues retains the different sources of the moral and theological virtues, but it binds them together in a unified moral life. It also integrates the life of faith with life in political community.

In the course of history, however, both religion and politics fractured in ways that called this unity of the virtues into question and changed the conditions under which Christians lived their moral lives. Luther's Reformation began not with the unity of the virtues, but with a proclamation of complete dependence on God's grace. Virtues, even infused and theological virtues, began to seem too much like possessions that people could hold on to in order to convince themselves of their own righteousness. The moral life had to begin with convincing people of their sinfulness, then restraining their evil. If there were a third use of the law, as Calvin argued, to guide the moral life, that guidance would have to come from daily reading of scripture, rather than from habits that became engrained in our ways of thinking and acting.[34] It would not do to claim so much for the virtues that we might lose sight of the underlying human sinfulness.[35] Religious disagreements also led to political conflicts, which had to be met by rulers who spelled out more precisely what was expected of all parties. When disorder threatened, virtue might seem less important than obedience. Finally, when Catholic religious leaders formulated their own response to the Protestant Reformation, they kept the theology of virtue, but they put more emphasis on rules in determining the details of the Christian life. As we have seen, the result was a shift in emphasis from virtue to duty that shaped both Catholic and Protestant ethics from the sixteenth century onward.[36] Only recently have theologians who represent many of the variations on the Christian stance begun to rediscover the importance of virtue for their own ways of thinking about the moral life. For our last chapter, we turn to these contemporary understandings of virtue to see what they may tell us about the future of Christian ethics.

Additional Reading

Cessario, Romanus. *The Moral Virtues and Theological Ethics.* 2nd ed. Notre Dame, IN: University of Notre Dame Press, 2009.

Herdt, Jennifer A. *Putting on Virtue: The Legacy of the Splendid Vices.* Chicago: University of Chicago Press, 2008.

Luongo, F. Thomas. *The Saintly Politics of Catherine of Siena.* Ithaca, NY: Cornell University Press, 2006.

Pieper, Josef. *The Four Cardinal Virtues.* Notre Dame, IN: University of Notre Dame Press, 1966.

Pope, Stephen J., ed. *The Ethics of Aquinas.* Washington, DC: Georgetown University Press, 2002.

Porter, Jean. *Recovery of Virtue: The Relevance of Aquinas for Christian Ethics.* Louisville: Westminster John Knox Press, 1990.

CHAPTER NINE

VIRTUE AND RESPONSIBILITY

The new moral problems people face today raise questions about systems of ethics built on goals and rules. Christian ethics has begun to speak less of right and wrong measured by goals and rules and more about responsible human action, which can also be understood in light of Christian traditions about virtue. Different versions of the Christian stance, however, have different ideas about how we acquire these virtues and which virtues are important. Each of these ways of thinking can help to provide a responsible interpretation of events that guides us to the right choice of action. What we need is a kind of virtue that gives us the habit of choosing the right way to think about the problem at hand.

People who face difficult moral choices often feel very much alone. Confronting a dishonest co-worker or speaking up against an unfair policy can leave you isolated, wondering whether you are doing the right thing and whether anyone appreciates the risks you are running. Resisting authority or making an end-of-life medical decision is a lonely task, even when you are surrounded by other people who offer you advice. You want to know what the goal is, and whether it is a good one. You want to think critically about the rules, and you want to know how a good person would think about your choices. Information and strategies are easy to come by. Thoughtful moral reflection is usually in shorter supply.

What we have seen through this introduction to Christian ethics, however, is that people facing such decisions have lots of company, if they know where to look for it. If you think about whether to punish dishonesty, or if you think about how to prevent it, you are asking about what Calvin called the three uses of the law. If you want to know what kind of medical outcome is worth seeking, or what kind of outcome should be avoided, you will be thinking in terms of a natural law understanding of the human person, as developed by Thomas Aquinas and subsequent Catholic theology. When you think about the kind of person you want to be when everybody is pulling you in different directions, you are rehearsing themes of virtue that go all the way back to Augustine and Aristotle. Ways of thinking about moral problems that have developed in the past can give direction to your thinking today. Whether or not you share the Christian faith, the study of Christian ethics provides ways to think about goals, duties, and virtues that may help you resolve your own problems. As we have seen, all of us answer our moral questions in these three ways, and many other people have done so, through a long history.

Recently, however, some people have questioned whether the ways of thinking that have been most important in the history of Western ethics are adequate to the choices we now have to make. For one thing, science and technology now pose questions that Christians and others have never faced before. Medicine can cure diseases that were previously incurable. We can unravel the intricacies of the human genome, prolong life, and delay the changes brought on by aging. Instant communication enlarges our knowledge and expands our circle of acquaintances, but it also threatens our privacy and our safety. Knowledge has always been power, but today we rely almost completely on people with specialized knowledge who manage the systems of finance, government, energy, and transportation on which our security and prosperity depend. It is not surprising that recent years have seen rapid growth in the study of medical ethics, the development of codes of ethics in many professions, and a proliferation of advisory boards, review panels, and special commissions that try to keep track of the moral choices that business managers, technical experts, and government officials have to make every day. We have entrusted other people with great power, but we are not quite sure that they, or we, know how to use that power ethically.

Understandably, people facing these issues begin to ask whether the patterns of ethical reflection found in textbooks like this one still fit the circumstances in which we now have to make our moral decisions. Most of us find it easier to identify with Dietrich Bonhoeffer than with Luther and Calvin. Calvin was sure about the uses of the law. Luther had no doubt that unruly people need restraint, so that even a bad ruler deserves obedience from Christians, because a bad ruler is better than no ruler at all. Bonhoeffer, by contrast, found himself living in a legal order that spread evil instead of restraining it. Good people found it difficult to do anything, precisely because they did not want to break the law or violate the oaths of loyalty that they had taken. What was needed, Bonhoeffer concluded, was not people who were trying to do their duty, but people who were willing to risk guilt by stepping outside of a failed system of rules.[1]

Bonhoeffer's situation was dramatic, and because his resistance to Hitler led to his death, he is remembered today as a martyr. But his understanding of the limitations of our preoccupation with doing the right thing and the importance of risking guilt has relevance to more familiar situations in which we often find ourselves. Moral problems often arise precisely when the rules have become outdated, or when they have been rewritten to serve some narrow interest instead of the common good. Situations of rapid change in businesses, universities, or community organizations are too fluid to allow us to formulate rules that we then might follow. Even a convinced deontologist will have to find some other way to make a decision in such cases.

Goals provide no more certainty. It is easy to think that we might get beyond the limitations of laws, oaths, and duties by focusing on the results. Surely, if we do the most loving thing or seek the greatest good for the greatest number, we will avoid many evils that might come from following bad rules. And who could think us guilty for trying to do the most loving thing? We have seen in some detail in chapter 5 how modern teleology tried to shape these alternatives to legalism in Bentham's utilitarianism and Fletcher's situation ethics. But the future is difficult to predict, as the proponents of every form of teleological ethics have learned.[2] Even if we get the results we want, we may find that subsequent events leave our achievements morally ambiguous. If the goal is peace, a compromise that brings the parties to agreement and prevents open warfare may seem like a good goal, and the people who achieve it may be hailed as peacemakers. But what if compromise now merely delays the conflict, perhaps until a date when the opponents have the resources and the appetite for an even more bloody battle? If that were to happen, the negotiators of the failed peace would probably regard themselves as unlucky, but still right. They might not be regarded so favorably by the victims of the subsequent conflict, however, and these reversals are so common in history that we might conclude that they were not even particularly unlucky. The Christian realist Reinhold Niebuhr argued that leaders must be prepared for such outcomes, since it is impossible to avoid them. What we need is not better goals or better luck, but humility to accept the ironies of history and forgiveness for those who bear the guilt of results that they could not have anticipated.[3]

Responsibility

A more systematic reflection on the limitations of rules and goals in Christian ethics is found in the work of H. Richard Niebuhr, whose *Radical Monotheism* we have already considered in connection with Augustine's idea that all goods must be understood in relation to God.[4] At a time when many philosophers were still arguing that teleology and deontology exhausted the possibilities for systematic moral thinking, H. Richard Niebuhr wrote *The Responsible Self* to suggest that these two ways of approaching moral problems grow out of the two dominant images that modern people have of themselves. First, there is the image of "man-the-maker," who successfully organizes lives and societies to reach goals. Utilitarian moral philosophy thinks in these terms, but so do the popular psychologists and television personalities who advise us on how to plan our lives, the engineers who tell us how to connect the pieces so that we get the products we want, and the regulators who tinker with interest rates and government securities purchases to produce the optimum rate of economic growth. "Man-the-maker" is deeply embedded in our modern sense of ourselves, but Niebuhr reminded his readers that the idea goes back to Aristotle and Thomas Aquinas, who told us that all human action must be directed toward an end. This, of course, is the starting point for teleological ethics.[5]

Another image, equally ancient and powerful, is the image of "man-the-citizen." Individuals living in society do not have their surroundings entirely at their disposal for whatever goals they want to pursue. They live in a space delimited by other people's projects. Their aims can extend no further than the next person's rights, and they must plan their actions in light of a framework of law that delineates those rights and identifies their responsibilities as citizens. Modern citizens, of course, participate in making laws as well as obeying them, but the question is still "by what law or system of laws shall I govern myself and others? How shall I administer the domain of which I am the ruler or in which I participate in rule?"[6] This is the image that gives rise to deontological ethics.

Niebuhr suggested that neither of those dominant images is fully adequate to the way people think of themselves, especially in today's world. The person is neither a maker, acting in a world in which all things are available for use according to human plans, nor a citizen, acting within a framework of law that sets determinate limits. We are above all *responders*. We are aware of the actions of other people that affect us and require some action from us in return. We respond to the homeless person who approaches us for a handout, to the friend who has a plan for next Friday night, and to the professor who announces an assignment with a due date. In larger groups, we respond to threats from nations whose global interests differ from our own, to appeals from fellow citizens who have no access to medical care, or to the promises of politicians who seek our votes. We are aware of a kind of demand in these forces that bear in on us. Some response must be made. At the same time, we are aware that we have some scope for freedom and creativity in that response. There is more than one thing that we could do.

So how do we know the right thing to do? If rules and goals will not tell us what to do, how do we choose the right course of action? Here, Niebuhr notices something that he finds extremely important: We do not react only to the external actions on us. We interpret what is happening to us. We find meaning and purpose in events, and we respond to the directions and intentions we see behind the appearances. We have a hunch that the ethics professor might be more flexible with the assignment if she knew that there is a biology midterm the same day. Our diplomats guess that the other side's belligerence is actually a signal that they are willing to talk.

Making the right choices requires developing responsibility—literally, the ability to respond—to interpret the actions on us and take appropriate actions in return. We cannot be responsible by sticking literally to the rules or plowing ahead with our goals, regardless of what anyone else does.

> Purposiveness seeks to answer the question: "What shall I do?" by raising as prior the question "What is my goal, ideal, or telos?" Deontology tries to answer the moral query by asking, first of all: "What is the law and what is the first law of my life?" Responsibility, however, proceeds in every moment of decision and choice to inquire: "What is going on?"[7]

The right action, Niebuhr suggests, tries to fit a response to what is happening, as best we can interpret it. We act responsibly when we seek the fitting response to events, as best we can interpret them.

To arrive at that interpretation, we must pay close attention to the immediate situation, to the people and forces that are acting on us here and now. But we must also think about these events in light of everything else we know and the whole reality of which they are a part. "Our interpretation of the immediate depends on our sense of the ultimate community of interaction," Niebuhr writes.[8]

For Christian ethics, that implies seeing all events in light of the Christian stance. As Charles Curran puts it, a stance "gives us the angle of vision from which we can put all the aspects of reality together and give some unity and order to what we see."[9] The Christian stance understands all events as part of the narrative of God's action through which history moves from creation, to sin and the Fall, to incarnation, redemption, and resurrection destiny. Niebuhr's radical monotheism suggests something similar. Because the ultimate community of interaction is God's relationship to the whole of reality and history, every event can be interpreted as part of God's action on us. No event is lacking in meaning, no matter how difficult it may be to see it in the moment.

The Christian stance thus provides a background interpretation for all events that helps us to make a fitting response to each of them. But as we have seen, the Christian stance does not make our decisions for us. When we act responsibly, fitting our choices to an interpretation of events, we must be responsible in another sense, too. We must *take responsibility* for our interpretation of events. A stance gives us a way of seeing our ultimate community of interaction, and it may be widely shared with a whole tradition. The details of our interpretation of the immediate, by contrast, are always our own.

Synergy

Catholic theologians shared many of the concerns that led H. Richard Niebuhr to write *The Responsible Self*. Especially in the years around the Second Vatican Council (1962–1965), theologians put new emphasis on the moral lives of Catholic laity, who were making their own moral decisions, without the help of the trained casuists who had been the arbiters of Christian ethics in the past. Catholics in the modern world were involved in family life, political leadership, and complex professional roles, where theologians often lacked the expertise to guide them. Responsibility to the specific places in which they lived and work and responsibility for their own moral choices became central to Catholics seeking to live their faith in the modern world, and the writings of a new generation of moral theologians reflected this new understanding of the Christian life. Bernard Häring (1912–1995) summed up this transformation in Catholic ethics with a work that rewrote the old works of casuistry. Unlike the manuals of moral theology that had been intended exclusively for the guidance of clergy, *Free and Faithful in Christ* was written for both clergy and laity, and its three volumes emphasized the theme of responsibility, rather than a list of acts to be done or avoided.[10]

These changes in Catholic moral theology also coincided with a renewed interest in virtue ethics among philosophers and theologians. Elizabeth Anscombe had already questioned the deontological foundations of modern moral philosophy in a way that suggested that a return to the virtue ethics of Aristotle might be required for a philosophical account of the way that people actually understand their moral lives. Since that time, many others have shared Anscombe's doubts, and some have concluded that we cannot know what we ought to do unless we know what kind of people we want to be. About the same time Gérard Gilleman suggested that moral theology should be recentered on Thomas Aquinas's understanding of the virtue of *caritas*, love or "charity." New ways of thinking about responsibility and virtue thus enter contemporary Christian ethics from several different sources, but developments since the middle of the twentieth century have tended to see moral choices as made by responsible individuals living in relationships that involve them as whole persons.[11]

From this background, Charles Curran has developed an approach to virtue ethics that he describes as a "relationality-responsibility model" of moral decision-making.[12] In his work, the emphasis on virtues and relationships in moral choice is combined with the variation on the Christian stance we have called Synergy.[13] The relationality in Curran's model ties ethical reflection to the actual relationships in which people respond to others around them and make moral choices. Describing an isolated action, apart from this web of relationships, will not enable us to call it right or wrong. An act of violence, a sexual encounter, or an apparently false statement cannot be evaluated apart from the other actions to which it is a response and the relationships within which the action has meaning for the person who does it. Synergy, however, sees relationality in widening circles of human connections. Precisely because all of reality is God's creation, moral thinking cannot be confined to an isolated relationship between two people, nor to a single family, group, or nation. Relational thinking that is shaped by the Christian stance pays close attention to what is going on in the immediate situation, but as H. Richard Niebuhr suggested, it connects the immediate to the ultimate context of God's relationship to history and humanity.

This gives the virtues a dual role in Curran's ethics. Some virtues are attitudes and dispositions that characterize good people in particular relationships. Others are general virtues that are relevant to all of our relationships and help us to see particular relationships in the larger reality of which they are a part. A complete account of virtue in Christian ethics will include both kinds of virtue.[14]

We can begin to build a list of particular virtues by considering the various relationships in which we find ourselves. Most obviously, these include relationships to other people. Some of these are intimate and personal, but if we are to sustain a moral life beyond the circle of close personal relationships, **justice** will be a primary virtue. Justice enables us to understand what we owe to others, whether it is simple courtesy to strangers in the supermarket or the tricky mix of friendship, accountability, and cooperation that we owe to the people we work with every day on the job. The person who imposes too much intimacy on the next person in the checkout line is lacking in justice, and so is the co-worker who always puts personal advancement above teamwork on the job. Justice is perhaps most important, however, in relationships with the many people who make up a society with us whom we will never meet or know personally. The way we care for other people when they are in need, the way we share the costs of public services, participate in the benefits of economic life, and meet the responsibilities of government together show whether we are just people, as much as or more than what we do in face-to-face relationships.

There are other relationships that have their own particular virtues. Increasingly, we understand that our relationship to nature requires the virtue of **stewardship**, if we are to avoid ecological catastrophe. While God is present in all relationships, the Christian also has a particular relationship to God that is sustained by virtues of **humility, openness,** and **gratitude**. Also among the particular relationships that each of us has is a relationship to ourselves. We sustain it by virtues that enable us to maintain our health and well-being, including the familiar moral virtue of **temperance**. However, the relationship to self also requires virtues of **honesty** and **integrity**. We have to be able to look at our own attitudes and actions without self-deception, and we need to care about whether we are the same person in all of our relationships with other people. Otherwise, we will soon begin to deceive some of them, and we will end up unable any longer to be honest with ourselves.

The general virtues that are important to all relationships are the familiar virtues of **faith, hope,** and **love**. As in Thomas Aquinas and the tradition of moral theology that comes down to us from him, these three virtues are for Curran closely related to each other and to the Christian stance as a whole. Curran places a special emphasis on the virtue of hope for our time, because the forces of history and limits of nature often seem to threaten all of our particular relationships and everything we do to sustain them. For Christian ethics, a hope that rests on the goodness of God's creation and the expectation of resurrection destiny enables us to make new commitments despite the failure of particular relationships, and to continue an honest relationship with ourselves, even when it is difficult to face our own shortcomings.

Virtues sustain relationships, but it is in relationships that we learn virtue. This in itself shows the importance of relationality in Curran's ethics. Without the virtues of parents, teachers, friends, and family who invite us into relationships, we would have no way to learn the virtues that we need to continue in those relationships and initiate new relationships

217

with others. Once we are in a particular kind of relationship—to other people, to God, to the world, or to ourselves—we see the virtues that make the relationship work, and we are in a position to develop them for ourselves. Virtues thus are habits of a sort, learned by practice just as they were in the ideas of Aristotle and Thomas Aquinas. But the Thomistic distinction between moral and theological virtues[15] has been largely replaced by the distinction between general and particular virtues. Where Thomas distinguished the virtues from one another by how we acquire them, Curran distinguishes them according to where we use them.

SYNERGY

CHARLES CURRAN thinks about virtue in terms of SYNERGY.
What virtues are important for Synergy? Particular virtues like justice, openness, stewardship, honesty, and integrity. General virtues of faith, hope, and love.
How are virtues acquired? By living in the relationships where these virtues are needed.

In this, Curran reflects another important change in Catholic moral theology that followed the Second Vatican Council. The sharp distinction that earlier theology made between natural and supernatural is now replaced by a single understanding of the moral life that reflects both common human experience and a theological understanding of the Christian stance. Christians can no longer offer two different accounts of the moral life, a natural one in which the virtues are explicable by reason and acquired by practice and a theological one in which the necessary virtues are given by God. What we know by reason includes an apprehension of the faith, hope, and love that are required in all relationships, and what we learn in relationship with God includes an understanding of the particular virtues that can also be learned by paying attention to all of our particular relationships.[16]

Curran's Synergy makes it possible to understand the connections between the virtues in Christian ethics and virtues as they are understood in other religious traditions, in philosophical ethics, or in the codes of practical and professional ethics drawn up by those who share a common way of working together. A synergist would expect that we would be able to understand the virtues that sustain particular relationships in other cultures and traditions, even when they are separated from us by great distances in space and time; and in fact, the study of virtues across traditions has become an important topic in comparative religious ethics.[17]

Integrity

Synergy emphasizes that virtues connect Christian ethics to shared human experiences and provide points of contact with other religious traditions. Integrity, by contrast, seeks out what is distinctive in Christian ideas of virtue and warns that superficial resemblances to other traditions may conceal deep differences. Because the integrity of the Christian witness is the most important thing for this version of the Christian stance, those who look at virtues in this way focus on the virtues that are essential to Christian community. We can see this way of thinking in the work of Stanley Hauerwas.

Hauerwas draws a connection between virtue and narrative. A synergist might call attention to the experiences of family life, work, or citizenship in which people generally take part in relationships and activities that teach them how a good person lives. What we learn in politics or on the job is much the same for everyone who participates, and the synergist expects that the virtues acquired there will be comparable, too. Hauerwas suggests, however, that what we learn from these activities comes not from the experiences themselves, but from the narratives in which we locate and explain the experience. Each of us has a story about our life, which we tell ourselves in an effort to tie the different parts of our experience together. Relationality has us being family members, citizens, co-workers, and worshippers, all at different times and in different places. Our activities would be a meaningless confusion without a narrative that ties them together and puts each of them in its place. The virtues learned in various separate relationships take on quite a different meaning as we locate them in the story that unifies our lives.[18]

For Christians, that narrative is provided by the biblical account of God's dealings with history and humanity. This world, Hauerwas writes, "is the creation of a good God who is known through the people of Israel and the life, death, and resurrection of Jesus Christ."[19] Through that story, the stories of individual Christian lives take on meaning and purpose. Their activities make sense in relation to God's activity. In this, Hauerwas's areteology is much like Augustine's.[20] Just as Augustine orders all the things that a Christian might love in relation to love for God, Hauerwas orders all of a person's relationships and experiences in a unified story and then orders all of these individual stories in the unifying narrative of the Christian stance. In the same way, just as Augustine says that the familiar virtues of the ancient world take on a different meaning when they are related to love for God above all things, Hauerwas says that familiar virtues like hope, justice, or patience take on different meanings when they are understood as part of the Christian narrative. The experiences may appear very similar to an outside observer, and the words may be familiar, but upon closer inspection, knowing what these virtues are and how they are to be lived requires thinking about them in distinctively Christian terms. The idea of the good person that is available in this way may even seem unintelligible to those who do not share the narrative.[21]

Hauerwas is, nonetheless, prepared to suggest to his readers what virtues are most important in this way of life shaped by the Christian narrative. He does not begin with lists of cardinal or theological virtues like the lists shaped by the logical requirements of Thomas Aquinas's *Summa theologiae* that we studied in the previous chapter. The answer has to come from the biblical narrative. What Hauerwas means by this, however, is deeply influenced by Karl Barth.[22] Just as Barth does not mean, when he says that we find the command of God in the Word of God, that Christians can locate a set of words in the Bible that tells them what to do, Hauerwas does not mean that the story of Jesus includes a definitive list of virtues that Christians ought to practice. The point is rather that the virtues Christians require are the ones that allow them to remember and retell the story of a savior who does not come with power, but willingly suffers crucifixion and death.

Peaceableness is a central virtue in this way of looking at the Christian life. Like Curran's "general" virtues, peaceableness is important to the Christian in every relationship, not just those that involve questions of pacifism, violence, and military service. Both within and beyond the community shaped by the biblical narrative, Christians are to cultivate the attitudes and dispositions that allow them to live without using force to protect themselves. They do not use coercion to get their way with others, and they do not resist evil when it is done to them. Peaceableness is the virtue that allows them to sustain that way of life, even in the fragmented and violent world in which we live.[23] **Patience** is important, too, because people often resort to violence when they cannot achieve their goals quickly. Peaceable people have to understand that peace is God's ultimate purpose, not something that they will accomplish by their own efforts. Those who trust in resurrection destiny know how to wait. Patience is not a strategy, but it is closely related to **hope**. Patience and hope are essential virtues for "living out of control," that is, living as people who refuse to use force to gain control over events, but who nonetheless seek constantly to witness to peace as a real possibility.[24]

Hauerwas also emphasizes the virtue of **justice**, lest those who read his account of peaceable, patient, and non-resistant Christians conclude that these people do not care when wrong is done to others. Justice is to be sought without violence, but also without fear. Christians therefore reject abstract concepts of "social justice" that provide blueprints for an ideal society but ask nothing of those who study them. Because Christians measure their witness by its integrity, rather than by its results, they do not hesitate to make what seem to be impossible demands on behalf of those who suffer from injustice and violence, even when this risks offending those who have power.

Clearly, these virtues which are essential for the integrity of the Christian community can only be acquired by living in it, participating in the life of the church through which the Christian narrative is retold, learned, and understood in relation to contemporary life. Hauerwas does not deny that other communities have their own virtues, too. In an interesting variation on the theological virtues of Thomas Aquinas, he even suggests that **faith, hope,** and **love** are "natural" virtues, in the sense that every community needs them to survive.[25] But the virtues that Christians share with other communities, even when they are as important as the virtues of faith, hope, and love, cannot do what peaceableness, patience, and justice do. They cannot sustain a community that remembers and retells the story of a crucified savior.

INTEGRITY

STANLEY HAUERWAS thinks about virtue in terms of INTEGRITY. What virtues are important for Integrity? The virtues that make it possible for a community to remember and retell the story of a crucified savior. These include especially peaceableness, patience, and justice. How are virtues acquired? By living in the Christian community and learning to see life in relation to the Christian narrative.

Liberation

Like Integrity, Liberation relates virtue to the lives of people who are bound together in a particular kind of community. Liberation theologians typically begin their work by locating themselves in a community that gives them a distinctive moral identity. This community may be African-American, Hispanic, or Asian-American by birth and heritage. They may belong to a people who have experienced colonial exploitation or organized discrimination by powerful forces in their own society. They may be despised for the disease that they have or the work that they do. They may be united by experiencing any of the many forms of oppression that are imposed on women in societies and cultures all around the world. Indeed, the community of identity may be built on a unique combination of these experiences. Liberation takes the form of Black theology, feminist theology, Hispanic theology, Womanist theology, *Minjung* theology, *Mujerista* theology, Dalit theology, and many more.

What links these particular experiences to the more general concern of Liberation is the experience of oppression. These communities participate in realities of sin that the Christian stance sees as inevitable in human experience, but they are also the victims of sin in brutal, persistent, and institutionalized forms. They anticipate the process of redemption with a special hope. Though their community is formed around incarnation, just as the Christian community Hauerwas describes is, liberation theologians relate to incarnation differently. For Hauerwas, the Christian community identifies itself with the peaceable kingdom proclaimed by Jesus. For the liberation theologians, the good news is that Jesus identifies himself with the community of the oppressed. "There can be no Christian theology that is not unreservedly identified with those who are humiliated and abused," James Cone writes. "For it is impossible to speak of the God of Israelite history, who is the God revealed in Jesus Christ, without recognizing that God is the God *of* and *for* those who labor and are over laden."[26] Taking incarnation seriously in that way would require a radical revision of the familiar forms of Christian theology and ethics. We have seen how it led Cone to a critical analysis of deontological ethics,[27] but it equally implies a new way of thinking about virtue.

We have already seen much of this new way of thinking in the work of Katie Cannon. Womanist ethics explains the moral life of women who are shut out from the fields of action that virtue ethics usually describes. They are not people who control their own destiny, but they survive with dignity in spite of limited opportunities and exploitation by the men in their lives. Their courage must be laced with duplicity to avoid provoking the violence that might destroy them and their children. Their temperance must sometimes include exuberant indulgence in pleasures while they are available, knowing that happiness is always fleeting and in short supply.[28]

We should be cautious about coming up with a general list of Liberation virtues that would apply to all of these places where distinct communities of identity create alternative ways of life under the shadow of oppression. Understanding these virtues requires immersion in the life of a particular community of oppressed people. However, theologians like Emilie Townes and Ada María Isasi-Díaz have described a process by which a community of oppressed people comes to awareness of its situation and begins to move toward some form of empowerment and social transformation. Townes, like Cannon, begins by calling into question the commitment of modern Christian ethics to autonomy. The idea of autonomy as an individual achievement, based on disciplined self-control and providing the starting point for a self-chosen way of life, simply has no meaning in the situation of the oppressed. As we move beyond a description of the lives of the oppressed to a prescription for policy, we must be guided by virtues of **mutuality** and **care**, not independence and individualism.[29]

Ada María Isasi-Díaz incorporates mutuality and care into a virtue of **solidarity**, which is for her the central virtue required for the liberation of the oppressed to begin to take shape under their own direction. Solidarity is a process, as Isasi-Díaz describes it. It begins with the "cry of the oppressed," rather than with an observer's account of their situation, but solidarity does not remain for long in the mode of lament. It continues through a development that Latin-American liberation theologians called *conscientization*, or *consciousness-raising*. The oppressed must become aware of their situation in the sense that they understand its causes. They know the economic mechanisms and the political powers that keep them oppressed, and they no longer see their plight as inevitable, as though it were a part of nature, or as right, as though they had done something to deserve their oppression. This awareness grows into genuine solidarity, however, when the oppressed begin to rely on each other. "This going beyond the isolated self is followed by creating strategies to carry out their struggle for liberation. Implementing these strategies keeps hope alive and, together with the vision of their own liberation, gives the poor and oppressed the **courage to risk** that sustains the struggle."[30]

It is particularly important, however, that the process of solidarity includes another step, in which at least some of the oppressors are incorporated into this community of solidarity, too. These "friends" of the oppressed begin to recognize the common interests they share with their partners in this new relationship, and they find themselves newly distant from the communities in which they had lived. There is now mutuality between the oppressed and these former oppressors, and both are able to participate together in devising strategies for social transformation.[31] This kind of community is not an easy achievement. Like the Christian community Hauerwas envisions, it is an eschatological sign, a reminder that something else is possible. Yet the actions that grow out of a commitment to mutuality are also "making parts of the future present now."[32]

LIBERATION

ADA MARÍA ISASI-DÍAZ and EMILIE TOWNES think about virtue in terms of LIBERATION.

What virtues are important for liberation? Solidarity, which enables the oppressed to rely on one another and take control of their own situation, and mutuality, which enables a dialogue that changes the relationships between the oppressed and the oppressors. Care and courage to take risks are also important.

How are virtues acquired? By a process of *conscientization*, in which people become aware of the forces and powers that are actually shaping their lives and learn what they must do to bring about real change.

Mutuality and solidarity thus belong to a process of learning and social transformation through which these virtues are acquired. Like the virtues Curran describes, mutuality and solidarity become part of a person's character through practice in a particular community, and like Hauerwas's virtues of peaceableness and patience, they are important because they are the virtues necessary to sustain the community in which they can be learned. What makes these virtues unusual is that the process of which they are a part goes on across the boundaries of community and culture within which descriptions of virtue are usually confined. Isasi-Díaz develops her account of conscientization, solidarity, and mutuality in the context of *Mujerista* theology, but she clearly intends us to see it as a strategy that can be employed wherever the oppressed may begin to understand their situation and speak a word so clear and compelling that at least some of their oppressors will hear it.

Realism

Both Integrity and Liberation stress the high demands of the Christian moral life, and those who are guided by the virtues of peaceableness and solidarity will not calculate the likelihood of success. This, of course, is precisely what Realism fears. Those who are so fearless as not to care whether their honest witness is effective may well accomplish nothing. Certainly they will accomplish less than those who engage in a more practical calculation of what is possible. Reinhold Niebuhr made this point clearly in his own introduction to Christian ethics, first published in 1935. The love of God and neighbor that Jesus taught is an impossible ideal. It reminds us, as Karl Barth was suggesting about the same time, that we live immediately under the judgment of the Word of God. But the ideal of love does not tell us very much about how to choose between the multiple possibilities, all of them imperfect, that give us our real choices. Even justice is at best approximate, something that we can only partly realize in any particular decision.[33] We need these impossible ideals, and the more impossible the better, for without them we quickly become satisfied with whatever we are able to accomplish without much risk to our own security and self-interest. The impossible ideal is always relevant, but not as a guide to actual moral choices. For that, we require a realistic calculation of possibilities.

It might seem, then, that Realism leaves little space for virtue in Christian ethics. Niebuhr stresses the calculation of actual results, and he dismisses as "sentimental" any talk about love when choices have to be made. Both his friends and his critics have interpreted his ethics as a strict consequentialism, aimed at obtaining the best results, or perhaps at avoiding the worst possibilities, by paying close attention to the facts.

Nevertheless, Reinhold Niebuhr is a virtue ethicist in his own unsentimental way. Virtues cannot tell us what we ought to do, but they can keep us from limiting our ideas of what is possible to what suits our own interests. **Faith** and **hope** maintain "the tension in which all moral action is grounded," and without them our calculations would merely be aimed at determining which course of action would cost us least personally. Much later, he would add that anything we can accomplish in history depends also on **love**, and on "the final form of love, which is **forgiveness**."[34]

We learn faith, hope, and love both in our experiences in relationship with other people and in the Christian scriptures that shape our expectations about those relationships. Like Curran's Synergy, Niebuhr's Realism resists drawing the sharp distinctions that earlier accounts of virtue sometimes made between virtues that are acquired in the Christian life and those that are available elsewhere. Faith, hope, and love are virtues that everyone needs to keep from dropping out of the moral discussion altogether. But are there virtues that enable us to ask what a good person would do? What would help us to see the right choice among the range of imperfect possibilities that are always before us? Niebuhr identified two attitudes that seem to perform that function in his realistic approach to moral choices. The first is a **critical attitude**. Like H. Richard Niebuhr, this attitude begins with the question, "What is going on?" But the critical attitude that Reinhold Niebuhr has in mind pushes far below a surface observation of events. Like the critical theories we considered earlier, it examines the interests at play in any political situation, testing claims against real possibilities and asking whether any system can deliver what it promises. If H. Richard Niebuhr wants to know what is going on, Reinhold Niebuhr's critical attitude asks, "What is *really* going on?"[35]

This tension between criticism and responsibility is present in all of our moral choices today, not only in our choices between different political and economic systems. We need to take a critical attitude toward every decision we make. This attitude pushes us to expand our vision and take in more of reality as we think about our choices. We want to think about all of the possibilities, the ones that are really before us and the ones that exist only as ideas, the ones that are familiar and the ones that have been tried only in distant places or in other cultures. Then we want to bring all our knowledge to bear on each of these possibilities, asking in detail how each of them would work. What kind of economic resources would each require? What has happened when similar ideas were tried at other times in history? What do psychologists, poets, and novelists tell us about how people have lived with each of these possibilities? What do philosophers and theologians and religious traditions tell us about human nature under each of these conditions? Is this possible world one in which real people could live together, or does it demand too much of them, or expect too little? Is this possibility sustainable, both for human beings and for their environment?

Every important choice requires that kind of imagination of us, because we want to choose with all the possibilities before us. The more we know, individually and collectively, the more possibilities we have and the more complicated our choices become. But our imagination must be a critical imagination. Otherwise, there is no difference between ethics and fantasy. To answer the question about human happiness that ethics has asked from the beginning, we have to know how each of these possible worlds would actually work.

What we will know after we have exercised this critical imagination, Reinhold Niebuhr tells us, is that no choice makes itself. The critical attitude shows us the limitations in each of the possibilities. It asks, "Will this choice deliver all that it promises, to the people to whom it makes these promises, when it promises to deliver them?" The answer, inevitably, will be no. Something will not arrive. Someone will be left out, and for some, the delivery will come too late. When we review all the possibilities with a critical attitude, each of them has its defects. At that point, some will refuse to choose at all. Revolutionaries will want to redraw the set of possibilities, insisting as Marxist theorists did through the nineteenth and twentieth centuries that given the right social and economic conditions, human nature itself can be changed. Some Christians will insist that we must wait for the Reign of God, when the limitations of sin will be removed and creation will be restored. The partial goods and partial evils that are characteristic of redemption within history are all the same from the perspective of resurrection destiny. Some will simply be so confused by the results of the criticism that they will be unable to choose. Comfortable within the narrow boundaries of their previous experience, they are shaken to discover how many possibilities there really are. They are shaken even more when the critical attitude is turned on what they already know, and they discover that it, too, is imperfect.

That is why Niebuhr insists that the critical attitude must always be paired with a "**responsible attitude**, which will not pretend to be God nor refuse to make a decision between political answers to a problem because each answer is discovered to contain a moral ambiguity in God's sight. We are men, not God; we are responsible for making choices between greater and lesser evils, even when our Christian faith, illuminating the human scene, makes it quite apparent that there is no pure good in history, and probably no pure evil, either."[36]

REALISM

REINHOLD NIEBUHR thinks about virtue in terms of REALISM. What virtues are important for Realism? Faith, hope, and love, which sustain moral commitments. A critical attitude and a responsible attitude, which enable us to understand the choices we face and to choose between possibilities which are always less than ideal.

How are virtues acquired? In the experiences of personal and political life shared with the whole society and in reflection on the Christian understanding of history and human nature.

The responsible attitude faces a much smaller range of choices than the critical attitude, because it is concerned only with the choices that are real options in the present. The resources are available. The cooperation of those who must work together on the choices can be secured. The results, while they can never be perfectly known, are predictable enough in the short run to allow us to take action, and we have a pretty good idea of the points at which we could make a new decision, if a change of direction were required.

The range of responsible choices is narrow, and all of them are imperfect. We know that from reviewing them with a critical attitude. Niebuhr suggests that this is also part of the Christian stance—"our Christian faith, illuminating the human scene," as he puts it. Living between incarnation and resurrection destiny, it is important not to expect too much from any historical possibility.

Still, there are choices to be made. Just as no one choice emerges from the scrutiny of the critical attitude as perfect in all respects, so the number of imperfect choices that are real options in the present is usually two or more. Indeed, it is part of the responsible attitude to look at choices in ways that multiply the number of real options, because where there are no choices, there is no way to be responsible. When we have considered the world from a particular stance, from any of the variations on the Christian stance, we still have a choice to make. The question is how we are going to make it.

Goals, Duties, and the Virtue of Responsibility

Responsibility, then, leads us back to those ways of moral reasoning that we examined earlier in this book: goals, duties, and virtues. This seems a strange place to end, because as we have seen, the search for responsibility grew out of dissatisfaction with those ways of making choices in the first place. Perhaps we have been travelling in circles on this long journey.

Perhaps. But there is one important difference between the images of "man-the-maker" and "man-the-citizen" that prompted H. Richard Niebuhr's dissatisfaction with the ethical theories that were available to him and the idea of responsible choice with which we are working now. As theoretical approaches to moral questions, deontology and teleology suggest that the choice of system determines what the responsible choice is in advance. Once I am a deontologist or a teleologist, I know how I will make all of my moral choices. The same might be said for areteology, or virtue ethics, though H. Richard Niebuhr did not specifically include it in his discussion. I begin with my image of what kind of person it is who makes the right choices, and then I know what kind of person I ought to be. Each image, "man-the-maker" or "man-the-citizen," implies its own set of characteristic virtues. Whether I choose the virtues first or choose the theory, I have one way of deciding all moral questions.

From this point of view, the study of ethics is about choosing the right theory, from which all the rest of the choices will follow. If I am a teleologist, I will ask only about goals. If I am a deontologist, I will only be concerned with knowing my duty. Likewise, in Christian ethics, a choice among the variations on the Christian stance will settle the question of which options among the available and imaginable choices are the real ones. A pacifist committed to Integrity cannot choose the use of force, any more than a Realist can rely on the power of love to change society.

But people do make such choices. Bonhoeffer, who at the beginning of the Third Reich grounded his resistance to the regime on the integrity of the Confessing Church, took the venture of responsibility that led him deeply into political involvement with the conspirators who were willing to risk guilt to end the war by Hitler's assassination. Martin Luther King, Jr., the Realist who studied Reinhold Niebuhr's social ethics at Boston University, "came to see for the first time that the Christian doctrine of love operating through the Gandhian method of nonviolence was one of the most potent weapons available to oppressed people in their struggle for freedom."[37] We would not be impressed with the Integrity or the Realism of someone who constantly changed their stance to suit the needs of the moment, but when we look at those who have made major contributions to our understanding of Christian life, we often find that it is precisely because when they had crucial decisions to make, they could draw upon the Christian stance as a whole. They did not confine their choices to the ones marked out by the variation on the Christian stance with which they began.

It might seem after a glance at the way this book is organized that the moral life is a matter of selecting a stance and selecting a way of moral reasoning, and then making all of your choices within that framework. There are those who see the history of Christian ethics as a collection of pieces from which just such a framework might be selected and assembled. Connect Integrity and virtue, for example, and all the rest of the toolkit can be discarded. Or link Liberation and teleology—free the oppressed by any means necessary—and make that the principle of every subsequent decision. If you have your theory ready, you will make the right decision when the choice comes along. But for what Reinhold Niebuhr calls a "responsible attitude," the choice of theory is also part of the right decision.

Once the real options have been identified, the responsible attitude asks what sort of ethical theory will order those options appropriately for this decision. When the choice is primarily my own, a choice of vocation or marriage or friendship that is part of the good life as I understand it, a teleology like that used by Aristotle or Augustine may be the right way to make the decision. In decisions like these, I have to choose between goods that seem to be really different, and though it is difficult to bring many other people into a decision about what is truly good, it is almost impossible to make the choice for myself without employing some sort of teleology. Deontology applied to decisions like these frequently turns out badly. "You have a duty to carry on the family business" is a rule that many who live by it live to regret.

We want an Aristotelian or an Augustinian teleology when the decisions matter to us most, personally. But in other cases, where less is at stake for us personally, a more utilitarian teleology works perfectly well. I might like a really nice automobile, but if too many other people want that particular make and model, the price may be too high and keep me away from too many other things that I also want. A nice car and a nice trip abroad are very different kinds of good, but they are enough alike in the ways they fit into my life that I can treat them as commensurable. I can determine how much I am willing to pay for each of them and compare it with how much other people are willing to pay for similar things and let the market make my choices. It is a perfectly serviceable way to arrive at the greatest good for the greatest number in some cases, even if we would not want to go so far as Bentham's dictum that this sort of teleology should be the guide "not only of every action of a private individual, but of every measure of government."[38]

In other cases, however, a rule is what is required. Large groups of people make their decisions not so much by what they want to accomplish, but by a set of rules that set the boundaries within which different individuals can set their own goals and ensure that the rights of those who have different goals are protected. The more people are involved in a decision, especially if they disagree about goals and if we cannot be sure about the outcomes, the more likely we are to require some kind of deontology to arrive at a good decision.

One of the virtues we might want to develop, then, is a habit of choosing the right way to think about goals or about duties when we have a moral decision to make. Following H. Richard Niebuhr, we might say that such a virtue would enable us to ask "What is going on?" in a way that enables us to choose an appropriate form of moral reasoning to decide between the real options before us. Such a choice would be responsible in both of the senses that Niebuhr suggested. It would be responsive to the actions of others upon us, providing a meaningful interpretation of those actions and not just a bare description of them. It would also take responsibility for the decisions that follow, recognizing that both the framing of the choices and the moral reasoning that go into the decisions involve our own judgments. In deciding what our goals and our duties are and deciding when to make each kind of moral decision, we become responsible people.

We might think of responsibility, then, as a virtue, but a particular kind of virtue, rather like the virtue of prudence in Thomas Aquinas, which was for him both a moral and an intellectual virtue.[39] Like a moral virtue, responsibility enables us to control our emotions and desires. By exercising responsibility, we overcome the desire to unload our decisions on someone else or some other power, excusing ourselves by saying that we did what we did because we had no other choice. We also overcome the temptation to identify ourselves too closely with a higher power. But responsibility is also an intellectual virtue, for when we have acquired it, we will regularly—habitually—hit upon the right framework among the many different moral frameworks available to us to make the decisions we have to make. As with other intellectual virtues, these good decisions will not be the results of luck or intuition. They will begin with study and practice. Responsible people make good moral decisions because they have available as part of their own character the full range of ways of understanding goals, duties, and virtues.

That might be said by way of conclusion to any study of ethics that begins with Aristotle's question about what it is that everyone seeks and proceeds through all the ways to answer that question that Western philosophy and religion have provided. We have covered many of those ways in this book, but we have left a larger number out. Our concern has been focused more specifically on a tradition in Christian ethics that takes Jesus' teaching about love of God and neighbor through the work of Augustine, and then through Thomas Aquinas, Martin Luther, and Jean Calvin, until we come to the variations on the Christian stance that are familiar to us today. To conclude that study, we must add that when responsible Christians ask, "What is going on?" they interpret the immediate in light of their sense of the ultimate community of interaction, as H. Richard Niebuhr put it.[40] For that, they will need the whole Christian stance, from creation to resurrection destiny, and they will each of them draw on Synergy, Integrity, Realism, and Liberation as responsibility requires.

Additional Reading

Foot, Philippa. *Virtues and Vices.* Berkeley: University of California Press, 1978.

Harris, Melanie. *Gifts of Virtue, Alice Walker, and Womanist Ethics.* New York: Palgrave Macmillan, 2010.

Hauerwas, Stanley. *Character and the Christian Life: A Study in Theological Ethics.* San Antonio, TX: Trinity University Press, 1975.

Keenan, James F. *Virtues for Ordinary Christians.* Franklin, WI: Sheed and Ward, 1996.

Kotva, Joseph. *The Christian Case for Virtue Ethics.* Washington, DC: Georgetown University Press, 1996.

May, William F. *Beleaguered Rulers: The Public Obligation of the Professional.* Louisville: Westminster John Knox Press, 2001.

Ottati, Douglas. *Hopeful Realism: Recovering the Poetry of Theology.* Cleveland: Pilgrim Press, 1999.

Schweiker, William. *Responsibility and Christian Ethics.* Cambridge: Cambridge University Press, 1995.

VIRTUES: A Test Case

There are many virtues, and the list varies as we move through time and between cultures. Nearly always, however, a tradition or an author identifies some virtues as more important than the rest. Both Stoic and Christian authors list the "cardinal" virtues of temperance, courage, prudence, and justice. Other Christians focus on the "theological" virtues of faith, hope, and love. Stanley Hauerwas identifies peaceableness and patience as essential for life in the Christian community, while Charles Curran identifies stewardship as an important virtue in our relationship to nature.

To decide which virtues are necessary and why they are important, we have to know something about the community or group in which these virtues are lived. Some groups are narrowly focused on a task, like a military unit or an election campaign staff. Others, like cities and nations, must provide the context in which many diverse people live out their whole lives. Some communities are small social or family groups. Others, like religious organizations, maintain a tradition that endures across centuries and extends around the world.

Suppose that you have been invited to give moral advice to one of these many different types of community. It can be any type of community you choose, but you should think of a specific example of the type. If the community you have in mind is a nation, you will want to discuss the United States, Afghanistan, or some other specific country. If you have a smaller social or working community in mind, you might think about a specific fraternity or sorority or a specific company. A university campus might count as a community in this sense, too. If you are thinking about a religious community, you should be thinking of a specific tradition, though the community itself might be as large as the global Roman Catholic Church or as small as a sub-group in a local congregation.

Whatever community you have in mind, you will want to know something about its history and its purpose, if it has one. You should also consider how large it is, and how it is related to other communities. You will want to think about whether there are other, similar communities with which this one must compete or cooperate.

Once you have formed a clear picture of the group you have in mind, consider what you would say to that community if they asked you to name the virtues that are most important for them. What are these virtues, and why is each of them important to this kind of community?

Questions

1. How many different virtues does it take to sustain a community? Can a group's identity be defined by a few virtues that it holds to be very important? Or does a community require many different virtues to cover the range of problems that may arise in its life?

2. If your group is built around more than one virtue, how are these different virtues related to one another? Are they "natural" virtues that any successful group must encourage? Or are these virtues specific to the group you are considering? Or is your list a combination of both?

3. How are the necessary virtues acquired in this community? Does the group sustain the virtues by itself, or do people bring the necessary virtues to the community from their experience in other places?

4. What specific authors and traditions in Christian ethics would help you to formulate your list of virtues for the group you are considering?

A POSTSCRIPT FOR THE INSTRUCTOR

S tudents bring a wide range of ideas, questions, and commitments to an ethics course. They have ideas about right and wrong and a basic sense of what it means to live a good life that give them a starting point for thinking about the questions of ethics. They know what some of those questions are. More than most of their professors, today's students live in a social world where they are confronted every day with competing answers to questions about personal relationships, honesty, effort, and commitment. They know that each of those decisions may have incalculable consequences for their future, and each of them makes an impact on their personal identity. They are familiar, too, with an expanded horizon of choices. Most of them have far more opportunities than their parents had. They know from experience how new technologies, new media, and global connections can change lives. They have lived their whole lives within a rapidly changing international order, full of new risks and new possibilities, and they are convinced that the choices about the environment, energy, and disease control that will have to be made by their generation will shape the human future, perhaps determine whether there is a human future. They know in world events and in their own lives how difficult it is to distinguish between what is best, what is possible, and what is right.

All this gives some urgency to the task of teaching an introduction to Christian ethics, but it is not new. As I pointed out in the preface to this book, Aristotle told us long ago in the *Nicomachean Ethics* that one of the peculiarities of teaching ethics is that the students already know a great deal about the subject before the lectures begin. Professors are apt to complain that today's students know less than their predecessors about history, literature, and their own religious traditions, but the chances are that they know more than previous generations about the questions of ethics, and they have learned what they know from a wider range of sources.

But the question for the instructor is also whether this background of knowledge and experience adds up to anything coherent. Perhaps what students bring to class are mere fragments of a moral vocabulary that has lost its meaning.[1] If that is the case, there would be little to be gained from a comprehensive introduction to the confusion. Perhaps the way to teach Christian ethics is to identify a properly Christian way of thinking about moral questions. Our task would then be to get the right way to do Christian ethics before our students as quickly as possible, avoiding other ways of thinking except perhaps to explain why they ought to be rejected.

There are introductions to Christian ethics that seem to proceed on those terms, but I think that this underestimates the vitality of the moral concerns that our students bring into the classroom. The words and ideas they have available may not always be completely coherent, but they are sufficient to support lively arguments about what they ought to be doing and how their communities ought to be organized. They are also well aware, even if they have a personal commitment to the Christian faith, that there are other ways of approaching these questions and real differences among Christians, too. The greatest risk of disappointment is that what they hear in the lectures and read in their textbooks will not connect with the full range of moral concerns and ideas they bring with them into the class. Our task in the classroom is not to proclaim the Word or to defend our own idea of Christian ethics, even though many of us do both of those things in other settings. Our task is to make students aware of the moral thinking they are already doing, to help them see that they have arguments as well as opinions and learn that those arguments have a history.

To do this, we have to provide them with a great deal of information that they probably do not know about the people who have shaped Christian ethics in the past, the moral problems that these people faced, and the traditions on which they drew, which often have a history that reaches well back before the beginnings of Christianity. A good deal of what can be made up into exam questions or researched for a term paper in a Christian ethics class will come from those materials. We also have to make sure that they are aware of the range of possibilities in contemporary Christian ethics, for although many of the students who register for an introduction to Christian ethics will have one or two of these possibilities in their own backgrounds, few will have a comprehensive view of the diversity in recent thinking or know enough about the other possibilities to understand clearly how their own convictions take shape against that background.

Most important, they will need to see that although Christian convictions can shape the way that people understand moral problems, their answers to these questions rarely follow directly from Christian convictions alone. Patterns of moral reasoning that are more widely shared among those who have tried to answer the questions of ethics—thinking in terms of goals, duties, or virtues—give shape to normative thinking in Christian ethics, too, and a large part of any comprehensive introduction to Christian ethics will be devoted to considering the ways that these approaches to moral questions interact with the main ways of thinking about Christian convictions.

What I have tried to do in this introduction to Christian ethics is to present this essential information in an organized and understandable way. I begin with five key ideas about God's relationship to humanity and history that shape what we will here call the "Christian stance."[2] I show how those ideas took shape in relation to other ways of thinking about ethics in the world of early Christianity, and I identify four major variations on the Christian stance found in Christian ethics today: Synergy, Integrity, Realism, and Liberation. These topics take up the first three chapters of the book. The six remaining chapters cover historical and contemporary developments in the three ways of thinking about moral choices that I mentioned a moment ago: teleology, deontology, and areteology. Not surprisingly, the last six chapters are often organized to show how the four variations on the Christian stance relate to each of the three ways of moral reasoning, though I have not rigidly adhered to that way of organizing the material.

The purpose of all of this is to indicate what is possible in Christian ethics, rather than to prescribe one way that it ought to be done. Students who use this introduction will have to figure out how to make use of these resources to arrive at their own ways of thinking about moral problems, just as they were doing their own thinking with whatever resources they had in hand before they began taking the course. The aim is not to get them to choose one among the Christian possibilities and use it exclusively. We need to look at the history and variety of Christian ethics the way that Albert Jonsen and Stephen Toulmin suggested we look at moral theory generally:

> If general, abstract theories in moral philosophy are read against their historical and social backgrounds, they will need to be understood not as *making comprehensive and mutually exclusive* claims, but rather as offering us *limited and complementary* perspectives on the whole broad complex of human conduct and moral experience, personal relations, and ethical reflection. So interpreted, none of these theories tells us the whole truth (even the only fundamental truth) about ethical thought and moral conduct. Instead, each of them gives us part of the larger picture we require, if we are to recognize the proper place of moral reflection and discussion, ideas and rules, in the world of human interactions and in our relations to the larger scheme of things.[3]

By providing the historical and social background that Jonsen and Toulmin see as essential for understanding and appreciating moral theories, I hope I have made it possible for students who use this book to see the different views of Christian ethics that compete for their attention as limited and complementary in the way that Jonsen and Toulmin suggest.

Having previously written a much shorter introduction to Christian ethics organized along these same lines,[4] I am conscious of how much more information I have tried to fit into these pages. Having taught this introduction to Christian ethics to undergraduates and to graduate theological students for twenty years, I am also aware of how much I have left out. There are textbooks in religious ethics that aspire to provide in one place all the resources you will need to teach the course, but I warn you that this is not one of them. It is perhaps only fair, however, to give you a brief inventory of what is missing.

Primary texts. A good introduction to the history and variety of Christian ethics requires opportunities to read Augustine, Thomas Aquinas, Luther, Calvin, and key contemporary figures in their own words, or at least in good translations. A collection of primary texts that matches the exposition in these chapters can easily be assembled by following my footnotes. In general, I have tried to focus on a limited number of representative authors and to draw the ideas of each author out of one or two important texts. It seems to me preferable that these works should then be read at some length, rather than assigning short excerpts from a wider range of sources.

Newspapers—also magazines, websites, video clips, blogs, and a variety of other media that have not been invented yet. Students need to learn to identify moral arguments in daily life, as well as in this textbook and the primary texts. This involves learning to distinguish moral arguments from predictions, threats, and exhortations and learning to identify similar patterns of deontological, teleological, and areteological reasoning, even when they are separated widely in time and concerned with quite different issues. Students learn to run these connections in two directions. Once they figure out how Thomas Aquinas appeals to the natural law, or how Luther argues for the necessity of a strong secular authority, they will quickly learn to spot the same line of reasoning in today's media. They can also strengthen their understanding of how moral arguments have worked historically by taking a contemporary argument and trying to decide who among the historical sources has made similar arguments.

Test cases. Students not only need to be able to identify moral arguments when they see them. Even an introductory course should give them practice in constructing a moral position of their own. This often proves surprisingly difficult for introductory students to do. Often it is quite different from the kind of thinking and writing they are required to do in other classes, and though they may regularly make moral judgments of surprising sophistication, articulating that case for someone else to follow may be the hardest assignment in the course. Carefully constructed hypothetical situations may make it easier to identify the key elements of the moral problem, and I have provided three such exercises following chapters 5, 7, and 9. Advanced students and students in graduate and professional programs, on the other hand, should work with the complexities of real cases when possible.

Reference works. These include not only dictionaries of ethics that provide concise summaries of key terms and concepts, but also the variety of "companions," "handbooks," and other guides published in recent years that provide more lengthy articles on ideas, historical events, and authors. We are all increasingly aware that an introductory text like this one cannot provide a comprehensive survey of Christian ethics. What an introduction to Christian ethics introduces, at least in the classrooms of Western Europe and North America, is almost always the Western Christian tradition as I have followed it here, developing from ancient sources, splitting into Catholic and Protestant branches, wrestling with the questions of modern moral philosophy, and incorporating the experiences of those who live on the margins of modern Western culture. Some students will want to explore the moral traditions of Eastern Christianity or the ways that Christianity has taken root in non-Western cultures. All of them should know that these variations on Christian ethics exist and where to find information about them. Specialized reference works that deal with bioethics, law, and business ethics in relation to Christian ethics are also important, especially for students who will deal with more fully developed case studies in their classwork.

Making good use of these resources in an introductory course will no doubt require some selectivity in the use of this text, emphasizing some chapters and supplementing them with primary texts and test cases while giving less attention to other chapters, or omitting them altogether. Like the theories they cover, these chapters are not intended to be *comprehensive and mutually exclusive*, but *limited and complementary*. As I suggest in the final chapter of this book, knowing what to emphasize and what to omit requires an intellectual and moral virtue something like prudence, both in the doing of ethics and in the teaching of it. This book comes into your hands as the instructor, then, not as a complete and indivisible guide to the teaching of Christian ethics, but as another resource for you to use along with those others I have just suggested in constructing your own way of introducing the subject. I hope you enjoy using it as much as I have enjoyed the teaching and writing that went into it.

Of course, I have had many companions in those labors. Special thanks are due to my colleagues in ethics at SMU. Charlie Curran's influence is evident in every chapter, and this book would be quite impossible without his contributions to the way that all of us in the discipline think about Christian ethics. Rebekah Miles and Theodore Walker, Jr., have been conversation partners as we have devised curriculum and catalog language and thought about the deeper issues of theological education. I have learned much from them directly, and even more that has been mediated from them through the students we have shared over the years.

Much of this book was written during a semester in residence at the

Center of Theological Inquiry in Princeton, New Jersey, and I am especially grateful for the scholarly resources and good colleagues I found there. John Burk and Larry Stratton read many of these chapters as they were written, and they helped me not only by critical reviews of the substance but also by talking with me about how they teach their own introductory courses. Mark Tarpley was my research assistant during the early stages of the writing, and Josh Mauldin was an invaluable assistant and collaborator in bringing it to a conclusion. I am also grateful to Kathy Armistead and the editorial staff at Abingdon Press for encouragement, and for patience.

It is said that there is no end to the making of books, and I have concluded that this means not only that more books are always being written, but also that those that have been written are never really completed. The author just has to stop at some point, and that is the point which I have now reached. I will be interested to learn what you have to add.

NOTES

A Preface for the Student

1. Charles E. Curran, *The Catholic Moral Tradition Today: A Synthesis* (Washington, DC: Georgetown University Press, 1999), 30.

1. The Origins of Ethics

1. See, for example, Barbara Mertz, *Red Land, Black Land: Daily Life in Ancient Egypt* (New York: HarperCollins, 2008).

2. In addition to the texts that are now in the New Testament, other letters and writings circulated among the early Christians with advice on how to live this new way of life. These include the Didache, the Epistle of Barnabas, and the Epistle to Diognetus. See Andrew Louth, ed., *Early Christian Writings: The Apostolic Fathers* (New York: Penguin Books, 1987).

3. For Aristotle's introduction to the study of ethics, see Book I of his *Nicomachean Ethics*, ed. Roger Crisp (Cambridge: Cambridge University Press, 2000), 3-22.

4. Aristotle, *Nicomachean Ethics*, 10-11.

5. Ibid., 5, 16-17.

6. Plato, *Republic*, trans. Robin Waterfield (Oxford: Oxford University Press, 1993), 133-58. These four virtues, translated into modern English in various words, are important for many writers in the history of ethics. A common translation calls them prudence, courage, temperance, and justice, which are often identified as the four "cardinal" virtues. See chapter 8 for more on these virtues in Christian ethics.

7. Plotinus, *The Enneads*, Stephen MacKenna, trans. (New York: Penguin Books, 1991), 45-55.

8. See Martha Nussbaum, *The Fragility of Goodness: Luck and Ethics in Greek Tragedy and Philosophy*, rev. ed. (Cambridge: Cambridge University Press, 2001).

9. Lucretius, *On the Nature of the Universe*, trans. Ronald Melville (Oxford: Clarendon Press, 1997).

10. Epictetus, *Discourses and Selected Writings*, trans. Robert Dobbin (New York: Penguin Books, 2008), 7.

11. See chapter 6.

12. Louis E. Newman, *An Introduction to Jewish Ethics* (Upper Saddle River, NJ: Pearson Prentice-Hall, 2005), 40.

13. James Gustafson, *Christ and the Moral Life* (Louisville: Westminster John Knox Press, 2009), 242.

14. Charles E. Curran, *The Catholic Moral Tradition Today: A Synthesis* (Washington, DC: Georgetown University Press, 1999), 30-33.

15. Ibid., 30.

16. Ibid.

17. "Epistle to Diognetus," in Louth, ed., *Early Christian Writings*, 144-45.

2. The Good Life and the Christian Life

1. See page 6 above.

2. Charles E. Curran, *The Catholic Moral Tradition Today: A Synthesis* (Washington, DC: Georgetown University Press, 1999), 33-34.

3. Marcus J. Borg, *The Heart of Christianity* (San Francisco: HarperSanFrancisco, 2003), 170.

4. Augustine, *Confessions*, trans. Henry Chadwick (Oxford: Oxford University Press, 1991), 40.

5. Ibid., 124-26.

6. See above, page 18.

7. Augustine, "The Catholic Way of Life and the Manichean Way of Life," in Boniface Ramsey, ed., *The Manichean Debate*, The Works of Saint Augustine, pt. 1, v. 19 (Hyde Park, NY: New City Press, 2006), 32-33.

8. Augustine, *The City of God against the Pagans*, ed. R. W. Dyson (Cambridge: Cambridge University Press, 1998), 632.

9. Augustine, "The Catholic Way of Life and the Manichean Way of Life," 49.

10. Augustine, *City of God*, 950-52.

11. Ibid., 928.

12. Ibid., 940.

13. Ibid.

14. Matthew 22:35-40. See page 6 above.

15. Augustine, *City of God*, 941.

16. Augustine, "Homilies on the First Epistle of John," in Boniface Ramsey, ed., *The Works of Saint Augustine*, pt. 3, v. 14 (Hyde Park, NY: New City Press, 2008), 110.

17. Augustine, *City of God*, 960-62.

3. Variations on the Christian Stance

1. John Courtney Murray, *We Hold These Truths: Catholic Reflections on the American Proposition* (Lanham, MD: Rowman and Littlefield, 2005). Murray's book was originally published in 1960.

2. Ibid., 101-22.

3. See chapter 6 for a more complete discussion of Thomas Aquinas and natural law.

4. Murray, *We Hold These Truths*, 37-39.

5. Ibid., 38.

6. As the sociologists Robert Putnam and David Campbell remind us, people today have far more contact with other ideas and other religions than they did even in the recent past. See Robert D. Putnam and David E. Campbell, *American Grace: How Religion Divides and Unites Us* (New York: Simon and Schuster, 2010), 519-40.

7. Lisa Sowle Cahill, *Between the Sexes: Foundations for a Christian Ethics of Sexuality* (Philadelphia: Fortress Press, 1985), 105-22; *Sex, Gender, and Christian Ethics* (Cambridge: Cambridge University Press, 1996), 46-55.

8. Charles E. Curran, *The Catholic Moral Tradition Today* (Washington, DC: Georgetown University Press, 1999), 40.

9. Stanley Hauerwas, *The Peaceable Kingdom* (Notre Dame, IN: University of Notre Dame Press, 1983), xxvi.

10. Ibid., 76.

11. H. Richard Niebuhr, "The Grace of Doing Nothing," in *The Christian Century* (March 23, 1932), 378-80.

12. Reinhold Niebuhr, *Moral Man and Immoral Society: A Study of Ethics and Politics* (Louisville: Westminster John Knox Press, 2002); *The Nature and Destiny of Man: A Christian Interpretation* (Louisville: Westminster John Knox

Press, 1996). *Moral Man and Immoral Society* was originally published in 1932. *The Nature and Destiny of Man* was first published in two volumes, in 1941 and 1943.

13. Reinhold Niebuhr, *An Interpretation of Christian Ethics* (New York: Seabury Press, 1979), 62.

14. Reinhold Niebuhr, *The Children of Light and the Children of Darkness* (New York: Charles Scribner's Sons, 1964).

15. Ibid., xiii.

16. Consider, for example, John Patrick Diggins, *Why Niebuhr Now?* (Chicago: University of Chicago Press, 2011); Speaking of Faith: "Obama's Theologian: David Brooks and E. J. Dionne on Reinhold Niebuhr and the American Present." http://speakingoffaith.publicradio.org/programs/2009/obamas-theologian/

17. Katie G. Cannon, *Black Womanist Ethics* (Atlanta: Scholars Press, 1988).

18. Katie Geneva Cannon, *Katie's Canon: Womanism and the Soul of the Black Community* (New York: Continuum, 1995), 60.

19. Ibid., 91-100.

20. Cannon, *Black Womanist Ethics*, 105.

21. James H. Cone, *A Black Theology of Liberation*, 20th Anniversary Edition (Maryknoll, NY: Orbis Books, 1990), 5. *A Black Theology of Liberation* was originally published in 1970 by J. B. Lippincott Company.

4. Goods, Goals, and God

1. Richard Dawkins, *The Blind Watchmaker* (New York: Norton, 1986).

2. See above, pages 9-13.

3. The familiar translation of the sayings of Jesus known as the Beatitudes reads "*blessed* are the peacemakers," etc., but the Greek *makarios* could also be translated as "*happy* are the peacemakers." As with *eudaimon*, the English word "happy" seems too light for the deeply satisfying life that the Greek term indicates, but the English word "blessed" may seem too otherworldly for a life that provides real and lasting happiness.

4. Andrew Louth, ed., *Early Christian Writings: The Apostolic Fathers* (New York: Penguin Books, 1987), 148.

5. Augustine, "The Catholic Way of Life and the Manichean Way of Life," Boniface Ramsey, ed., *The Manichean Debate*, The Works of Saint Augustine, pt. 1, v. 19 (Hyde Park, NY: New City Press, 2006), 49.

6. Augustine, *The City of God against the Pagans*, ed. R. W. Dyson (Cambridge: Cambridge University Press, 1998), 927-30.

7. Augustine, "The Catholic Way of Life and the Manichean Way of Life," 43.

8. Augustine, *Confessions*, trans. Henry Chadwick (Oxford: Oxford University Press, 1991), 221-72.

9. H. Richard Niebuhr, *Radical Monotheism and Western Culture* (Louisville: Westminster John Knox Press, 1993), 24-37.

10. Niebuhr explains how this transformation works in Augustine's theology in *Christ and Culture* (New York: Harper and Bros., 1951), 206-18.

11. Augustine, *Confessions*, 124-25.

12. H. R. Niebuhr, *Radical Monotheism*, 100-113.

13. Augustine, "Sermon: The Sacking of the City of Rome," in E. M. Atkins and R. J. Dodaro, eds., *Augustine: Political Writings* (Cambridge: Cambridge University Press, 2005), 205-14.

14. Augustine, *City of God*, 941.

15. Aristotle, *Nicomachean Ethics,* ed. Roger Crisp (Cambridge: Cambridge University Press, 2000), 5.

16. Augustine, "The Catholic Way of Life and the Manichean Way of Life," 49.

5. The Greatest Good for the Greatest Number?

1. See above, pages 89-90.

2. Jeremy Bentham, *An Introduction to the Principles of Morals and Legislation,* J. H. Burns and H. L. A. Hart, eds. (London: The Athlone Press, 1970), 12.

3. John Stuart Mill, *Utilitarianism*, Roger Crisp, ed. (Oxford: Oxford University Press, 1998), 64.

4. Ibid., 105.

5. Bentham, *Principles of Morals and Legislation*, 40.

6. Peter Singer, *How Are We to Live?* (Amherst, NY: Prometheus Books, 1995), 222-25.

7. Singer does allow that individuals may have special responsibilities for the ordinary needs of their families, because others will be unlikely to take care of those needs.

8. Ibid., 222. For Singer's view of theology, see *How Are We to Live?* 188. He is more sympathetic to Buddhism, which expresses a concern for suffering in non-theistic terms, but he believes Buddhism has failed to make that concern effective in social terms.

9. William Paley, *Natural Theology*, Matthew Eddy and David Knight, eds. (Oxford: Oxford University Press, 2006), 7-10. Many people found Paley's argument persuasive until Charles Darwin (1809–1882) proposed his theory of natural selection, which suggested that very intricate forms of life could arise from random variations over time, without any need for a purpose to guide the design.

10. William Paley, *Principles of Moral and Political Philosophy* (New York: Garland Publishing, 1978), 60. Paley's *Principles*, published in 1785, was immediately popular with students and professors and remained the required text for many courses in ethics in Britain and America well into the nineteenth century.

11. Ibid., 65.

12. Joseph Fletcher, *Situation Ethics: The New Morality* (Louisville: Westminster John Knox Press, 1997), 30.

13. Joseph Fletcher, "Love and Utility," *Christian Century* 95 (May 31, 1978), 592-94.

14. Paley, *Principles*, 64.

15. Fletcher, *Situation Ethics*, 79. See page 40 above.

16. See pages 72-74 above.

17. Adam Smith introduced the idea of an "impartial spectator" in 1759. See Adam Smith, *The Theory of the Moral Sentiments*, ed. D. D. Raphael and A. L. Macfie (Oxford: Oxford University Press, 1976), 109-10.

18. See above, page 88.

19. See above, page 12.

20. Jeremy Bentham, "Anarchical Fallacies," in Jeremy Waldron, ed., *Nonsense upon Stilts: Bentham, Burke, and Marx on the Rights of Man* (London: Methuen, 1987), 53.

21. Joseph Butler, "Upon the Love of Our Neighbor," in *Fifteen Sermons Preached at the Rolls Chapel* (London: G. Bell and Sons, 1949), 199-200.

6. Natural Law and Human Law

1. See page 69 above.

2. See page 11 above.

3. For more on Kant, see chapter 7, pages 149-53.

4. John Rawls, *A Theory of Justice*, rev. ed. (Cambridge, MA: Harvard University Press, 1999), 28.

5. See page 9 above.

6. *Summa theologiae*, I-II, QQ. 90-108. See Thomas Aquinas, *Treatise on Law*,

trans. Alfred Freddoso (South Bend, IN: Saint Augustine's Press, 2009). Quotations from the *Summa* in this chapter are taken from this translation.

7. *Summa theologiae*, I-II, Q. 94, a. 2.

8. *Summa theologiae*, I-II, Q. 95, a. 2.

9. See Timothy C. Potts, *Conscience in Medieval Philosophy* (Cambridge: Cambridge University Press, 1980), 135-36.

10. See pages 36-41 above.

11. *Summa theologiae*, I-II, Q. 94, a. 4.

12. Ibid.

13. *Summa theologiae*, I-II, Q. 94, a. 5.

14. Ibid.

15. Gustavo Gutiérrez, *Las Casas: In Search of the Poor of Jesus Christ* (Maryknoll, NY: Orbis Books, 1993).

16. We will consider the Liberation view of deontological ethics in more detail in the next chapter.

17. See page 47 above.

18. See page 19 above.

19. Thomas Aquinas, *Summa theologiae*, I-II, Q. 94, a. 6.

20. See page 37 above.

21. Martin Luther, "On Secular Authority," in Harro Höpfl, ed., *Luther and Calvin on Secular Authority* (Cambridge: Cambridge University Press, 1991), 8.

22. Ibid., 9.

23. Luther makes the important exception that Christians must not obey if the ruler attempts to tell them what to believe; but even then they must be prepared to lose their property, and even their lives, if the ruler persecutes them for this disobedience.

24. Luther, "Secular Authority," 15.

25. See above, page 38.

26. Luther, "Secular Authority," 11-12.

27. Jaroslav Pelikan and Valerie Hotchkiss, eds., *Creeds and Confessions of Faith in the Christian Tradition* (New Haven: Yale University Press, 2003), vol. 2, 698.

28. Ibid., 700-701.

29. Stanley Hauerwas, *The Peaceable Kingdom* (Notre Dame, IN: University of Notre Dame Press, 1983), 61.

30. See pages 124-25 above.

31. Reinhold Niebuhr, *The Children of Light and the Children of Darkness* (New York: Charles Scribner's Sons, 1964).

32. Reinhold Niebuhr, *The Nature and Destiny of Man: A Christian*

Interpretation (Louisville: Westminster John Knox Press, 1996), vol. 1, 271-72.

33. Jean Calvin, *Calvin: Institutes of the Christian Religion*, ed. John T. McNeill (Louisville: Westminster John Knox Press, 1960), 417-18.

34. Ibid., 360.

35. Ibid., 1518.

36. Ibid., 1519.

37. See Emil Brunner, *The Divine Imperative* (Philadelphia: Westminster Press, 1947), 208. Different theologians give different names to this basic list of family, work, government, and religion. For some, they are "orders of preservation." Dietrich Bonhoeffer called them the "divine mandates." Some include additional orders, such as the institutions of culture or education, in the list. Amidst the variations, the basic idea remains that a workable society is composed of different centers of authority that the society as a whole needs to maintain itself and provide for the people who live in it.

38. See page 124 above.

7. Principles, Casuistry, and Commandments

1. W. D. Ross, *The Right and the Good* (Oxford: Oxford University Press, 1930).

2. See pages 130-32, 141-42 above.

3. Immanuel Kant, "An Answer to the Question: What Is Enlightenment?" in Pauline Kleingeld, ed., *Toward Perpetual Peace and Other Writings on Politics, Peace, and History* (New Haven: Yale University Press, 2006), 17.

4. Kant's actual formulation of this principle is "Act only in accordance with that maxim through which you can at the same time will that it become a universal law." See Immanuel Kant, *Groundwork of the Metaphysics of Morals*, Mary Gregor, trans. (Cambridge: Cambridge University Press, 1997), 31.

5. See page 5 above.

6. Kant, *Groundwork*, 7. See page 10 above.

7. See page 127 above.

8. Dietrich Bonhoeffer, *Ethics* (Dietrich Bonhoeffer Works, vol. 6; Minneapolis: Fortress Press, 2005), 115-16.

9. Dietrich Bonhoeffer, *Letters and Papers from Prison* (Dietrich Bonhoeffer Works, vol. 8; Minneapolis: Fortress Press, 2010), 424-31.

10. *Summa theologiae*, I-II, Q. 94, a. 2.

11. See page 129 above.

12. Immanuel Kant, "On a Supposed Right to Lie from Altruistic Motives," in

Lewis White Beck, ed., *Critique of Practical Reason, and Other Writings in Moral Philosophy* (Chicago: University of Chicago Press, 1949), 346-50.

13. "Casuistry," in *The Oxford English Dictionary*, 2nd ed. (Oxford: Clarendon Press, 1989), II, 961.

14. John Paul II, *Veritatis splendor*, in John Wilkins, ed., *Considering Veritatis Splendor* (Cleveland, OH: Pilgrim Press, 1994), 151. An *encyclical* is a letter written by the Pope to provide instruction on matters of faith and ethics. They are usually known by the first two words of their Latin text, in this case, "The splendor of truth…"

15. See, for example, Paul Ramsey, *The Patient as Person: Explorations in Medical Ethics* (New Haven: Yale University Press, 1970); *The Just War: Force and Political Responsibility* (New York: Charles Scribner's Sons, 1968); *Christian Ethics and the Sit-In* (New York: Association Press, 1961).

16. Paul Ramsey, *Deeds and Rules in Christian Ethics* (New York: Charles Scribner's Sons, 1967), 112.

17. Albert R. Jonsen and Stephen Toulmin, *The Abuse of Casuistry: A History of Moral Reasoning* (Berkeley: University of California Press, 1988).

18. John Rawls, *A Theory of Justice,* rev. ed. (Cambridge, MA: Harvard University Press, 1999), 18.

19. See page 150 above.

20. See the description of the realist version of the Christian stance on pages 55-59 above.

21. Martin Luther King, Jr., "Letter from Birmingham Jail," in James M. Washington, ed., *A Testament of Hope: The Essential Writings of Martin Luther King, Jr.* (San Francisco: Harper and Row, 1986), 293. For King's reference to Thomas Aquinas, see page 127 above.

22. Ibid.

23. Donal Dorr, *Option for the Poor: A Hundred Years of Vatican Social Teaching* (Maryknoll, NY: Orbis Books, 1992).

24. James H. Cone, *A Black Theology of Liberation*, 20th Anniversary Edition (Maryknoll, NY: Orbis Books, 1990), 5; Gustavo Gutiérrez, *We Drink from Our Own Wells: The Spiritual Journey of a People* (Maryknoll, NY: Orbis Books, 2003).

25. Rosemary Radford Ruether, *Sexism and God-Talk* (Boston: Beacon Press, 1983), 61-68.

26. Karl Barth, *Church Dogmatics* (Edinburgh: T. & T. Clark, 1961), III/4, 4.

27. Ibid., 9.

28. Bonhoeffer, *Ethics*, 284.

29. Jaroslav Pelikan and Valerie Hotchkiss, eds., *Creeds and Confessions of*

Faith in the Christian Tradition (New Haven: Yale University Press, 2003), vol. 3, 504-8. For Barth's exchange with Emil Brunner on natural theology, see Peter Fraenkel, trans., *Nature and Grace* (Eugene, OR: Wipf and Stock, 2002).

30. Barth, *Church Dogmatics*, III/4, 26.

31. See Reinhold Niebuhr, *Essays in Applied Christianity*, ed. D. B. Robertson (New York: Meridian Books, 1959), 141-47.

8. Virtues, Natural and Theological

1. See page 118 above.

2. Aristotle, *Nicomachean Ethics*, ed. Roger Crisp (Cambridge: Cambridge University Press, 2000), 3-4.

3. See Aristotle, *Nicomachean Ethics*, 68-72.

4. In the nineteenth century, temperance became narrowly connected with avoiding alcoholic drinks as part of healthy living.

5. See page 20 above.

6. See above, pages 78-79.

7. Augustine, "The Catholic Way of Life and the Manichean Way of Life," Boniface Ramsey, ed. *The Manichean Debate*, The Works of Saint Augustine, pt. 1, v. 19 (Hyde Park, NY: New City Press, 2006), 43.

8. Ibid., 52.

9. See, for example, Augustine's sermon on the sacking of Rome, in E. M. Atkins and R. J. Dodaro, eds., *Augustine: Political Writings* (Cambridge: Cambridge University Press, 2001), 205-14.

10. Augustine, *Confessions*, trans. Henry Chadwick (Oxford: Oxford University Press, 1992), 201.

11. *Augustine: Political Writings*, 2-3.

12. Augustine, *The City of God against the Pagans*, ed. R. W. Dyson (Cambridge: Cambridge University Press, 1998), 924.

13. See above, pages 10-12.

14. See above, pages 126-28.

15. Aristotle, *Nicomachean Ethics*, 194-96.

16. Thomas Aquinas's discussion of virtue is found in *Summa theologiae,* I-II, QQ. 49-67. This part of the *Summa* is often called the *Treatise on the Virtues*. See Thomas Aquinas, *Treatise on the Virtues*, trans. John A. Oesterle (South Bend, IN: University of Notre Dame Press, 1966). Quotations from the *Summa* in this chapter are taken from this translation.

17. Thomas Aquinas, *Summa theologiae*, I-II, Q. 57. Prudence is required for

successful application of casuistry in Christian ethics, as described above on pages 158-60.

18. Ibid., I-II, Q. 60.

19. Ibid., I-II, Q. 55, a. 1; Q. 58, a. 3.

20. Ibid., I-II, Q. 60, a. 5. See Aristotle, *Nicomachean Ethics*, 78. (The translation "quick-witted" comes from Roger Crisp.)

21. Thomas Aquinas, *Summa theologiae*, I-II, Q. 51, Q. 64.

22. See page 193 above.

23. The Latin word Thomas uses is *caritas*, which is often translated into English as "charity." Like the Greek word *agapē*, *caritas* refers to a spiritual relationship, as opposed to sexual love or affection between persons.

24. Thomas Aquinas, *Summa theologiae*, I-II, Q. 61, a. 2.

25. 1 Corinthians 13:13. See *Summa theologiae*, I-II, Q. 62, a. 4.

26. *Summa theologiae*, I-II, Q. 62, a. 4.

27. Ibid., I-II, Q. 55, a. 4.

28. Ibid., I-II, Q. 64, a. 4.

29. See page 193 above.

30. Thomas Aquinas, *Summa theologiae*, I-II, Q. 61, a. 5.

31. Ibid., I-II, Q. 65, a. 3.

32. See above, page 78.

33. Catherine of Siena, *The Dialogue*, trans. Suzanne Noffke (New York: Paulist Press, 1980), 37-38.

34. See above, page 140.

35. Jean Calvin, *Calvin: Institutes of the Christian Religion*, ed. John T. McNeill (Louisville: Westminster John Knox Press, 1960), 292-94.

36. See above, pages 148-49.

9. Virtue and Responsibility

1. Dietrich Bonhoeffer, *Ethics* (Dietrich Bonhoeffer Works, vol. 6; Minneapolis: Fortress Press, 2005), 283-85. See also page 175 above.

2. See above, pages 88, 109-10.

3. Reinhold Niebuhr, *The Irony of American History* (Chicago: University of Chicago Press, 2008), 61-64.

4. See above, pages 78–94. Note again that H. Richard Niebuhr and his brother Reinhold Niebuhr are two different persons.

5. H. Richard Niebuhr, *The Responsible Self: An Essay in Christian Moral Philosophy* (Louisville: Westminster John Knox Press, 1999), 48-51.

6. Ibid., 53.

7. Ibid., 60.

8. Ibid., 109.

9. Charles E. Curran, *The Catholic Moral Tradition Today: A Synthesis* (Washington, DC: Georgetown University Press, 1999), 30.

10. Bernard Häring, *Free and Faithful in Christ: Moral Theology for Clergy and Laity*, 3 vols. (New York: Seabury Press, 1978–81).

11. See G. E. M. Anscombe, "Modern Moral Philosophy," in *Ethics, Religion, and Politics* (The Collected Philosophical Papers of G. E. M. Anscombe, Vol. 3; Minneapolis: University of Minnesota Press, 1981), 26-42; and Gérard Gilleman, *The Primacy of Charity in Moral Theology* (Westminster, MD: Newman Press, 1961). Anscombe's essay was originally published in 1958, and Gilleman's book appeared in French in 1959.

12. Curran, *The Catholic Moral Tradition Today*, 73-77.

13. See above, pages 46-50.

14. Curran, *The Catholic Moral Tradition Today*, 113-30.

15. See above, pages 199-204.

16. Curran, *The Catholic Moral Tradition Today*, 41-42.

17. See, for example, Lee Yearley, *Mencius and Aquinas: Theories of Virtue and Conceptions of Courage* (Albany, NY: State University of New York Press, 1990).

18. Stanley Hauerwas, *The Peaceable Kingdom* (Notre Dame, IN: University of Notre Dame Press, 1983), 24-34.

19. Ibid., 15.

20. See above, pages 193-96.

21. Stanley Hauerwas, *With the Grain of the Universe: The Church's Witness and Natural Theology* (Grand Rapids: Brazos Press, 2001), 15.

22. See above, pages 173-74.

23. Hauerwas, *Peaceable Kingdom*, 1-15.

24. Ibid., 105.

25. Ibid., 103.

26. James H. Cone, *A Black Theology of Liberation*, 20th Anniversary Edition (Maryknoll, NY: Orbis Books, 1990), 1.

27. See above, pages 167-68.

28. See above, pages 60-62.

29. Emilie M. Townes, *Womanist Ethics and the Cultural Production of Evil* (New York: Palgrave Macmillan, 2006), 125-38.

30. Ada María Isasi-Díaz, *Mujerista Theology: A Theology for the Twenty-first Century* (Maryknoll, NY: Orbis Books, 1996), 95.

31. Ibid., 96-100.

32. Ibid., 100.

33. Reinhold Niebuhr, *An Interpretation of Christian Ethics* (New York: Seabury Press, 1979), 22-24.

34. See ibid., 64; also *The Irony of American History*, 63.

35. See above, pages 212-14.

36. Reinhold Niebuhr, *Faith and Politics*, ed. Ronald Stone (New York: George Braziller, 1968), 56.

37. Martin Luther King, Jr., "Pilgrimage to Nonviolence," in James M. Washington, ed., *A Testament of Hope: The Essential Writings of Martin Luther King, Jr.* (San Francisco: Harper and Row, 1986), 38.

38. Jeremy Bentham, *An Introduction to the Principles of Morals and Legislation*, J. H. Burns and H. L. A. Hart, eds. (London: The Athlone Press, 1970), 12.

39. See above, page 199.

40. *Responsible Self*, 109.

A Postscript for the Instructor

1. Alasdair MacIntyre raises this possibility in the "disquieting suggestion" with which he begins his critical view of contemporary moral thought. See Alasdair MacIntyre, *After Virtue: A Study in Moral Theory*, 3rd ed. (Notre Dame, IN: University of Notre Dame Press, 2007), 1-5.

2. I owe this terminology to my colleague Charles Curran, who has influenced this introduction in many other ways that will be apparent simply by comparing it with his book, *The Catholic Moral Tradition Today: A Synthesis* (Washington, DC: Georgetown University Press, 1999). For his presentation of the Christian stance, see especially pages 30-47.

3. Albert R. Jonsen and Stephen Toulmin, *The Abuse of Casuistry: A History of Moral Reasoning* (Berkeley: University of California Press, 1988), 293.

4. Robin W. Lovin, *Christian Ethics: An Essential Guide* (Nashville: Abingdon Press, 2000).

INDEX